ALAIN LOCKE
AND
PHILOSOPHY

Alain Locke. *Courtesy of Moorland-Spingarn Research Center, Howard University.*

Alain Locke

AND

Philosophy ———

A QUEST FOR CULTURAL PLURALISM

Johnny Washington

CONTRIBUTIONS IN AFRO-AMERICAN AND
AFRICAN STUDIES, NUMBER 94

GREENWOOD PRESS
NEW YORK • WESTPORT, CONNECTICUT • LONDON

Library of Congress Cataloging-in-Publication Data

Washington, Johnny.
  Alain Locke and philosophy.

  (Contributions in Afro-American and African
studies, ISSN 0069-9624 ; no. 94)
  Bibliography: p.
  Includes index.
  1. Locke, Alain LeRoy, 1886-1954.
2. Afro-Americans—Biography. 3. Afro-Americans—
Politics and government. 4. Afro-Americans—
Education. I. Title. II. Series.
E185.97.L79W37 1986   191   85-9873
ISBN 0-313-22957-0 (lib. bdg. : alk. paper)

Library of Congress Catalog Card Number: 85-9873
ISBN: 0-313-22957-0
ISSN: 0069-9624

First published in 1986

Greenwood Press, Inc.
88 Post Road West
Westport, Connecticut 06881

Printed in the United States of America

The paper used in this book complies with the
Permanent Paper Standard issued by the National
Information Standards Organization (Z39.48-1984).

10 9 8 7 6 5 4 3 2 1

PRISM

Protest, preserve, protect—
        the pagan in search of the Puritan
        the humanist wanting the pragmatic sense

And there it hovers, the mirrored prism
        of his mind, suspended somewhere
        between conflicting worlds

Reflecting . . . rejecting . . .
        each side but a part of the whole
        he cannot bind

And like the seasons, sides
        come and go as one by one
        each is spent—

Yet each face, kissing at angles,
        streaks to the vortex
        where energies collide—

In "the quest for uncertainty"
        only paradox survives
        to anoint his struggle

Harriette Allen Insignares

CONTENTS

CONTENTS

FOREWORD

Dr. Johnny Washington's work on Alain Locke is a very significant and pioneering contribution to the literature on the thoughts of Black philosophers. It is significant in two main respects: First, it is a comprehensive formulation and evaluation of the thoughts of a Black philosopher by a professional Black philosopher. In our time books of this kind are extremely rare, both in Africa and the Diaspora. Second, given its scope, logic, and style, it successfully demonstrates the existence and seriousness of Black philosophy.

We perhaps ought to remind ourselves that an enterprise of this nature is fraught with many temptations. It is, for instance, understandable, though unscholarly, for a philosopher to employ such new opportunity merely to castigate a society which has long suppressed the thoughts of a significant section of itself. Professor Washington's care in not only recognizing but avoiding such temptations justifies my view that here is a work that deserves a wide readership on its own merit.

Alain Locke, as Dr. Washington has shown, concerned himself not merely with political issues affecting justice and freedom for Blacks, but he was equally concerned with analysis of philosophical questions of values, art, and knowledge in general. In this regard Locke's axiology, as formulated in "Values and Imperatives," makes him a precursor of the non-cognitive twentieth-century ethical theorists who emphasize feelings and attitudes as the basic modes in ethical judgments.

This brings us to a question that is as interesting as it is important: Is there a need for Black philosophy beyond the need to search for the Black past and formulate an ideology that rejects racial domination? For in a very important sense, the larger society has regarded questions of the past, and of racism, as important only insofar as certain members of that society often raise such questions mainly to deny philosophy to the Blacks. If, on the other hand, such questions become part of the subject matter of Black philosophy, it is mainly because Black philosophers view these as obstacles to be cleared to allow freedom and dignity, as a foundation for philosophic thought. This may help explain why, as Dr. Washington writes, "Black philosophy usually originates within the community and seeks to examine issues of justice." Those who employ Black philosophy to search for justice and truth are no less relevant than Socrates and Jesus who were gadflies of their times.

Black philosophy and African philosophy have an affinity to the extent that Black philosophy is the production of Black philosophers who themselves are Africans in the Diaspora, whereas African philosophy is the product of Africans. There is another common ground between the two: both are currently struggling to assert themselves as serious and rationally unavoidable aspects of human thought. It is then possible to merge the two philosophies and to describe them together as Africana Philosophy, an expression which Professor Lucius Outlaw has used to describe the merger. In July 1982, Professor Outlaw organized a conference at Haverford College in Philadelphia with the general theme of "Africana Philosophy." It brought together leading professional African and African-American philosophers. One of the main concerns of the conference was the question of what should constitute the nature of a philosophical contribution that deserves the adjective "Black" or "African." Prior to this conference, however, several philosophy conferences had been held in Africa to discuss similar themes, and valuable contributions came from both the Continent and the Diaspora.

Intellectual contact and exchange between Africans and African descendants abroad is, of course, nothing new. Indeed, Alain Locke' anthology, *The New Negro* (1925), was a kind of manifesto of the Negro Renaissance movement in the 1920s. This movement inspired Aimé Césaire's concept of *Negritude*, an idea popularized by Leopold Sedar Senghor, the first president of Senegal. Traces of this inspiration are also available in Dr. Kwame Nkrumah's notion of African Personality. (Nkrumah was the first president of Ghana.)

Alain Locke and Philosophy is a bold and pioneering work which should compel us to emphasize one important point: a further development of Black and African philosophies requires that Black philosophers take themselves and their predecessors seriously. In doing so, they will find that a scholarly work on a fellow Black philosopher need not be less deserving and philosophic than a work on a celebrated European philosopher. The advice then is contained in Booker T. Washington's metaphor, "Cast your buckets where you are!"

Perhaps I should end on a note of prophecy: Washington's *Alain Locke and Philosophy* will mark the birth of professional Africana Philosophy, just as *The New Negro* signalled the beginning of the Negro Renaissance.

H. Odera Oruka
University of Nairobi
Kenya, Africa

PREFACE

In the broadest sense this volume is about Alain Locke's philosophic interpretation of Black Americans' prolonged, historical experiences, their contributions to culture, and their struggle for social justice. Thus, this work covers two distinct, although related, social epochs. The first epoch pertains to the Black experience from the turn of the century, when Locke began writing, up to the 1960s, a few years before Locke's death. The second epoch is marked by the social transformations that occurred in the 1960s through the 1970s to the present.

Prior to the 1960s, the term "Negro" was used to refer to Black Americans, whereas in the 1920s the term "New Negro" became popular. In the 1960s, when Blacks were assuming a new identity, they rejected "Negro," a notion they felt the larger society had forced on them. They began referring to themselves as Afro-Americans or Blacks. Because Alain Locke died before the last two interchangeable terms came into vogue, throughout this volume I have tried to remain true to Locke's spirit and times by using "Negro" where appropriate. In many instances, however, I have used "Negro" and "Blacks" or "Black Americans" interchangeably.

At this time I wish to thank the following persons, without whose assistance this volume would not have been possible: Frances D. Anderson, Victoria R. Lee of Rensselaer Polytechnic Institute; Peggie Rowland of Tennessee State University, who typed and retyped various parts of this manuscript; Jean E. Houghtaling of Rensselaer Polytechnic Institute, who was quite helpful in obtaining materials through interlibrary loan; Deborah Schwartz, one of my former students at Rensselaer Polytechnic Institute, who proofread the entire manuscript; Maureen Melino of Greenwood Press, who in kind ways provided useful suggestions; Esme E. Bhan of Howard University, who guided me through the Alain Locke collection; and, finally, Richard A. Long of Atlanta University, who stimulated my interest in the study of Alain Locke's works. I alone, however, am responsible for any defects this book may possess.

INTRODUCTION

The 1950s was a decade of peace and prosperity relative to the profound social crises we have undergone since then: the civil rights movement, the Vietnam War, campus unrest, Watergate, the oil shortage, the women's movement, the nuclear freeze movement, inflation-recession, and the volatile political situation in the Middle East and Central America. Such crises and social transformations have forced both the academic and lay communities to reexamine their basic values. Among the masses there has been a rekindling of interest in religion, which seems to offer hope to people in search of more meaningful normative standards. Among certain educators the response to these crises has been equally telling; they have begun to establish centers to study the "interface" of values and technology, and to devise programs that make a greater effort to incorporate normative issues into existing programs.

Whereas philosophers and other humanists have always been interested in value issues, their interest in normative issues dwindled with the beginning of modern science in the seventeenth century. They have instead aligned themselves closely with science which claims to be value neutral, Kant notwithstanding. In the early twentieth century John Dewey, William James, and other American Pragmatists, although they wrote much about values, strengthened the alliance between philosophy and science and accepted its criteria of truth.

A contemporary of the early Pragmatists, Alain L. Roy Locke was also concerned with value issues, but he refused to align himself so closely with the scientific method. Locke argued that the source of values and their standards lay in attitudes, feelings, and preferences. As is shown in Chapter 2, he criticized American philosophy and other philosophic traditions for basing the criteria of values on experimental or scientific results, and for neglecting a value theory that had feelings, attitudes, and preferences as its basic elements. Locke also criticized American society for believing that the white race was superior to any other.

As a member of a racially oppressed minority, Locke knew what it was to be treated unjustly because of race or color. He knew what it was to be a Black person living in racist America, and he felt and understood the dynamics of pervasive conflict, both potential and actual, that yoked together the Black and white races and other ethnic groups. Locke sought to understand the deep-seated attitudes, feelings, and prejudices that perpetuated the racial tension that characterized America. Throughout his life, he also attempted to identify the mechanism, rooted in the hearts of individuals, groups, organizations, and institutions, that would defuse racial tension and produce a more tolerant society.

Alain Locke was born in Philadelphia on September 13, 1886, only two decades after the nation had ended its most bitter crisis, the Civil War. He died on June 9, 1954, the year Martin Luther King, Jr., initiated the civil rights struggle in Montgomery, Alabama. During his career as a scholar, writer, social critic, literary critic, educator, philosopher, and Socratic gadfly and midwife, Locke strove to advance the principles of social justice for Blacks and other oppressed people. Chapter 1 demonstrates that Booker T. Washington, W.E.B. Du Bois, Marcus Garvey, Martin Luther King, Jr., and others, were also midwives and gadflies in the cause of Blacks and other minorities.

Locke had been intellectually well prepared for his philosophical career. He entered Harvard University in 1904 as a philosophy student and earned his B.S. degree in 1907. His Harvard teachers included William James, H. M. Sheffer, Hugo Münsterberg, George Herbert Palmer, George P. Adams, Josiah Royce, George Santayana, and Horace M. Kallen. Between 1907 and 1910, Locke studied as the first Black Rhodes scholar at

Oxford. From England he went to the University of Berlin where he remained until 1911; among his teachers there were Frantz Brentano, Alexius Meinong, and Paul Natrop. At this time he also studied in Paris under the tutelage of Henri Bergson. Locke received his Ph.D. degree from Harvard in 1918; somewhat earlier, in 1912, he had become associated with Howard University in Washington, D.C., where he remained as a philosophy teacher until his retirement in 1953.

Locke's initial philosophic interest was in value theory, and, in developing his own value views, he drew on the works of most of his teachers. Aside from his Ph.D. dissertation, "The Problem of Classification in the Theory of Values" (1918), and "Values and Imperatives" (1935), Locke devoted little attention to problems that preoccupy professional or academic philosophers, and although his axiological views are limited in volume, they are striking. (This matter is discussed in Chapter 2.)

Locke's value theory was a product of his reflections on racial problems, but the application of his view is not limited to racial issues. His value views are applicable to any human situation in which conflicts and the potential for conflicts between individuals and groups are found.

In Chapter 4, for example, Locke's value views are related to the problem of the nuclear arms race, and it is argued that a consideration of Locke's views sheds light on the problems which the United States and Russia are facing in their attempts to reach an agreement about world peace.

Chapters 3, 4, and 5 discuss the ways in which Locke's views are applicable to current political problems by integrating his views with those of Hannah Arendt (1906–1975). As a Jew, Hannah Arendt experienced racial oppression, much as Alain Locke did. This she experienced directly while she was living in Nazi Germany before escaping to the United States in 1941.

It will be seen that Arendt and Locke's philosophic orientations are similar in many respects, although there is no evidence that the two knew each other's works. Just as Locke's philosophic views were in part shaped by the oppression experienced by Blacks, so were Arendt's views in part shaped by the oppression the Jews suffered in Nazi Germany. Locke, who was a cultural pluralist and a value relativist, opposed any philosophy that rested on absolutist principles because he felt that absolutism was antithetical to the ideals of democracy. These ideals allow for a plurality of standards and values. He felt that the best society was one that was organized around the principles of pluralism so that ethnic minorities could maintain their cultural differences and enjoy freedom. Today he would argue that the United States and Russia would come closer to attaining peaceful relations if both would realize that absolutes are largely the source of the tension. Each side needs to abandon absolutes, embrace pluralism, and respect each other's cultural and national differences.

Arendt was quite sympathetic toward other groups that suffered oppression; in the 1950s she wrote about school desegregation as it pertained to Black Americans. During the Little Rock, Arkansas racial struggle of that period, Arendt wrote an article about school desegregation, which generated much debate, drawing in people like Ralph Ellison. As Elisabeth Young-Bruehl observed:

Though her Little Rock article was strenuously attacked by many people, most of them liberals, Arendt gave ground to only one—Ralph Ellison. Ellison referred in passing to Arendt's essay as he replied in 1963 to a *Dissent* article by Irving Howe entitled "Black Boys and Native Sons." Arendt's "Olympian authority" was, Ellison thought, alienating; he realized that her tone was largely responsible for the intensity of her critics' responses. But it was not this sort of criticisms to which Arendt replied. In an interview granted to Robert Penn Warren for a 1965 volume entitled *Who Speaks for the Negro?*, Ellison offered an explanation of Negro parents' attitudes towards the integration struggle that Arendt found compelling.[1]

Similarly, she opposed any absolutist doctrine. In her book *The Human Condition* (1958), she went so far as to deny the existence of human nature, presumably on the grounds that such a notion suggested that human beings had absolute features in common, the existence of which denied the uniqueness and freedom of each individual. She believed that any form of absolutism in political discourse was dangerous because absolutism could easily be used to support a totalitarian ideology which, for example, governed Hitler's Germany, where only Hitler had the freedom to act and issue absolute laws to which the masses were forced to conform.

Arendt's own conception of politics, which she worked out in *Between Past and Future* (1961), *The Human Condition*, *On Revolution* (1963), and *Crises of the Republic* (1972), was modeled on the ancient Greeks' political experiences and on U.S. political institutions. She prized the American Revolution of 1776, an event to which she dedicated her book, *On Revolution*. She, like Locke, had great faith in American democracy, although she recognized its limitations, one of which was that the two-party system did not provide adequate room for the masses to participate in the political arena.

As a remedy in *On Revolution* and *Crises of the Republic* Arendt introduced a new concept of the state which she called the council system. It would require no party affiliation, and it would have the shape of a pyramid, with power, freedom, and authority originating in its bottom layer, constituted by the grassroots people who took the initiative to engage in politics. This concept of the political community would allow concerted, free action and would open political discourse among the citizens.

This notion of the council system encompasses a federated council system which involves a plurality of councils. Chapters 3 and 4 describe how this notion of councils can be incorporated into Locke's pluralistic society, giving Blacks and other minorities greater opportunity to exercise freedom and to protect their cultural differences.

In the 1960s and early 1970s, Black Americans, inspired by the activities of Malcolm X, the Black Panthers, Martin Luther King, Jr., and the Black Muslims, worked to underscore their cultural differences from the larger society. Some even spoke of the need to create a separate Black state within American society. The Blacks expressed their political energies through mass protests, sit-ins, voter registration drives, and race riots. Black students enrolled in white educational institutions and demanded the institution of Black Studies courses which would emphasize the cultural experiences of Africans and Black Americans. The literary works of such people as Eldridge Cleaver, W.E.B. Du Bois, Malcolm X, and Stokeley Carmichael were popular. Ironically, however, little, if any, mention was made of the pioneer in the study of Black and African cultures: Alain Locke, who, more than a half century earlier, emphasized the intellectual and aesthetic importance of Black Americans' cultural heritage. It is difficult to explain why Locke was virtually ignored in the 1960s. Today, scholarly interest in Locke is high and is growing at a rapid pace. This is true not only in the United States, but also in Africa, especially among philosophers. Currently, the Philosophy Department at Howard University is planning a centennial to commemorate the birth of Locke. The growing community of Black professional philosophers, virtually nonexistent two decades ago, is largely responsible for this rediscovery of Locke.

Black people, ignorant of the breadth and depth of Locke's works, ignored Locke in the 1960s partly because they felt he was not sufficiently militant. In search of an historic hero, they instead turned to people like Du Bois and Frederick Douglass. It will be seen, however, that Locke's philosophic attitude was just as militant as that of Du Bois or Douglass, but people such as Douglass, Booker T. Washington, Du Bois, and Marcus Garvey were politically more visible than Locke. Each placed greater emphasis than Locke on the importance of political and economic equality for Blacks. As will be shown, Locke was more concerned with cultural equality, which, he believed, was to be achieved through the concerted effort of a Black cultural Elite— what Du Bois called the Talented Tenth. Arendt, Locke, and Du Bois all shared the view that an Elite was important for leadership in the realm of human affairs. Locke placed greater emphasis than Du Bois and Arendt, on a cultural Elite rather than on a political Elite. Chapter 5 argues that if an Elite is to advance the Black community as Locke desired, his notion of cultural leadership and equality is inadequate. Without belittling the importance of artists and their products, the Black community, if it is to advance itself politically, must rely on a political Elite. In fact, the political Elite and the cultural Elite need to unite.

Today a number of authorities are beginning to realize the need to combine political and cultural resources, including scientific inquiry and scholarship, in an effort to establish global peace. They are realizing the limits imposed by the technological and military approaches to world problems. This is not to suggest that statesmen need to become artists or vice versa. Rather, they have important roles to play in their respective fields, both nationally and internationally, in promoting world peace. Locke echoed this position in his examination of the problems of world peace, a problem with which he was concerned in most of his works, especially in the area of education.

A social reformer can choose among four alternatives in an effort to produce social change: bribery, force, political persuasion, or education. These, of course, are not mutually exclusive; Locke, however, placed greater emphasis on education. Most of his writings on education focused on the problems which a segregated education system engendered. Although he wrote much about Black education, his message was directed not only to Blacks, but also to whites, whom he regarded as being largely responsible for the Blacks' low-quality education. He also felt that the educative process could materially reduce conflict among the races and thus promote harmony. As already noted, he argued that most conflicts originated from absolutist thinking. A form of absolutist thinking, he maintained, was reflected in the dogmatic attitude shared by the larger society that its value creed was superior to the creeds of ethnic minorities and Third World people. He urged educators to dispel such an attitude and in its place encourage an attitude of openness among students, so that the principle of value reciprocity, not the principle of domination, would become the ideal that directed action. In this regard, Locke held that it was important for students to acquire knowledge about the history of various ethnic groups, to gain a greater appreciation of other cultural values. His views on this issue are explored in Chapter 6.

Today many educators and legislators are debating the need to desegregate Black colleges, and a few mergers have already begun to take place. As early as the 1930s, Locke explored this issue and concluded that Black colleges should remain segregated, so that Black people could further develop their own unique culture. In this connection, he argued that Black colleges should be directed by Black leaders who would provide role models for Black youth. He also suggested that an important element in the goal of Black colleges should include the training of Black youth for leadership. That is, the colleges should train the Black Elite. These views are examined in Chapter 7.

This Elitism represents only one side of Locke's thought; the other side is his non-Elitist position, evidenced in part by his concern for the education of the Black masses. Chapter 8 demonstrates that Locke's views on education straddled the opposing educational views of Booker T. Washington, who wanted to educate the Black masses, and of W.E.B. Du Bois who wanted to educate the Black Elite. Thus, Locke's struggle to reconcile in his own mind the views of Washington and Du Bois represents a paradox in Locke's thought. This and other paradoxes are discussed in Chapter 8.

At the turn of the century, Washington and Du Bois were also divided on the question of whether Black Americans should adopt the principle of racial integration; in particular, they were at odds on whether education in America should be integrated, segregated, or desegregated. As noted, Locke was also drawn into this controversial issue. But here again he was inconsistent. He shared Washington's feeling that Black colleges should remain segregated. When, as early as 1935, Locke turned his attention to secondary education, he demanded that the schools be desegregated in order to establish parity for Blacks. The year 1984 marks the thirtieth anniversary of the Supreme Court's decision that enjoined the desegregation of public schools; how much progress has taken place within the past thirty years? Locke's writings on education might serve as a standard against which to measure this progress, if any. If he were writing today, he would probably support both bussing and Affirmative Action. Chapter 9 examines Locke's views on desegregation.

While Locke was developing his views on school desegregation, he was also discerning the rise of what he called the New Negro. Harlem was the mecca for Locke's New Negro who discarded the ways and values of the Old Negro, the "Uncle Tom" of the South. The Harlem Renaissance marked an outburst of creative activity among Black Americans, such as Jessie Fauset, James Weldon Johnson, Langston Hughes, Claude McKay, Garvey, Du Bois, and Locke. Du Bois and, perhaps to a greater degree, Locke were the leaders of this movement. Locke is widely known for the role he played in the Harlem Renaissance; without him it is unlikely that it would have achieved the glory it did. Locke was to the Harlem Renaissance what Martin Luther King, Jr., was to the civil rights movement of the 1960s. If the claim can be made that significant historical events are causative factors affecting the development of subsequent historic events, it is likely that the civil rights movement of the 1960s had its roots in the Harlem Renaissance. The works of the Black artists and writers of the 1920s and 1930s provided the basis for the Black Studies programs that grew out of the civil rights movement, just as the available evidence indicates that the Harlem Renaissance, the Garvey movement, and the civil rights movement, inspired the liberating movements on the continent of Africa in the 1960s. Today the second generation of the New Negro has begun to intensify its political aspirations. More Blacks today hold high political office than ever before. Chapter 10 is devoted to a discussion of Locke's New Negro.

Historical evidence and traditions indicate that, since time immemorial, Africans have made great cultural contributions to their own and to other civilizations of the world. In spite of slavery and other negative factors, Black Americans, too, have made great contributions to art, as is evidenced by the achievements of the New Negro. One may ask whether Black American artists genetically inherited this cultural capacity from their African ancestors, or whether they acquired this creative faculty from environmental conditions. Locke's answer to this question and others is explored in Chapter 11. The final chapter shows how Locke's views are relevant to today's world by returning to the issue of desegregation and the related problem of ethnic identity.

A prolific writer, Locke published hundreds of articles and edited or authored a number of books. His works focused on the Black experience, its music, art, literature, poetry, drama, and education. He even devoted a few articles to religion, namely, the Baha'i faith. During the latter part of his career, he accepted the Baha'i faith and attempted to integrate it into his own philosophy of values. His major books include *The New Negro* (1925), *Plays of Negro Life: A Source-Book of Native American Drama* (co-edited with Montgomery Gregory) (1927), *The Negro and His Mu-*

sic (1936), *Americans All: Immigrants All* (1939), *The Negro in Art* (1940), and *When Peoples Meet: A Study of Race and Culture Contacts* (co-edited with Bernhard J. Stern) (1942). The major English-speaking journals to which he contributed included: *The World Tomorrow, Howard Review, The Nation, Survey Graphics, The Forum, Harvard Education Review, Journal of Adult Education, Opportunity, Phylon,* and *Crisis.*

Because of the diversity and volume of Locke's works, the present book cannot, of course, do justice to him. I have not attempted the Herculean task of examining the scope of Locke's view, nor have I devoted much attention to the Harlem Renaissance, which has already received considerable scholarly attention. Rather, the core of this volume is made up of Locke's views on values, cultural-political pluralism, education, Black and African culture, and the many paradoxes, inconsistencies, contradictions, and ambiguities that surface in his considerations of these themes.

Locke was not a systematic philosophical thinker in the sense of Royce or Santayana; he was interested in neither building nor defending a philosophic system. Nor did he approach his subject matter with preconceived assumptions to be forced on reality. Locke regarded himself as a realist: he wanted to keep his feet on the solid rocks of reality and avoid the trap of the systematic thinker who, in the quest for certainty, tends to escape the problems of life by formulating systems and ideologies with his own inherent logic. An author as prolific as Locke would have benefited from the unity which a system can give to the thinker's work. Because Locke's works lack an adequate systematic framework, his basic insights are not altogether coherent. His basic insights are scattered throughout his diverse writings, and as a consequence, many of his notions are contradictory and paradoxical.

In another sense, the paradoxes and contradictions characterizing Locke's thoughts go beyond the fact that his views are not integrated into a system. They are derived from the social contradiction rooted in the racist society which he tried to understand—the contradiction that Du Bois said created in him a double consciousness. This contradiction originates from the tension between the two societies of America, one Black and the other white. Locke regarded his own life as a paradox:

I should like to claim as life-motto the good Greek principle,—"*Nothing in excess*," but I have probably worn instead as the badge of circumstance,—"*All things with a reservation.*"Philadelphia, with her birthright of provincialism flavored by urbanity and her petty bourgeois psyche with the Tory slant, at the start set the key of paradox; circumstance compounded it by decreeing me as a Negro a dubious and doubting sort of American and by reason of the racial inheritance making me more of a pagan than a Puritan, more of a humanist than a pragmatist.

Verily paradox has followed me the rest of my days: at Harvard, clinging to the genteel tradition of Palmer, Royce and Munsterberg, yet attracted by the disillusion of Santayana and the radical protest of James: again in 1916 I returned to work under Royce but was destined to take my doctorate in Value Theory under Perry. At Oxford, once more intrigued by the twilight of aestheticism but dimly aware of the new realism of the Austrian philosophy of value; socially Anglophile, but because of race loyalty, strenuously anti-imperialist; universalist in religion, internationalist and pacifist in world-view, but forced by a sense of simple justice to approve of the militant counter-nationalisms of Zionism, Young Turkey, Young Egypt, Young India, and with reservations even Garveyism and current-day "Nippon over Asia." Finally a cultural cosmopolitan, but perforce an advocate of cultural racialism as a defensive counter-move for the American Negro, and accordingly more of a philosophical mid-wife to a generation of younger Negro poets, writers, artists than a professional philosopher.

Small wonder, then, with this psychograph, that I project my personal history into its inevitable rationalization as cultural pluralism and value relativism, with a not too orthodox reaction to the American way of life.[2]

Thus seen in the larger perspective, the paradoxes found in Locke's work represent not so much a weakness in his views, but, in part, the depth and complexities of the racial problems he tried to face. Furthermore, if any unity can be attributed to Locke's thoughts, such unity lies in the paradoxes that pervade his works, just as contradictions established unity in the works of a dialectical thinker such as Hegel or Marx. It is difficult to detect a single, unifying paradox in Locke's thought. Locke was a pluralist who, like William James, appreciated the diversity of human experience. In the absence of a single, unifying paradox, Locke's works are unified by a cluster, a plurality of paradoxes, some of which are considered in this volume.

Locke left behind several hundred boxes of unpublished papers—manuscripts, letters, essays, and so on,—currently located at Howard University. But he did not apparently leave behind a fullfledged autobiography; had he done so, we would have deeper insights into his personality and works, and would be able to decipher some of the paradoxes on which his life and works largely rested.

At Locke's funeral, held in New York City on June 11, 1954, his friends and colleagues made some revealing remarks about him as a person, friend, philosopher, and teacher. Among these were Ralph J. Bunche, Y. H. Krikorian, William Stuart Nelson, William Stanley Braithwaite, Benjamin Karpman, and W.E.B. Du Bois. Here, at length, are their respective comments.
Bunche:

It is with a sense of deep personal loss that I contemplate the death of Alain Locke. As a colleague and friend I have known him, worked with him, sought and taken his sage advice and profoundly respected him for more than a quarter century. How much inspiration I have derived from his life and works I cannot possibly measure, but it has been great, for in my younger days, in the Twenties and Thirties, Alain Locke was a strong and unique beacon lighting an exciting new course for aspiring young Negroes. . . . Alain Locke's large influence and work survive though his frail little body and his very big heart are gone. Too few, perhaps, well understood or adequately appreciated Alain Locke. Those of us who did have lived a richer life for it.

Krikorian:

To his [Locke's] studies he brought his keen intelligence, his sense of wonder, his sense of human values. His whole mind was saturated with the best thoughts and traditions of our civilization. As a philosopher he had a critical mind, breadth of vision and a fine sense of values . . . Finally, Alain Locke had an inspiring, beautiful personality. I know of no one in whom courtesy, kindness, and courage were so harmoniously patterned. To be with Alain Locke was an experience— an enlightening and civilizing experience.

Nelson:

It is with a deep sense of community and personal loss that I bring to this occasion a word on behalf of Howard University; for in speaking of Dr. Locke I speak of one who for a very long time was for us teacher, philosopher, and friend. The number of years Dr. Locke spent at Howard University has its own significance, for he touched nearly ten generations of students and was equalled or exceeded in this length of service to the institution by very few. . . . It was the quality of his presence that left its mark upon us. . . . He did not detach himself from concern with practical issues and the hurley burly. But he did not succumb to the event. He walked among the affairs of men with the eyes and mind of an educated man, of one who bore the obligation and possessed the ability to make choices. He was no unwilling victim of this movement or that. He was no faddist. If he was enthusiastic about an idea or a trend, it was by deliberate choice and not by unwitting conformity. To use his own words, he was determined to be free from "blind partisanship." He understood the "puzzling paradoxes" which enshroud certain great human problems and the "long range perspective required to see and understand them."

Braithwaite:

I knew Alain Locke for over forty years, the roots of our friendship and associations being embedded in the year of his studies for his doctorate at Harvard. He had returned from Oxford and his Rhodes scholarship, flushed with the spirit of European culture. Having chosen philosophy as the instrument of his intellectual survey of human conduct and aspiration, he decided upon teaching as the profession in which to put his enlightened spirit to service. The cornerstone of the philosophic ideal was the determination of values and by them the estimation of conduct which affects human lives and relationships. Through teaching Alain Locke, during the long tenure of his professorship at Howard University, became a force and inspiration in the lives of young people for more than two generations. But it is as a man of letters that his most enduring reputation will rest. I would say a few words in regard to this aspect of his shining career because it was unique.

His philosophy developed into a study of aesthetic values, and he applied these values to confirm racial integrities. His aesthetic sensibilities might well have prompted him to manifest his ideals in the creative forms of verse, the drama, or fiction, if his intellectual necessity had not urged him to correct long-standing fallacies by applying a critical and interpretative wand to their misconceptions. He saw beyond the local, and detached the universal spirit of man, and sought to bring these segments of social and economic racial differences into a universal spiritual balance.

Karpman:

In Dr. Locke, intelligence, culture, and wisdom have combined in an unusual synthesis reflecting the finest of his race. But his contributions go beyond his race; they belong to all humanity. Dr. Locke was a multi-faceted personality which like a shining diamond brilliantly reflected many rays of light. Nothing reflects so much his versatility as the expressions given today by his friends, each one reflecting a different aspect of his personality.

He was the most cosmopolitan man I ever knew. He was cultured to the very tips of his finger nails. He had all but completely emancipated himself from the consciousness of color. In his presence, one did not feel that he was speaking to a Negro or to a particular human known as American, however intelligent, but to an urbane cosmopolitan. He was an unusual personality, a great man even among the great. His achievements are not conspicuous or spectacular, or of the type for which people arrange parades or erect monuments. But his influence has penetrated millions of human souls. His achievements are durable and lasting, and their influence will carry him for many generations to come . . . He gave the Negro an individuality to a greater degree than the race had ever known before. He gave him dreams to dream, but dreams that could be fulfilled, visions that could be attained; he gave him a sense of belonging, a cause to struggle for. More than anyone else, he contributed to removing from the Negro the stigma of inferiority and gave him social and human dignity as Emerson and Thoreau a century before gave it to the American. He gave the Negro a consciousness of being a part of mankind in general, a partner in man's creative progress. Many a Negro today walks with straighter gait, holding his head high in any company, because of Alain Locke.

Du Bois:

Alain Locke was a man who deliberately chose the intellectual life; not as a desirable relief from reality, but as a vocation compared with which all else was of little account. In a land like America and among a group as inexperienced as American Negroes this was simply not understandable. That a man in the midst of money-making or gambling should at intervals devote some time to thought itself or to the bases of human reason, is to our day possible if not profitable. But to give a life to thinking and its meaning, that is to most Americans quite inexplicable. So that to many this lonely figure, who spoke quietly and smiled with restraint, became often an object of pity if not evil gossip and ridicule.

Yet in truth Alain Locke stood singular in a stupid land as a rare soul who pursued for nearly half a century, steadily and unemotionally, the only end of man which justifies his living and differentiates him from the beast and bird; and that is the inquiry as to what the universe is and why; how it exists and how it may change. The paths pointed out by Socrates and Aristotle, Bacon and Descartes, Kant and Hegel, Marx and Darwin, were the ones Locke followed and which inevitably made him unknown and unknowable to a time steeped in the lore of Micky Spillane. And yet in Locke's life lay a certain fine triumph. He knew life's greater things: pictures and poetry, music and drama, conversation which was not filth, laughter not clownish, and appetites which never fell to cheap lust. His severe logic, his penetrating analysis, his wide reading gave him a world within, sparsely peopled to be sure, but finely furnished and unforgettable in breadth and depth. It built a man not fit for war, but nobly courageous and simply consistent, who could bear pain and disappointment and yet live and work. For his dark companions he had faith and fellowship; for their smaller problems advice and guidance. But for himself he had only truth . . . .

His quest for truth and logic was no easy task. It was often contradictory and disappointing. It either appealed in vain to understanding or found no understanding to which it could appeal. It was a thankless task to those who see life as money, notoriety or dirt. And yet its faithful pursuit is more than living. It is more than death.

We may mourn that his latter days of hard-earned leisure could not have lasted longer. But perhaps he would say if he spoke now, that life is not length of days nor plethora of pleasure but satisfaction of work attempted, and that surely he had.[3]

Indeed, Locke was a great person; some of his friends were tempted to call him Saint Locke.

NOTES

1. Elisabeth Young-Bruehl, *Hannah Arendt: For Love of the World*, (New Haven: Yale University Press, 1982), pp. 315–316.

2. This biographical sketch prefaced Locke's essay, "Values and Imperatives," in *American Philosophy, Today and Tomorrow*, eds. Sidney

Hook and Horace M. Kallen (New York: Lee Furman, 1935), pp. 313–333.

3. Locke's funeral orations' entitled ''The Passing of Alain Leroy Locke,'' were published in the 1954 issue, Volume 15, of *Phylon*.

ALAIN LOCKE
AND
PHILOSOPHY

1   WHAT IS BLACK PHILOSOPHY?

I

It is difficult to render a precise definition of philosophy. Its meaning varies from culture to culture and from philosopher to philosopher. To Plato philosophy meant one thing, to Hume it meant another, and to Dewey, still another. To a Black philosopher such as Alain Locke, philosophy takes on a meaning and a function entirely different from that ascribed to it by any of the above. These differences are the focus of this chapter: specifically, what constitutes Black philosophy? The answer to this question is considered in this chapter and in chapter 12.

People normally think of philosophy as primarily an academic discipline, differentiated into specialized areas such as logic, epistemology, aesthetics, ethics, and metaphysics. This conception of philosophy was in large part promulgated by Plato and Aristotle, in whom the entire intellectual tradition of the Western world has its origin. In modern times, this specialization and the resulting fragmentation of philosophy have increased. Contemporary philosophy, especially the Pragmatic branch, has for the most part modeled itself on the experimental method of science, a development for which Charles Peirce (1839–1914) is largely responsible. Since the times of Plato and Aristotle, and especially since the first part of this century, there has been increased interest in ''analytic philosophy'' which relies heavily on the scientific method.

During this time, there has been a correspondingly decreased interest in the study of values, examined within the social context. This trend is one of Locke's main criticisms of contemporary philosophy. Philosophers seem to have become disinterested in making philosophy practical, as Socrates had tried to do in his own time and as Black philosophers have tried to do since the turn of the century. Associating Socrates with Black philosophers is not an attempt to mislead the reader. Over 2,000 years separate the life of Socrates and the lives of Black American philosophers, and there are admittedly sharp differences between ancient Greek and Black American cultures. Nevertheless, ideals such as freedom and justice, which concern both Socrates and Black philosophers, are timeless and cut across cultures. The two cultures have more in common than might initially be expected.

Socrates is of particular interest in this context because he provides a model for understanding Black philosophy. Few people question Socrates' status as a philosopher, yet many people are so accustomed to think of philosophy as a specialized academic discipline, from which, traditionally, most Black thinkers have been excluded, that they may have problems understanding the nature of Black philosophy. Such people may even doubt the existence of a "Black philosophy." This chapter posits that a Black philosophic tradition exists and that it has much in common with the tradition of Socrates.

We begin with a brief consideration of the basic activities and philosophic orientation of Socrates, followed by an examination of the activities of certain Black thinkers. This examination will offer a better sense of what constitutes Black philosophy, by demonstrating that Black philosophy usually originates within the community and seeks to examine issues of justice.

Unlike Plato and Aristotle, Socrates was not a wealthy man. He owned few material goods, mingled with the poor, for whom he felt compassion, and spent much of his career pointing out to the rich and powerful in particular that they were living lives of illusion and ignorance. He saw ignorance as the ultimate evil, the source of all wrongdoing; he saw knowledge as an intrinsic good toward which everyone ought to strive.

Socrates lived during a period when Athens was undergoing political, social, and moral crises associated with the Peloponne-

sian War. Athens attempted to provide a political solution to
the crises by instituting a dictatorship of the Thirty Oligarchs,
of whom the Sophist Critias was the key leader. This government
was repressive and viewed Socrates' philosophic activities as a
threat to its stability. Socrates was criticized and punished for
being a social critic. The government ordered him to refrain from
his diatribes: it is reported that Critias told Socrates "to give your
clobbers and donkeys a rest."[1]

Critias and others had diagnosed Athens' crises as a political
problem which required a dictatorship for its solution. The heart
of the problem as Socrates saw it, however, was human ignorance and prejudice; the solution lay in knowledge, the application of reason to understanding human nature and society.
Reason, he believed, would enable the individual to gain self-
mastery by discovering the principles that govern actions. Socrates believed that an individual had to learn to master himself/
herself before mastering others. In this view, reason has a twofold function: it liberates persons from the tyranny of ignorance
and at the same time binds them to principled normative standards. By using reason to overcome ignorance and prejudice, the
individual can develop his or her unique potential. Socrates felt
that the state had prevented the development of human potential because the state was ruled by ignorant men whose actions
were motivated by power, passion, and wealth, creating injustices against the ruled.

Socrates thus saw the Athenian state as problematic because
it was ruled through ignorance, force, and might rather than
through reason. His philosophic program, therefore, was directed toward the state, which he set out to change by practicing
civil disobedience. He violated what he called "the unjust laws
of the state" in order to expose these laws. In doing so, he
appealed to the higher law of conscience or reason.

The state became the classroom where Socrates practiced his
social philosophy, and the Athenian citizens were his students.
Ironically, he admitted that he had nothing to teach, no philosophic truth to impart. He admitted that, unlike the gods, he
was not a wise man; rather, he was wise only insofar as he knew
that he knew nothing. His teaching took the form of midwifery
whereby he assisted people in exposing their ignorance, in de-

livering their own insights, and in reexamining their stereotyped assumptions.

In describing his ethical mission in relation to the state, he saw himself as a gadfly. According to this metaphor, the state, because of human ignorance, laziness, and social habits, had a tendency to become sluggish, as if recovering from a long sleep and injustices crept in. The gadfly awakened the state, as a horsefly awakens a lazy horse. The awakened state might fulfill its ethical obligations to its citizens and reciprocally benefit its citizens. Socrates believed that the state must constantly be prodded into performing right actions.

Socrates was much more revolutionary in his political outlook than Plato and less utopian. Socrates challenged the society in which he lived and took risks; Plato was less practical and sought security in philosophic contemplation. Plato's political philosophy, as expressed in *The Republic*, insists on the importance of the strong ruler, the philosopher-king, who alone, through the use of reason, grasps the principles of conduct and imposes those principles on the earthly state. In Plato's state there was less need for the gadfly and for civil disobedience because, if the philosopher-king ruled well, in conformity with the light of reason, there would be little or no need for change and revolution. If the state were organized according to the vision of the ruler, Plato postulated, justice would almost automatically prevail provided all persons found their place in the state and performed functions best suited to their nature.

Because of Socrates' revolutionary view, coupled with his insistence on the importance of reason in criticizing society, it will become clear that his political philosophy provides a model for examining Black philosophy. Or, as the case may be, Black philosophy provides a model for understanding Socrates. Most of the Black philosophers, like Socrates, were concerned with the problems of social injustice, and, also like Socrates, most Black thinkers carried out their philosophic programs within the social context. Social philosophy, including ethics, political philosophy, aesthetics, and the philosophy of education, is thus characteristic of both Socrates' thought and of Black philosophy. Human beings are the primary focus. (It should be noted that the available evidence does not indicate that Socrates himself was a slaveholder, although he lived in a slaveholding society, which we may assume he found acceptable. Most Black philosophers would doubtless criticize Socrates for not aggressively attacking the Greeks' practice of slavery.)

Most of the Black philosophers, except perhaps Martin Luther King, Jr., and Locke, were not consciously imitating Socrates. We may doubt whether Booker T. Washington studied the works of Socrates carefully, although W.E.B. Du Bois knew Socrates well but probably did not intend to copy him. That these two did not consciously follow Socrates, however, does not make them less Socratic in their philosophic activities. Locke, on the other hand, specifically referred to himself as a Socratic midwife,[2] and in King's civil rights activities, he clearly exemplifies the Socratic gadfly.

There is another sense in which Socrates saw the relationship of philosophy to the social realm. Plato and Aristotle defined philosophy as the "love of wisdom" which "begins in wonder"; they understood philosophy to be a luxury which the isolated individual enjoys at leisure. Plato built his Academy and Aristotle his Lyceum to provide for such luxury and leisure. In contrast, Socrates saw philosophy as beginning in perplexities and social crises. And so, for Black philosophers, philosophy is neither luxury nor leisure for the isolated individual. It involves a struggle against the unjust society from which it arises and against which it is primarily directed.

The social dimension of Socrates' philosophy is evident in his use of the dialectic method: philosophic activity involves dialogues between the thinker and the community. At the expense of risking his or her own life, the thinker investigates and criticizes the beliefs, assumptions, and prejudices of the community. The dialectic unfolds in the following way: thesis, antithesis, and synthesis resulting in a social harmony whereby conflicts are reconciled and universal harmony prevails. Such philosophic activities generate tensions, conflicts, and contradictions within the community and within the individual. As Hegel and Marx subsequently insisted, such conflicts and contradictions are the means by which social changes are brought about and justice established. King also made use of the social dialectic in his attack on racial segregation.

II

Individualism, as encouraged by both the Protestant ethos and capitalism, is pervasive in American society. Because of slavery, segregation, and group suffering, the spirit of individualism is less pervasive among Blacks than within the larger society. Thus among themselves, American Blacks as a race tend to be more cooperative and less competitive than their white counterparts. In the 1920s Locke observed the feeling of unity among Blacks:

With this generation of Negro poets, a folk temperament flowers and a race experience bears fruit. Race is often a closer spiritual bond than nationality and group experience deeper than an individual's: here we have beauty that is born of long-suffering, truth that is derived from mass emotion and founded on collective vision. The spiritual search and discovery which is every artist's is in this case more than the personal; it is the epic reach and surge of a people seeking their group character through art.[3]

Although Locke made this comment in reference to Black poets, it is equally applicable to Black philosophers. The most revealing aspect of this passage, in reference to the above remarks about the nature of social philosophy, is that he holds that truth is "founded on collective vision." What he means by this phrase will be made clear in the sequel. His observation coincides with the thesis advanced here that Black philosophic activity arises out of the Black community and that it attempts to deal with problems that both the Black community and American society face.

Although Black freedom fighters during the slavery era engaged in philosophic activities in the broad sense described above, my present purpose is to examine Black philosophy as it emerged at the turn of the century and as it developed to the present. The contrasting views of Booker T. Washington and W.E.B. Du Bois, as well as those of King and Locke require consideration. Washington, Du Bois, and King will be studied in turn, with occasional reference to Locke. Because this book is mainly about Locke, this first chapter is devoted primarily to outlining the views of the above-mentioned thinkers.

Washington appeared at a critical time in American history. Like Socrates, he emerged amidst cultural crises. The South had been defeated by the North, and the smoke from the Civil War guns still lingered in the air. The Congressional Act of Reconstruction had disillusioned Southerners and especially Blacks. Because of such political failures, the country was still in the process of deciding what to do with its newly freed Blacks. They had been excluded from political participation. The cotton industry had continued to thrive, and, as a result, there was increasing demand for Black laborers.

Blacks were attracted to factories in the North which they thought offered them economic opportunity; between 1900 and the end of World War I, Southern rural Blacks migrated to industrialized Northern cities, where they faced additional problems. They encountered racial prejudice and resentments from which they had tried to escape by leaving the plantation South, and they experienced joblessness, overcrowded housing, street crime, and other social ills typical of urban industrial life. These problems affected American people generally, not just Blacks. Although Pragmatism emerged as a response to these problems, it failed to address the problem of racial injustice.

The Southern-born Washington, a former slave, offered a philosophy of hope for these Blacks, although his main interest was in the rural Black masses. Washington shared in the American dream that success could come through hard work, conviction, and initiative. He inspired rural Blacks with this dream, and he believed that Blacks, both as individuals and as a race, could ultimately overcome the ill effects of slavery.

The development of Washington's philosophy parallels the development of indigenous American philosophy, notably Pragmatism. Pragmatism sought to give a formal philosophic justification to the American dream. Pragmatism is basically a theory of meaning, concerned primarily with offering a novel method for clarifying and ascertaining the meaning of beliefs. It emerged at a time when America was facing problems, some already mentioned, brought on by rapid industrialization. These included clashes between old and new beliefs and values, and tension between tradition and technological-scientific progress. Pragmatism assumed that in order to solve such problems a new

way of thinking was needed, that people needed to think scientifically about social problems.

Pragmatism as conceived by Charles Sander Peirce (1839–1914),
William James (1842–1910), and John Dewey (1859–1952) stresses
the practical side of human experience. Each, in various ways,
insisted that the meaning of a belief is ascertained by seeing
what practical effect the consequences of the belief might have
on the environment. A belief is meaningful if the consequences
of the action to which it gives rise work—that is, if its consequences enable the individual to enjoy success. A meaningless
belief, on the other hand, is one whose consequences do not
work and do not lead to success. By emphasizing the practical
side of experience, Pragmatism essentially echoes the basic ethos
of pioneering America: success, self-confidence, belief, conviction, action, and progress.

Washington probably never read the works of the Pragmatists,
but the spirit of Pragmatism was in the air during his time. As
will become evident shortly, his philosophy is in the spirit of
that of the American Pragmatists, notwithstanding the remarkable differences between the two. It will be seen that most views
of the Black philosophers are in effect a mixture of Socrates'
philosophy and Pragmatism, which results in a novel philosophy reflecting the Black experience. This mixture, however, is
in part coincidental. It is not strange that Black philosophy has
affinities with Pragmatism, for both originated in American culture. Du Bois and Locke were influenced by Pragmatism, but
each sought to outline his own philosophy of value in which
attitudes and feelings had a central place. Both beliefs and attitudes have a central place in Washington's philosophy, but he
gives no rigorous, formal analysis of them.

The core of Washington's philosophy was reflected in his celebrated 1895 Atlanta Address. There he outlined his thoughts
on economics and on the relationship between the races. His
speech began:

One-third of the population of the South is of Negro race. No enterprise
seeking the material, civil, or moral welfare of this section can disregard
this element of our population and reach the highest success. . . .

Not only this, but the opportunity here afforded will awaken among us a new era of industrial progress. Ignorant and inexperienced, it is not strange that in the first years of our new life we began at the top instead of at the bottom; that a seat in Congress or the state legislature was more sought than real estate or industrial skill; that the political convention or stump-speaking had more attractions than starting a dairy farm or truck garden.[4]

Then he introduced his metaphor of the "lost ship" which had an ambiguous meaning. Was it applicable to whites or Blacks, or both? He suggested that it had reference to both.

A ship lost at sea for many days suddenly sighted a friendly vessel. From the mast of the unfortunate vessel was seen a signal, "Water, water; we die of thirst!" The answer from the friendly vessel at once came back, "Cast down your bucket where you are." A second time the signal, "Water, water; send us water!"ran up from the distressed vessel, and was answered, "Cast down your bucket where you are."[5]

He was telling Black people that they were surrounded by opportunities among Southern whites; he felt that Blacks had no need to migrate to other places. Nor did Southern whites have the need to turn to other people or things as a source of labor. Washington, however, did not foresee the day when the farming industry would become mechanized—tractors replacing mules, automated cotton pickers replacing Black hands—and Southern Blacks would be forced off the land. Automation and high technology have also replaced many factory workers, Blacks included, in the North. Neither Washington nor, for that matter, Dewey and other advocates of technology anticipated this consequence of technology.

Washington insisted that both races should recognize the importance of the principle of reciprocity in economic life. Blacks would offer their labor and service to whites who owned most of the material resources and the means of production, whereas whites would give Blacks the opportunity to utilize their labor in agriculture and in industry, and to acquire property and skills so as to develop their own economic base and create their own community. Only in this way could both races move progressively forward.

Indeed, Washington believed in progress, as did John Dewey

and Henry Ford, yet he differed from the Pragmatists in that he was not a professional or academic philosopher and was not concerned with the narrow epistemological problem of clarifying the meaning of beliefs. Washington, Du Bois, and King were all men of action. They were concerned with the problem of meaning in the widest sense, such as in the question of what Blacks and people generally must do to enjoy meaning in life. Certain Pragmatists were also concerned with this broad question, but they were more preoccupied with the limited sense of meaning mentioned above, that is, ascertaining the practical effect of beliefs.

Washington also told whites and Blacks that, although they should work together in the American economy, they should remain separate in social matters. He thereby ruled out racial integration. He suggested that Blacks and whites traverse parallel paths, and he used the "hand" metaphor to convey this message: "In all things that are purely social we can be as separate as the fingers, yet one as the hand in all things essential to mutual progress." This statement reflected Washington's position on race relationship: Blacks and whites were to accept racial segregation. Most Blacks agreed with his position, but some, such as Du Bois, found it totally unacceptable. Du Bois and his followers thought this view compromised the political and civil rights of Blacks. This relationship between Washington and Du Bois is discussed below.

Washington applied his philosophy in concrete ways through his educational program and his political activities. In 1881 he founded Tuskegee Institute, which was designed to train Blacks in industrial and agricultural skills so that they might become useful citizens. Philosophy and other humanities courses did not have any importance in Tuskegee's curriculum and were emphasized much later and only after Washington's death. Washington glorified the craftsman and had little interest in those who possessed only "book-learning." Socrates also prized the craftsman, whom he considered less pretentious than the poet and the politician. Here again Du Bois disagreed with and criticized Washington; Du Bois insisted that humanities courses were as important as vocational and technical courses.

Between 1895 and 1915, Washington exercised enormous political power, influencing both whites and Blacks, Northerners and Southerners. Whites credited him with being a leader of both races, and several Presidents of the United States often turned to him for advice on issues pertaining to Blacks.

Washington's midwifery role is manifest in his political activities. His speeches and deeds were intended to help whites realize who Blacks were and who they could be if allowed the opportunity to be truly free. His speeches also helped whites and Blacks discover who they were in relationship to each other. People tend to develop an image of themselves based on how they appear to others. As Hegel suggests, the slave and the master define themselves in terms of each other; each confirms the identity of the other. Washington intended his famous autobiography, *Up From Slavery* (1900), to play this midwifery role. Both races widely accepted this work, but Washington's critics questioned his effectiveness in delivering accurate knowledge about Black people. Du Bois repeatedly suggested that Washington only reinforced the whites' belief in their superiority to Blacks and the Blacks' belief in their inferiority to whites.

As a philosopher and educator, Washington wrote no systematic philosophical treatise. Like Socrates he was interested in taking philosophy directly to the people, in order to route the injustices Blacks suffered. He especially wanted Blacks to realize their own potential, which he thought could be facilitated through the acquisition of industrial and agricultural skills. The skilled Black masses would become Socratic midwives by disseminating skills to the community.

Washington was also a gadfly, but he played this role in a mild and careful manner so as not to offend whites and he admonished Black "militants" not to offend whites. He recognized lynching and the Jim Crow laws as unjust, yet he did not openly, aggressively advocate changing these practices and laws. He believed that once Blacks and whites were educated and Blacks had acquired an adequate economic base, these injustices would automatically be abolished and whites would accept Blacks as citizens. Hence, Blacks had no need to advocate political and civil rights, or at least, so he told whites. Yet he quietly took steps to support anti-lynching laws. Thus, unlike Socrates and King, Washington was behind the scenes, a kind of invisible gadfly. Because of this invisibility, many Blacks and most whites came to look on Washington as a "yes-man," as an "Uncle Tom." Some of his critics maintained that many whites saw this "Uncle Tom" image as an accurate representation of Blacks. Locke and other Harlem Renaissance writers tried to dispel this image, replacing it with what they called the "New Negro," a concept discussed later in this book.

III

The ideas of Washington and Du Bois present many parallels and contrasts. Du Bois was born to free parents in Great Barrington, Massachusetts, in 1868; Washington, whose mother was a slave and whose father was a free white, was born in Virginia around 1863. Du Bois' political base was the industrial North. Both men attained major social leadership roles: Du Bois emphasized the importance of what was called the "Black Elite" or the "Talented Tenth" whose job was to inspire and uplift the Black masses; Washington attributed leadership to the masses, insisting that they alone, not the Elite, would uplift the Black community. Ironically, Washington's role in the Black community demonstrated the opposite; he alone was perceived as *the* Black leader. In contrast, Du Bois thought that social leadership trickled down to the masses from the Elite. Washington preferred manual training over art, science, and the humanities; Du Bois was more Elitist, perhaps because of his own educational experience at Harvard and in Berlin. "Education and work," Du Bois wrote,

are the levers to uplift a people. Work alone will not do it unless inspired by the right ideals and guided by intelligence. Education must not simply teach work—it must teach Life. The Talented Tenth of the Negro race must be made leaders of thought and missionaries of culture among their people. No others can do this work and Negro colleges must train men for it. The Negro race, like all other races, is going to be saved by its exceptional men.[6]

In emphasizing this notion of the Talented Tenth, Du Bois and Locke had more in common with Plato than with Socrates.

Their Talented Tenth was in some ways comparable to Plato's philosopher-king whose job was to uplift the masses from the Cave of Illusion, where they were enslaved by ignorance, unable to distinguish image from reality.

The institution of slavery that existed in this country can also be compared to Plato's Cave. Slavery stripped Blacks of their cultural heritage, because they lived in a segregated society where they were denied freedom and adequate education. The Talented Tenth was to liberate Blacks from the Cave of Ignorance which was slavery—hence the importance of educating the Talented Tenth. This position conflicted with Washington's and also contrasted sharply with that of King, who looked on the entire Black masses as the Talented Tenth. According to King, the Black masses had a spiritual mission to uplift humanity generally.

In spite of the Elitism in Du Bois and Locke, they treated philosophy as primarily an activity applicable to solving social problems and to creating a just society. Du Bois and Locke were trained in philosophy, although neither saw himself as a professional philosopher. Francis L. Broderick reports that William James, one of Du Bois' teachers, discouraged Du Bois from pursuing philosophy as a career; perhaps James thought that Du Bois did not have the intellectual power to be a philosopher. Apparently Du Bois accepted James' advice because he pursued social science, "with a view to the ultimate application of its principles to the social and economic rise of the Negro People."[7] Either James did not give this same advice to Locke, or Locke did not accept it.

Like Du Bois, Locke did not see himself as a professional philosopher; rather, he regarded himself "as a philosophic midwife to a generation of younger Negro poets, writers, artists." This description also applies to Du Bois, who, like Locke, worked with Black writers, artists, and scholars, assisting them in developing their works. Du Bois and Locke were especially instrumental in this midwifery role during the Harlem Renaissance and during their tenures at Atlanta University and Howard University, respectively. Du Bois' *Souls of Black Folk* (1903) and Locke's *The New Negro* (1925) may be seen as midwifery tools, intended to enable people, both Black and white, to develop a more accurate understanding of the experiences of Black people and to dispel the image of Blacks created by Washington and by slavery.

Like Washington, Du Bois was politically active and visible, much more so than Locke who seems to have been eclipsed by Du Bois. Although Du Bois saw the society as the source of the problems Blacks suffered, his philosophy was in part formulated in opposition to Washington, whom he felt had misdirected Blacks. In 1905, Du Bois formed what came to be known as the Niagara Movement. Its purpose was twofold: (1) to oppose Washington's political machine and (2) to agitate for the political and civil rights of Blacks. The National Association for the Advancement of Colored People (NAACP), formed in 1910, grew out of the Niagara Movement.

The NAACP's philosophic orientation and method were quite different from Washington's, and it was largely infused with Du Bois' ideas and character. Washington's program was steeped in the tradition and ethos of the South, which he was careful not to upset too much. Certainly Washington desired social changes, but he preferred that they occur quietly and gradually. To this end, he appealed mostly to the good-will of Southern whites. Du Bois and the NAACP adopted a much more aggressive, open strategy: legal agitation. The NAACP became an active Socratic gadfly, prodding society to practice its principles of democracy. Du Bois himself was a gadfly in his own right, although his personality was more reserved than Washington's, yet more outgoing than Locke's. More importantly, he felt that the Talented Tenth as a whole should act as midwives and gadflies. These were its philosophic missions.

The NAACP, as well as similar organizations and movements within the Black community, served as forums in which Black thinkers and leaders engaged in philosophic discussions which were not merely academic. Such discussions were intended to formulate policies keyed to directing social change. Such forums were often instrumental in initiating dialogues and action within the Black community, which led to the civil rights movements of the 1960s and early 1970s.

Du Bois, like Locke, was greatly influenced by the American Pragmatists, and like Washington he shared in the American dream of progress. Du Bois was a prolific writer, often incorporating philosophic views from many sources into his own works, always attempting to apply these to problems of racial injustice. His career extends nearly a century. In view of the diversity and complexity of Du Bois' philosophic activities, the bulk of the philosophic problems with which he was concerned cannot be covered here.

One of the basic philosophic problems which Du Bois explored was one that concerned American Pragmatists and Black philosophers: the nature of community life in America. Each in his own way recognized that community life in America was problematic. James, Royce, and Dewey agreed that the competitive spirit of capitalism, increased industrialization, and the principle of individualism, among other factors, militated against community life. Most Black philosophers, however, saw these as secondary, not primary, factors. In their eyes the primary factors had to do with racial oppression, the removal of which, as Du Bois clearly suggested, would do more to create a genuine community for all people. The American Pragmatists largely sidestepped the problems of race; neither Du Bois nor Locke ignored them. Additionally, both Du Bois and Locke focused on the Black Elite and the Black masses in explaining Black cultural contributions.

Like Du Bois, Locke subscribed to the principle of Elitism. Locke and, to a lesser degree, Du Bois argued that the Black masses or what he called the Folk were important in the development of cultural values. He considered the Folk to be the key source of cultural elements. During the Harlem Renaissance and throughout his career, Locke encouraged the Elite—artists, writers, and scholars—to draw from the folk experience in developing culture.

However, Du Bois and Locke differed in four important ways. First, Du Bois insisted that cultural values primarily pertained to the genteel tradition, and he encouraged the Elite to draw from that tradition.

Second, Du Bois insisted that Black art should be conscious propaganda, with a political message, whereas Locke in *The New Negro* held that Black art should be solely for the sake of art. Francis L. Broderick in his *W.E.B. Du Bois* notes the difference between Du Bois and Locke on this matter:

Locke's thesis pushed too far would turn the [Harlem] renaissance into decadence, DuBois warned, because if the Negro ignored the fight and tried to do pretty things, he would kill the beauty in his art. DuBois's prescription for short stories in the *Crisis* showed the gulf between him and Locke: he [DuBois] demanded fiction "clear, realistic and frank, and yet fiction which shows the possible if not the actual triumph of good and true and beautiful things." [8]

Third, Du Bois held that Blacks could be liberated from the Cave of Oppression or Ignorance by achieving political and civil equality through legal agitation. Locke did not deny the importance of legal agitation, nor did he deny the importance of political and civil equality, but he felt that cultural equality was equally important, provided such equality took place within a pluralistic society. His insistence on the cultural equality of Blacks provided a balance to the economic, political, and legal equality that Marcus Garvey, Du Bois, and King offered.

Fourth, Du Bois acted out his gadfly role in his association with the NAACP and in other political activities. Locke's gadfly role was manifested primarily through his scholarship, and as a philosopher he was interested in interpreting the Black cultural experience and in criticizing the larger society. Like Socrates, he was an inspiration to gifted Blacks, the Talented Tenth. He thought that the demonstration of their creative achievements would motivate whites to respect these gifted Blacks and their works and eventually to respect the Black masses generally.

Locke wrote:

For successful peoples are rated, and rate themselves, in terms of their best. Racial and national prestige is, after all, the product of the exceptional few. So when Negro life begins to produce poets, artists, thinkers and to make creative contributions that must be recognized not only as outstanding but as nationally representative, the old attitudes become untenable. [9]

IV

Like Du Bois and Locke, Martin Luther King, Jr., was trained in philosophy, but he differed from most traditional philosophers in also having formal training in theology. During his career he successfully combined these two fields and applied them to the racial problems in America. King admired certain traditional philosophers, such as Socrates, Kant, Hegel, Bentham, Mill, and Marx who were concerned with political and moral issues. Because of Marx's concern with the oppressed class, King held that Marx's theory possessed merit, but King never accepted it in its entirety; he felt it was incompatible with Christianity and with religion generally. He was also critical of most traditional philosophers for not making God the cornerstone of their ethical-political systems, for having neglected the spiritual side of human nature, and for downplaying the principle of love, as in the teaching of Jesus.

In the realm of religion and theology King was most influenced by Jesus, Gandhi, Reinhold Neibuhr, Martin Buber, and Walter Rauschenbuch. The last-named inspired King to make religion practical by relating it not only to the spiritual, but also to the social and economic dimensions. People cannot live by spirit alone, King insisted.

In King's capacity as a Socratic midwife, he was not interested in mere academic discussion or debate of philosophic issues. In some of his works, however, he did give a philosophic analysis of racism, and the provided philosophic justification for massive civil disobedience and mass demonstrations. As a midwife, King was interested in liberating Blacks and whites from myths created by racism and segregation. He particularly wanted to destroy the myth of the racial inferiority of Blacks and to replace it with a sense of pride and racial dignity; he wanted to disabuse whites of their notion of superiority and to replace it with a sense of respect and brotherly love for all people.

As a "social surgeon" King viewed racism as a social cancer, rapidly eating away at the moral fiber of the United States and affecting both Blacks and whites. Such was his diagnosis of the nation's major problem. As a social surgeon, he offered a prescription and performed the operation, which took the form of civil disobedience. His prescription called for the wholesale desegregation of all public facilities in the North and South, and granting Blacks their full political rights as citizens. He thought that these could best be achieved in a racially integrated society.

Here is a sharp difference between Washington and King. As

shown in his public addresses and writings, Washington, many of his critics claim, sought to exonerate whites and to blame Blacks for their problems. Du Bois and others criticized Washington for this position. In contrast, Du Bois, Locke, and King blamed whites for the Blacks' problems. King urged that the entire country must courageously struggle together to end social injustice.

Among Washington, Du Bois, Locke, and King, King came closest to fitting the description of the Socratic gadfly, and was one with Socrates himself. Hanes Walton, Jr., has observed the similarity between King and Socrates:

Martin Luther King, Jr., guided by a vision of a "beloved community" on earth, was a social critic of the sort whose role in relation to society was classically stated by the fifth-century teacher and founder of political philosophy, Socrates, who, when accused by the Athenian government of introducing new gods and of corrupting the youth, defended himself.[10]

Unlike King, however, Socrates played the gadfly role as a single individual. Socrates would probably have been less effective if he had struggled alone to change a society as complex and vast as the American society which King attempted to transform. Whereas Socrates had acted alone as a gadfly, King organized and involved thousands of Americans—Blacks, whites, Protestants, Catholics, and Jews—and encouraged them to be gadflies for the cause of justice. They were to practice civil disobedience and violate the unjust laws of segregation which had divided this country since the days of slavery. In doing so, they often suffered grave consequences such as imprisonment and even death. One wonders whether Socrates would have pressed on in the face of bullwhips, bombings, jail cells, firehoses, and George Wallace had he been in the prime of life as King had been. (Socrates was executed in old age.)

The other feature that distinguishes Socrates' philosophic activities from King's was that Socrates rested his activities on reason and knowledge. Although King did not overlook their importance, the principle of Christian love, not knowledge or reason alone, was the basis of his civil disobedience and nonviolence. Thus, he successfully combined Jesus' notion of love with Gandhi's notion of nonviolence, and these became the guiding ideals of the Southern Christian Leadership Conference. King attempted to eliminate racism through the use of nonviolent direct action. Only in this way, he believed, could the Beloved Community, modeled on the Christian concept of community, be established. He wanted to infuse the country with love, which he saw as an alternative to the hate, violence, and aggression which characterized the old order. He dreamed of racial integration, and he opposed such people as the American Black Muslims and the younger Malcolm X, who opted for a racially separated society. And he opposed all forms of revolution which involved violence such as the one envisaged by Frantz Fanon in his *The Wretched of the Earth.*

King saw nonviolence as a means and as an end in itself because he felt that nonviolence should be the principle around which the Beloved Community, once created, became organized. In his view, means and ends were intertwined. He also regarded love as both a means and an end in itself.

Neither Washington, Du Bois, nor Locke stressed love as a basis for community life to the same degree that King did. Neither did they emphasize integration as King had done. Washington evoked the principle of friendship, which he thought should govern the relations between Blacks and whites, and he suggested that the spirit of fraternity should thrive in a Black community which was to be separate from the white community. Much the same is true for Du Bois, although, it will be recalled, he wavered between the ideal of integration and separation. In Locke the principle of tolerance was basic for the Black community and for American society generally. He encouraged whites to be tolerant of the manifest differences of Blacks and other minorities and not attempt to destroy such differences.

King shared Washington's, Du Bois', and, to a lesser degree, Locke's belief in social progress. King believed that social progress would ultimately result in the Beloved Community. His notion of progress was derived from Hegel's sense of the dialectical process, which can ultimately be traced back to the Socratic tradition. In contrast, Washington's notion of progress was quite un-Hegelian because he did not place a positive value on social conflicts through which, in the Hegelian tradition, progress emerges. Locke's notion was similar to Washington's. King said that Hegel's conception of philosophic truth and his dialectic appealed to him: "His [Hegel's] contention that 'truth is the whole' led me to a philosophic method of rational coherence. His analysis of the dialectical process helped me to see that growth comes through struggle."[11] Hegel's world hero, as described in his philosophy of history, is comparable to the great men whom King admired, namely, Socrates, Jesus, Buddha, and Gandhi. Each was a cosmic agent of historical change, as was King himself. The chief difference between these and Hegel's hero is that Hegel's often employed violence to produce social changes, whereas the other figures did not.

Because King was committed to the philosophy of nonviolence, it is difficult to see how he could reconcile it with Hegel's view of social progress. In Hegel, good and evil, violence and nonviolence, creation and destruction are but moments in the historical flow. Thus, Hegel would say, and probably quite rightly, that the violence which King objected to and other negative elements are dialectically necessary, part of the logic of history, without which there can be no progress. It follows that one of the basic contradictions in King's philosophy was his insistence on an Hegelian conception of social progress while rejecting altogether the principle of violence.

Washington, Du Bois, Locke, and King made significant contributions to social and Black philosophy and were instrumental in improving social and political conditions for Black people and for people generally. But the struggle which these men generated must continue; as in a war, Blacks must hold the ground they have gained and whenever possible continue to strive collectively for higher ground. The struggle of Black people is an eternal one. The gadfly's task is never finished.

Traditionally, Black philosophers, especially those with whom we have been concerned here, were not philosophers in the same way as Plato, Aristotle, Thomas Aquinas, Kant, Hegel, Peirce, James, and Dewey. Admittedly, James and Dewey, like Alfred North Whitehead, saw difficulties with the overspecialization of philosophy and thought their own philosophic works avoided such difficulties. It is questionable, however, whether they altogether succeeded in overcoming such specialization. In many ways, for example, Dewey, who wrote extensively on social and moral problems, encouraged specialization: he was the high priest of technology and exalted the technological specialists, insisting that everyone should become specialists. Most of the Pragmatists accepted the methodology of science as the yardstick for all values, a view which Locke found objectionable.

The following chapter examines Locke's thoughts on values in order to clarify why he was critical of Pragmatism. But first let us briefly consider his overview of philosophy. In his "Values and Imperatives" he offers the following conception of philosophy:

All philosophies, it seems to me, are in ultimate derivation philosophies of life and not of abstract, disembodied "objective" reality; products of time, place and situation, and thus systems of timed history rather than timeless eternity. They need not even be so universal as to become the epitomized *rationale* of an age, but may merely be the lineaments of a personality, its temperament and dispositional attitudes projected into their systematic rationalizations.[12]

Most of the Pragmatists would probably accept certain aspects of Locke's conception of philosophy: namely, that "philosophies are not of abstract, disembodied 'objective' reality; products of time, place and situations," but they would have difficulty accepting other elements of Locke's conception according to which philosophies "may merely be the lineaments of a personality, its temperament and dispositional attitudes." Central to the philosophy of most Pragmatists is the notion of belief, of validity, which they maintain can be confirmed or refuted by the scientific method. As will be shown, Locke holds that all values, including ultimate values, are derived from attitudes.

Most Black philosophers would probably agree with Locke's entire conception of philosophy. Black philosophy here has been characterized as pertaining to the social and cultural settings of Blacks and as deriving largely from the personalities of Washington, Du Bois, King, and others. Does Locke not emphasize the social character of philosophy and the fact of personality from which it is derived? Although Locke does not try to define

Black philosophy per se and he speaks about philosophy in general, his view certainly coincides with my description of Black philosophy.

NOTES

1. Robert S. Brumbaugh, *The Philosophers of Greece* (New York: Crowell, 1964; Albany: State University of New York Press, 1981), p. 131.

2. See Alain Locke's autobiographical sketch, in "Values and Imperatives," *AmericanPhilosophy, Today and Tomorrow*, eds. Sidney Hook and Horace M. Kallen (New York: Lee Furman, 1935), p. 312.

3. Alain Locke, ed., *Four Negro Poets* (New York: Simon and Schuster, 1927), p. 5.

4. Booker T. Washington, *Up From Slavery* (New York: A. L. Burt Company, 1900), pp. 218–219.

5. Ibid., p. 219.

6. Cited in August Meier, Elliott Rudwick, and Francis L. Broderick, eds., *Black Protest Thought in the Twentieth Century*, 2d ed. (Indianapolis: Bobbs-Merrill Company, 1976), pp. 54–55. Originally cited in "The Talented Tenth," *The Negro Problem: A Series of Articles by Representative Negroes of To-day*, Booker T. Washington and others (New York: James Pott and Company, 1903), pp. 33–75 passim.

7. Francis L. Broderick, *W.E.B. Du Bois: Negro Leader in a Time of Crisis* (Stanford, Calif.: Stanford University Press, 1959), p. 16.

8. Ibid., 160.

9. Alain Locke, "The High Cost of Prejudice," *The Forum* 78 (December 1927): 503.

10. Hanes Walton, Jr., *The Political Philosophy of Martin Luther King, Jr.*, (Westport. Conn.: Greenwood Publishing Company, 1971), p. 5.

11. Martin Luther King, Jr., *Stride Toward Freedom* (New York: Harper and Brothers, 1958), p. 101.

12. Locke, "Values and Imperatives," p. 313.

2   ASPECTS OF ALAIN LOCKE'S AXIOLOGY

I

Alain Locke was a well-known cultural critic, scholar, teacher, writer, and interpreter of Black culture, roles enhanced by the publication of his *The New Negro* through which he provided leadership to the Harlem Renaissance. He was not as well known as a philosopher, however. This chapter shows that, in addition to his contribution to Black philosophy, he opened up new paths in professional philosophy, especially in the area of axiology. He outlined his views of axiology in his Ph.D. dissertation, "The Problem of Classification in the Theory of Values" (1918) and in his essay, "Values and Imperatives." Because the essay is a more mature formulation of the views considered in his dissertation, the focus here is on the essay in order to demonstrate not only how Locke may be regarded as a professional philosopher, but also how he contrasted with most Black philosophers: they did not attempt to make a formal analysis of a problem(s) in the same way that Locke did. Using this type of formal philosophy did not mean that Locke abandoned Black philosophy. He remained concerned with the Black experience and with applying philosophy to social conditions. The most pervasive theme in his works is the value conflicts among individuals and groups. "Values and Imperatives" illuminated the sources from which such conflicts arose and offered the means for reducing them.

Locke was able to penetrate to the core of a problem, interweave diverse ideas, and produce original insights. In discussing his "Values and Imperatives," the following problems are highlighted: (1) how objective values and their standards are grounded in subjective experience; (2) how value conflicts arise; and (3) how value conflicts can be reduced.

YES! (handwritten margin note)

II

"Values and Imperatives" was written with the conviction that American philosophy and other contemporary philosophical movements did not offer an adequate theory of values. One of Locke's objections to American philosophy was that in its flight from traditional metaphysics it associated itself too closely with experimental science. The criterion of values there stressed experimental results.

By placing a greater emphasis on the pragmatic consequences of the individual's actions, James and Dewey gave a different twist to American philosophy. They wrote that ideas, beliefs, and theories were merely tools for action and were to be tested in and through their consequences. This stress on practice, Locke felt, resulted in a certain type of absolutism which he called "a universal fundamentalism of values in action."[1] The common person, influenced by the virtues of Pragmatism, created absolutist attitudes toward the objects of his or her practical interests and projected these as valid "for all conditions, all times and all men."[2] Locke did not think that American philosophy in its reaction against traditional metaphysics had dispelled absolutes. American philosophy had merely transposed absolutes from the realm of being to the realm of practice, as manifested in the actions and attitudes of the intellectual and the common person. The trouble with this type of attitude, argued Locke, was that it bred value conflicts among individuals and groups and encouraged bigotry.

Both James and Dewey, and to some degree Royce, in formulating their value theories, attended to the emotional side of human experience, and both James and Dewey allowed for the principle of relativism. Against traditional philosophy, they agreed that normative principles were relative to individuals and groups. In this regard, Locke accepted their value theories, but he found their versions of Pragmatism problematic because they

dubious reading of Locke's perspective (handwritten margin note)

placed too much emphasis on consequences and not enough on preferences and attitudes. These, in Locke's view, were as important as pragmatic consequences:

Human behavior, it is true, is experimental, but it is also selectively preferential, and not always in terms of outer adjustments and concrete results. Value reactions guided by emotional preferences and affinities are as potent in the determination of attitudes [values] as pragmatic consequences are in the determination of actions. In the generic and best sense of the term "pragmatic", it is as important to take stock of the one as the other.[3]

Locke held that an effective value theory which paid attention to the emotional side of human experience should be developed along the lines of the works of Frantz Brentano, the father of modern value theory. Brentano's value theory demonstrated, as Locke himself wished to demonstrate, that objective values and their standards were in the subjective realm of the valuing processes, not in the realm of rational absolutes. Nor did they altogether lie in the empirical world.

Traditional value theories, including those in American philosophy, have erred in their search for objectivity by locating their standard outside the valuing process. The result has been two extremes, radical subjectivism and radical absolutism. The first, represented by the Protagoreans, holds that each individual is the measure of all things. The second, represented by the Kantians, maintains that certain values are universally valid for all rational beings. Locke's position lies between these two extremes:

The natural distinctions of values and their functional criteria surely lie somewhere in between the atomistic relativism of a pleasure-pain scale and the colorless, uniformitarian criterion of logic,—the latter more of a straight-jacket for value qualities than the old intellectualist trinity of Beauty, Truth and Good.[4]

III

Central to Locke's resolution of the subjectivism/objectivism problem is what he called feeling-reference or form-quality. These

refer to the basic feelings that underlie and create values and
their absolute norms. He often used feeling-reference and form-
quality interchangeably with attitudes and preferences; they corresponded to his other technical term value-mode. The moral,
religious, and aesthetic value-modes are normally used to distinguish between different types of value situations. These modes
are traditionally regarded as objective features of the world.

The relationship between attitudes and value-modes is that
one evokes or enjoys a certain attitude as one values a given
situation. The attitude in question creates, molds, and shapes
the value-mode and its standard, determines the nature of the
value, and induces us to regard the situation as good/bad, beau-
tiful/ugly, or holy/unholy. Locke identified four attitudes that
constitute the unity and diversity of values: exaltation, tension,
acceptance or agreement, and repose or equilibrium. These correspond, respectively, to different value-modes: the attitude (or
feeling) of exaltation creates the religious value and its norms;
tension creates the moral value and its norms; and so on. Stereotypes also play a fundamental role: they act as filters through
which a scene is judged, and they play a key role in acting as
mind-sets that sustain values. Locke maintained that values were
not fixed. They shifted as attitudes shifted; a given scene might
in one instance be regarded as ethical and in another instance
as religious. Hence the difference in value judgment.

Locke suggested that stereotypes were the means by which
values were fixed, stabilized and generalized. He seemed to be
using the term "stereotypes" much as traditional philosophers
such as Peirce, James, and Dewey used the term "habit"—James
regarded habits as the "fly-wheel of society." Hume, it will be
remembered, located the general principles of values in social
customs. He rejected the notion that the standards of values
were absolute. Locke, on the other hand, stated that in addition
to stereotypes, the categorical imperative, the universal element
of values, was given in the immediate context of the valuing
process. "It [the categorical imperative] supplies the clue to the
functional value norm,—being felt as good, beautiful, etc.—and
we have this event in mind when we say that in the feeling-
reference to some value-mode, some value ultimate becomes the

birthmark of the value."[5] Thus, each basic attitude of exaltation, tension, and so on, creates its own categorical imperative.

Kant's categorical imperative which was universal and absolute lay outside human nature; it existed in rationality alone and confronted the human will as a rational necessity. Locke's categorical imperatives were in human nature, in basic attitudes, and involved a psychological urgency or necessity "to construe the situation as of a particular qualitative form-character."[6] In this way we experience the categorical imperative which is a psychological absolute, yet functional and flexible; it is not an eternal principle derived from God or some other transcendent lawgiver.

Locke's conception of values and absolutes closely resembled Santayana's. Santayana explained how absolutes are created:

Our conscience and taste establish these ideals; to make a judgment is virtually to establish an ideal, and all ideals are absolute and eternal for the judgment that involves them, because in finding and declaring a thing good or beautiful, our sentence is categorical, and the standard evoked by our judgment is for that case intrinsic and ultimate. But at the next moment, when the mind is on another footing, a new ideal is evoked, no less absolute for the present judgment than the old ideal was for the previous one.[7]

Santayana's basic position was that all values spring from the irrational side of our nature. "If any preference or precept," Santayana maintained, "were declared to be ultimate and primitive, it would thereby be declared to be irrational, since mediation, inference, and synthesis are the essence of rationality."[8] Insofar as Locke emphasized the feeling side of values, which he regarded as primitive, he shared Santayana's view that values were largely irrational. Locke, however, did not hold the extreme position, that the rational faculty plays no role in the valuing process. His point seemed to be that in the initial stage of the valuing process feeling played a primary role, but in subsequent stages of the process feeling became secondary and rationality assumed a basic function.

If the comparison is not pushed too far, there is a resemblance between Kant's categories of the mind which make objective knowledge possible and Locke's categories of feelings which make objective values possible. Kant postulated the twelve categories of the mind, together with the formal conditions of space and time, to explain the conditions under which we organize our experience, in accordance with these *a priori* forms. Similarly, Locke postulated the four categories of feelings largely to explain the ways in which we organize our valuing experiences. Locke also suggested, but did not state, that the four categories of feelings are *a priori*, formal conditions for valuing the world. He never said that the forms of feeling are grounded in culture or customs alone, and he never spelled out the exact relationship between culture or customs and the forms of values.

In addition to explaining the ways in which we organize our valuing experience, Locke also wanted to explain the merger, transformation, transferral, and conflict of values. Consider this illustration: If while one is listening to Beethoven's Ninth Symphony one feels exalted, one is induced to regard it as possessing religious value. On the other hand, if one feels conflict or tension while listening to the Symphony, it then possesses moral or ethical value. The changed feeling results in changed value judgment of the same scene. Locke seemed to be suggesting that the forms under which feelings are felt remain fixed, but our feelings are flexible. Noting the ways in which values shift, Locke wrote:

The awe-inspiring scene becomes "holy," the logical proof, "beautiful," creative expression, a "duty," and in every case the appropriate new predicates follow the attitude and the attitude cancels out the traditionally appropriate predicates. . . . We are forced to conclude that the feeling-quality, irrespective of content, makes a value of a given kind, and that a transformation of the attitude effects a change of type in the value situation.[9]

Although Kant's forms of knowing bore certain similarities to Locke's forms of valuing, the two differed fundamentally on how the categorical imperative(s) functions: Kant's categorical imperative existed as a single absolute principle by which all rational wills were necessitated to conform. Locke claimed that a plurality of categorical imperatives corresponded to the various basic feeling-modes:

These modes co-assert their own relevant norms; each sets up a categorical imperative of its own, not of the Kantian sort with rationalized universality and objectivity, but instead the psychological urgency (shall we say, necessity?) to construe the situation as of a particular qualitative form-character. It is this that we term a functional categorical factor, since it operates in and through feeling, although it is later made explicit, analyzed and validated by evaluative processes of judgment and experimental test.[10]

IV

Locke's other technical notions involve two types of polarities: the value polarity and the Jungian polarity. To grasp the meanings of these notions, it will be instructive to study their functions and how they fit into the overall value scheme. These polarities were subdivisions for each value-mode—the religious, ethical, logical, and aesthetical. The value polarity discriminated for each value-mode negative and positive values. Similarly, the Jungian polarity discriminated for each value-mode "an introverted and an extroverted variety of value."[11] The latter type of value pertains to the end toward which the value is directed. Introverted value is directed to the individual where it is individualized. Extroverted value is directed to the community where it is socialized. Consider, for example, the religious value-mode whose underlying feeling-form is that of exaltation. When the value is of the introverted type, the value is centered on the individual, and the religious value is enjoyed as inner ecstasy. Its positive value is regarded as holiness and its negative value as sin. In this case, the predicates "holy" and "unholy" apply respectively. The religious mystic who withdraws from the world is representative of the introverted type of value. On the other hand, when the value is of the extroverted type, it is manifest in the community, socialized, and shared among members of the community. The value is shared by the community as religious zeal. Its positive value is regarded as salvation and its negative value as damnation. In this case, the predicates "good" and "evil" apply respectively. Locke claimed that the religious reformer who confronted the world, seeking to transform it, was representative of the extroverted type of value.

Let us take as our next illustration the ethical value-mode. Its underlying feeling is that of tension, which in Locke's view, is felt in situations of conflict and of choosing. When the value is the introverted type, individualized, the tension is felt in the realm of conscience and the situation is ethical. Its positive value is that of conscience and its negative value, temptation. By contrast, in the case of the extroverted value, the tension is felt as a duty, motivating the individual's or group's outer behavior, and the situation is of the moral type. Its positive value is that of right and its negative value, crime. To the introvert, the positive and negative predicates "good" and "bad" apply respectively; to the extrovert, the positive and negative predicates "right" and "wrong" apply respectively. And so on for the other two categories, the logical and the aesthetical.

The concept of feeling or attitude is the key to understanding Locke's view of values. He held that by focusing on a single factor, namely, feeling or attitude, he offered a novel explanation of how value mergers, transfers, and conflicts occurred, in both the individual and community. Dewey and other traditional value theorists attempted to explain value conflicts and convergences by focusing almost exclusively on ends, ideals, and consequences. In Locke's view, such theorists had difficulties in explaining why we often shift value predicates from one category to another; why, for example, we might apply the predicate "beautiful" to a logical proof or apply the predicate "noble" to an ethical deed.

Locke wrote:

We are aware of instances, for example, where a sequence of logical reasoning will take on an aesthetic character as a "beautiful proof" or a "pretty demonstration," or where a moral quality or disposition is appraised not as "good" but as "noble," or again, where a religious ritual is a mythical "reality" to the convinced believer but is only an aesthetic, symbolic show to the noncredal spectator.[12]

Locke held that the traditional way of accounting for the use of such predicates assumed that they were being used only metaphorically. Locke did not accept such an explanation; he thought that something else was at issue. In fact, he stated that the use of such predicates in these inappropriate ways was evidence in support of his alternative theory: that attitudes which created values were not fixed, that the value and its predicate varied with attitude. What may be regarded as an inappropriate predicate was in functional relations and agreement with the attitude or value in question.

Table 1 shows a graphic outline of Locke's value schema.[13]

V

To this point our primary concern has been with explaining the dynamic relations and interconnectedness among values. The analysis has centered on the individual seen in isolation. However, as was previously noted, one of Locke's main philosophic interests in "Values and Imperatives" was the nature of internal conflicts within the various value fields. He devoted attention to these in the latter part of the essay. He also alluded to the nature of "external conflicts" which arise when one group seeks to impose its value creed on others. He considered racial problems to be instances of such value conflicts. As Locke proposed his solution to value conflict, he seemed to collapse the distinction between internal and external conflicts.

Is there an effective way to resolve conflicts within and among the various value fields? The answer to this question depends a great deal on what is taken to be the source and nature of such conflicts. In his *Public and Its Problems*, Dewey explains in great detail that political and social conflicts which result in the destruction of community life arise out of the criss-crossing, clashing and overlapping of indirect consequences of individual and group behavior. People's interests and ideals tend to clash rather than harmonize in social situations in which consequences are not adequately perceived and controlled in accordance with the scientific method. Can science and technology solve most, if not all, value conflicts and other social problems?

Locke thought that science and technology helped make people aware that the traditional absolutes which he saw as the source of many problems were without validity. Science, he said, can teach us that values are relative and that all values are based "not upon priority and precedence but upon parity and reci-

Table 1

MODAL QUALITY Form-Quality and Feeling-Reference	VALUE TYPE or Field	VALUE PREDICATES	VALUE POLARITY	
			Positive	Negative
EXALTATION: (Awe-Worship) a. Introverted: (Individualized): Inner Ecstasy b. Extroverted: (Socialized): Religious Zeal	Religious	Holy—Unholy Good—Evil	Holiness Salvation	Sin Damnation
TENSION: (Conflict-Choice) a. Inner Tension of "Conscience" b. Extrovert: Outer Tension of "Duty"	Ethical Moral	Good—Bad Right—Wrong	Conscience Right	Temptation Crime
ACCEPTANCE or AGREEMENT: (Curiosity—Intellectual Satisfaction) a. Inner Agreement in Thought b. Outer Agreement in Experience	Logical Truth Scientific Truth	True (Correct) and Incorrect True—False	Consistency Certainty	Contradiction Error
REPOSE or EQUILIBRIUM a. Consummation in Contemplation b. Consummation in Creative Activity	Aesthetic Artistic	Beautiful—Ugly Fine— Unsatisfactory	Satisfaction Joy	Disgust Distress

procity.''[14] Beyond that, science can do very little to resolve conflicts within the value arena because the conflicts are inherent in human nature, rooted in our psychological makeup.

According to Hobbes, individuals inevitably clashed with one another, as a result of competition, greed, self-interest, and mutual distrust. These conflicts were sharpened and intensified in the state of nature. He believed that peace and security could be established only if people were forced to obey the absolute ruler, backed by the sword, and ultimately grounded in the natural, absolute law of reason.

The contrast between Hobbes and Locke is clear. Hobbes said that differences and conflicts among people could be settled, if they conformed to the absolute norm which is a necessary feature of the natural order of things. Locke would say that absolutes of the type Hobbes spoke were not given but were created by people and that people must recognize this in order to create harmony among themselves. Both Locke and Dewey would have agreed that Hobbes' absolute law had no basis in fact; both would have said that Hobbes' absolute ruler would create more problems than could be solved.

Locke perhaps would have gone so far as to say that the absolute political order which Hobbes envisaged was merely a projection of Hobbes' own attitudes and preferences. More specifically, in Locke's view Hobbes' absolute rule and ruler would be altogether ineffective in reducing conflict among people. The reasons would be that the Hobbesian proposal could in no way remove the value polarities mentioned above: ''Repose and action, integration and conflict, acceptance and projection, as attitudes, create natural antinomies, irresolvable orders of value.''[15]

If Locke's view about the nature of conflicts is related to the Black experience, a well-known example comes to mind: the historical conflicts that existed between Du Bois and Washington. As previously noted, their conflicts came to the fore in questions concerning the education of Black people, which, for the purpose of this discussion, may be subsumed under the rubric of the moral situation. It will be remembered that Washington was one of the most politically visible and active figures of both races. Du Bois was somewhat withdrawn from the Black masses. As a social leader and educator, Washington was directly in contact with the Black masses. Du Bois was representative of the introverted type and Washington of the extroverted type. If Locke's theory is correct, the value orientation of each pulled the Black community into opposite directions. In fact, the conflicts between Du Bois and Washington were, by their very nature, irresolvable. At times, both Du Bois and Washington acted as though their respective values were absolute mandates issued from God. According to Locke such values were to be understood as being preferences and attitudes projected as absolutes to which their respective followers expressed loyalty. A good dialectician would see the tension between these two absolutes as a vehicle for social change.

Hegel, Marx, Fanon, and other dialecticians placed a positive value on such conflicts, especially on external conflicts, without which, in their view, there would be no social progress and ultimately no social harmony. Locke was interested in social harmony, but he did not place a great deal of positive value on conflicts. In fact, as already noted, he held that society should organize itself around certain principles which would allow for the reduction of conflicts. Attention has already been brought to the importance he placed on the principles of pluralism, relativism, and loyalty, which he thought led to the reduction of conflicts. In view of the fact that value conflicts are rooted in our psychological makeup, Locke stated that we must find ways to control such conflicts "by understanding how and why, to find principles of control from the mechanisms of valuation themselves."[16]

VI

Although the various value-modes are inherently incompatible, Locke held that they were also complementary in human experience. The value-groups, including the values of ethnic groups and others, could be made complementary. Locke insisted that individuals and groups must develop attitudes of tolerance for the values of people outside their own value-field; for example, people in the value-field of religion should be tolerant of people in the value-field of morals. Whites must be tolerant of the cultural values of Blacks, and vice versa. This in effect meant being loyal to one's own group and at the same time being loyal to the cultural values of the larger society. Locke also evoked the principle of social reciprocity, which he regarded as the key principle required to reduce all types of conflict, internal as well as external. In order to effectively combat value conflicts and to allow for the complementary character of values, he suggested that it was not sufficient to develop a detached attitude toward the values of others; the principle of social reciprocity was also needed. Groups must share values: value-groups, cultural groups, and ethnic groups, for example, must give and receive from each other so that each may enrich the other. In this way, he hoped, the myths of value superiority and the attitudes that promote value-bigotry, value-monopoly, and racism could be dispelled and society could move in the direction of social harmony.

Locke believed that the principles of tolerance and social reciprocity, along with certain other principles mentioned above, would lead to the open society where universal harmony prevailed. It may be objected that Locke's notion of tolerance has a negative connotation, suggesting passivity and indifference. As a practical matter, however, the principle of tolerance might be effective in reducing internal conflicts within the various value-fields. In the field of religion, for example, despite their historical ideological differences, Protestants and Catholics alike in Ireland and elsewhere might come to enjoy a greater degree of unity, if they would increasingly recognize the need of each group to be tolerant of the values of the other. However, the principle of tolerance is less effective at the practical level when extended to the racial situation.

The racial situation in America is a complex one involving many factors: economic, social, and historical. The error in Locke's notion of tolerance is that it suggests that the larger society and ethnic minorities relate to one another on a "live-and-let-live" basis—which is the literal meaning of "tolerance." This live-and-let-live philosophy may signal to the larger society and to minorities messages that may forestall needed social changes. The larger society which treats Blacks and other minorities unjustly may come to interpret Locke's "tolerance" to mean that matters will automatically and gradually work themselves out in the best interest of all, providing society adopts such a policy in dealing with minorities. As many people have come to believe, such a policy will exonerate the larger society from its past wrongdoings. Similarly, Blacks and other minorities might come to interpret tolerance to mean that it is permissible to let the larger society "off the hook" as it were, that Blacks and other minorities need not remind the larger society that they were—and still are—victims, and seek redress. Will this tolerance principle work in South Africa?

Tolerance and mutual respect among the various ethnic groups in this society can be achieved only when the larger society acts to offset the injustices Blacks and other minorities have suffered. In this way, the larger society can gain a sense of self-respect and thus extend this feeling of respect to others. Such actions required to offset injustices have to be translated in terms of making it possible for minorities to obtain adequate housing, schooling, employment, and other essentials of life. Blacks and other minorities also have key roles to play before this mutual tolerance and respect can be enjoyed. They have to continue to struggle, so as not to lose the ground that was gained in the civil rights movement in the 1960s and early 1970s; by continuing the struggle Blacks and others may gain new ground, which they deserve, and may achieve a new sense of identity and purpose. These qualities are preconditions for self-respect; self-respect is a precondition for tolerance, and tolerance, like any other worthwhile aim, cannot be achieved without rigorous effort—without a struggle, in the words of Hegel.

In a capitalistic, pragmatic society such as the United States in which freedom and justice are denied to its minorities, it is not altogether clear that the larger society will readily express the attitude of tolerance toward Blacks and other minorities in the absence of creative conflicts or struggles. Nor is it altogether clear, as Locke seemed to suppose, that if the larger society develops an appreciation for the cultural values of minorities and if minorities do the same for the larger society, the attitude of mutual respect among the various groups will automatically follow. Furthermore, many of the tensions and conflicts within social groups in this society stem from the economic contradictions that pervade our capitalistic society. Society could move in the direction of reducing conflicts among certain social groups by reorganizing economic institutions so that people on all levels of society could enjoy its wealth. Economic reciprocity must come before cultural reciprocity.

Locke himself recognized the role of economic conditions in creating social conflicts. He thought his own position was not far removed from Marxism:

This sounds Marxian, and is to an extent. But the curtailing of the struggle over the means and instrumentalities of values will not eliminate our quarrels and conflicts about ends, and long after the possible elimination of the profit motive, our varied imperatives will still persist. Economic classes may be absorbed, but our psychological tribes will not thereby be dissolved.[17]

Although Locke's position seemed to border on Marxism, he did not think that the reorganization of economic institutions would make much difference in reducing conflicts among the "psychological tribes." This may be partly true. As he maintained, the value-polarities will remain in human nature.

NOTES

1. Alain Locke, "Values and Imperatives," in *American Philosophy, Today and Tomorrow*, eds. Sidney Hook and Horace M. Kallen (New York: Lee Furman, 1935), p. 314.

2. Ibid., p. 315.

3. Ibid., p. 318.

4. Ibid., p. 319.

5. Ibid., p. 320.

6. Ibid., p. 322.

7. George Santayana, *The Sense of Beauty: Being the Outline of Aesthetic Theory* (New York: Charles Scribner's, 1896; New York: Dover Publications, 1955), p. 9.

8. Ibid., p. 14.

9. Locke, "Values and Imperatives," p. 321.

10. Ibid., p. 322.

11. Ibid., p. 323.

12. Ibid., p. 325.

13. Ibid., p. 324.

14. Ibid., p. 326.
15. Ibid.
16. Ibid., p. 328.
17. Ibid., p. 331.

3 ALAIN LOCKE'S MODEL OF THE POLITICAL COMMUNITY

Alain Locke wrote no treatise on the body politic per se, although, in addition to examining Black culture, he was very concerned with analyzing and interpreting American culture and politics. Locke did not dichotomize culture and the body politic; they were related to the degree that producers of culture (for example, artists, scholars, and writers) determined how the realm of human affairs, the political, cultural community, was to look, feel, and sound. As is discussed in chapter 5, he believed that cultured persons had a political duty to uplift and lead the masses by, among other things, elevating the standards of taste. As is shown later in this chapter, Locke's view of culture and the body politic has much in common with Hannah Arendt's.

I

We will first examine Locke's view of culture and politics and of community by demonstrating the ways in which his notion of community was influenced by James, Dewey, and Royce. Although Arendt obviously had no influence on Locke, the two in many ways converged in their conception of politics. The latter part of this chapter, together with chapters 4 and 5, discusses their similarities and differences.

James, Dewey, Locke, and to a lesser degree Royce subscribed to the principle of relativism-pluralism, although James limited this principle to the isolated individual's psychological experiences. Unlike Peirce, James was more concerned with the concrete problem of the individual: one's hopes, aspirations, fears, doubts, and beliefs. Although James was less concerned with the general notion of community, he was not unconcerned with social issues. James was trained as a physician, established psychology as a science, and helped popularize Peirce's version of Pragmatism. However, James' own version of Pragmatism always regarded the unique individual as primary and collective humanity as secondary.

German Idealism reversed this position, positing that the isolated individual was nothing apart from collective humanity. James opposed German Idealism because he believed that it denied individuals their uniqueness and freedom. James, like Dewey, Locke, and certain other American philosophers, preferred a more open-ended universe. If Idealism, with its inherent absolutism and monism, denies the freedom of the individual, the relativism-pluralism principle on which Pragmatism rests provides the arena for the exercise of such freedom, a contention which Locke shared with most Pragmatists.

The type of pluralism which James endorsed was, Locke believed, a counterforce to traditional metaphysical pluralism, which merely allows for a plurality of principles and elements. This old-fashioned pluralism which James opposed presupposed a monistic, common substratum. According to both James and Locke, the trouble with this type of pluralism was that it lent support to political authoritarianism, which demands uniformity among groups and individuals and does not allow for cultural diversity among groups and individuals. In addition Locke believed that authoritarianism could easily lead to a totalitarian society—anti-thetical to a democratic society which prizes the diversity of individuals and groups. Locke thought that James' view of pluralism was more appropriate to a democratic society because such a pluralism provided the basis for cultural pluralism, thereby preserving group differences so that the various ethnic groups could coexist.

Locke praised James for introducing his novel form of pluralism because it was an attempt to disestablish authoritarianism and its absolutes. But in Locke's view James did not go far enough. "For the complete implementation of the pluralistic philosophy it is not sufficient merely to disestablish authoritarianism and its absolutes; a more positive and constructive development of pluralism can and should establish some effective mediating principles for situations of basic value divergence and conflict."[1] If a monistic-absolutist view engenders conflicts, a solution to this lies in cultural pluralism which provides the basis for ideological peace.

II

Like Locke and Dewey, Royce was interested in developing a concept of a viable community in which people could be free. But his approach was quite paradoxical. Although German Idealism and Pragmatism were opposing views, Royce tried to combine them into a coherent system, stressing the importance of the individual and the community. The paradox with which Royce grappled turns on this score. German Idealism as expressed by Hegel and others had little, if any, room for the unique individual. Rather, it emphasizes the organic relatedness with other individuals and with nature—each of which is inherently connected with the Absolute. Up to this point, Royce, for the most part, agreed with German Idealism. Here, the paradox comes to the fore to the degree he tries to reconcile the views of James and Hegel. Like James and Locke, Royce wanted to make Hegel's Idealism more compatible with Pragmatism which recognizes the plurality of facts, values, elements, and principles. In order to make a case for this position, he turns to James' notion of the individual will. As against Hegel, Royce insisted, as did James, that the individual was not only a rational, but also a willing being with hopes, desires, and beliefs that could be satisfied through the exercise of the will. Moreover, Royce believed that individuals achieved their uniqueness by exercising their will and by devoting themselves to a cause. Individual wills also often clashed, tending to disrupt community life, if the willing individuals failed to subscribe to the absolute principle of loyalty.

In most of Royce's writings the notion of community has a central place. But he differed from most of the American philosophers by grounding his community in German Idealism and by placing a great emphasis on the absolute, metaphysical principle of loyalty which is closely connected with his notion of cause. He held that the individual achieves authenticity only by making commitments to a cause. A cause moves the previously isolated individual into the public world which is populated by other willing individuals who are devoted to the same cause, and whose motivating factor is the principle of "loyalty to loyalty." For Royce, loyalty to loyalty is the basic ethical principle which underlies the community and which harmonizes individual conflicting wills. James found this view of community disturbing because, with emphasis on the absolute principle of loyalty, it denied the plurality of principles, facts, and values, and leaned too heavily toward a monistic, boxed-in universe. In such a universe, in James' view, the individual is predetermined by the Absolute's will.

As the following passage indicates, Locke did not find Royce's principle of loyalty altogether objectionable:

It is the Roycean principle of "loyalty to loyalty", which though idealistic in origin and defense, was a radical break with the tradition of absolutism. It called for a revolution in the practise of partisanship in the very interests of the values professed. In its larger outlines and implications it proclaimed a relativism of values and a principle of reciprocity. Loyalty to loyalty transposed to all the fundamental value orders would then have meant, reverence for reverence, tolerance between moral systems, reciprocity in art, and had so good a metaphysician been able to conceive it, relativism in philosophy.[2]

Royce's notion of community was also connected to his notion of interpretation and meaning. James had insisted that the individual acts and creates values in accordance with the principle of utility, and each individual enjoys meaning largely in isolation. All values, Royce held, are measured against the absolute principle of loyalty, and all actions must ultimately be motivated by that principle. The community of interpreters is needed to place the deeds of individuals in perspective and to ascribe meanings to those deeds.

Because Locke spent most of his career interpreting Black culture, it is safe to say that he was influenced by Royce's view that human experience required interpreting in order to make sense of it. But Locke was more than an interpreter; he also brought his critical mind to bear on human problems to which he always suggested practical approaches. He did not regard God as the interpreter. Rather, he looked on all inquiring minds as having a key role to play in determining the importance of human experience.

Dewey's notion of the community directs attention to worldly experience. Dewey opposed Absolute Idealism, for reasons similar to James' and Locke's but Dewey would perhaps have agreed with Royce that James devoted too much attention to the isolated individual. Dewey saw his own works as providing a balanced account of the individual and the community, yet most of Dewey's critics say that his social and political thought seems to have submerged the concrete individual in social and biological processes.

Dewey offers an in-depth formulation of his view of the community in the *Public and Its Problems*. There, his formulation hinges largely on the distinction between direct and indirect consequences. Direct consequences emerge from the transactions of two or more individuals but do not extend beyond those involved in the transactions; indirect consequences affect others not directly involved in the transaction which produced the consequences.

According to Dewey, in America's earlier history, the indirect consequences from which the state emerged were largely limited and manageable. The identities of states were secure and recognizable. Technological innovations, however, have changed the nature of these consequences. Today indirect consequences have begun to overlap and mutually inhibit one another, resulting in the destruction of community life in America. Public officials and the community at large can no longer control the fluctuations of indirect consequences. The public has moved into phases of perpetual eclipses, where individuals and groups no longer have control of their lives. People feel alienated, frustrated, and hopeless, like Marxian laborers.

Dewey believed that the intelligent application of science and technology would usher in what he called the Great Community, in which the ideals of democracy would become a living reality. He suggested that science could solve the problems of community life without creating additional problems which would be beyond its control; for him science had no limits. This is plainly untrue. In the first place, scientists cannot control all of the direct and indirect consequences of their discoveries. Genetic engineers are now technologically in a position to create and manufacture life in the laboratory. Who knows what adverse effect such a "manufactured organism" might have on human life, both now and in the future. Moreover, many of the consequences of this technology are both unpredictable and irreversible. It may therefore be asked how scientists can control consequences they cannot understand, predict, or reverse.

Yet another problem is involved: Dewey stated that in the Great Community, scientific findings would be disseminated and shared among the masses. In this way, the community would be integrated. But it is problematic how complicated findings could be translated from technical to natural language so that the public could understand them. It is difficult for experts in various specialties to communicate with one another, and the difficulty increases tenfold when specialists attempt to communicate to nonspecialists. Today scientists operate in a world far removed from common sense and the day-to-day experiences with which the masses and public officials are familiar. They live in a world of complicated formulas and instruments whose measurements may or may not correspond to reality as we know it. It is not evident then how scientists can be helpful in deciding the course of political and social events, as Dewey would have had us believe.

III

Although Locke did not have as much faith in science as Dewey, Locke's vision of community life was almost identical to Dewey's. Both prized the ideals of democracy, and both, no less than Thomas Jefferson, felt that education was necessary to prepare people to be effective, informed citizens.

A well-organized democratic society, Locke believed, would protect the cultural differences among groups. The belief that we should erase cultural differences is consistent with the American "melting pot" doctrine according to which every one is encouraged to conform to the same way of life. Many politicians once evoked this doctrine as a solution to social problems between racial groups. Locke considered the melting pot idea to be another form of absolutism. (Although Dewey was not an absolutist, his own view of community echoes the melting pot notion, in which science and technology would play a key role in fulfilling the community's aim.) If Americans, Locke insisted, wished to solve their problems of community life, they needed to change their attitudes toward minorities. They should not try to change the minorities themselves:

In spite of the leveling off of many present differences under the impact of science, technology, and increased intercommunication, we cannot in any reasonably near future envisage any substantial lessening of the differences in our basic value systems, either philosophical or cultural. The only viable alternative seems, therefore, not to expect to change others but to change our attitudes toward them, and to seek raprochement not by the eradication of such differences as there are but by schooling ourselves not to make so much of the differences. These differences, since they are as real and hard as "facts" should be accepted as unemotionally and objectively as we accept fact.[3]

Just as Locke believed that Royce's principle of loyalty should be used to protect cultural differences, so also he believed that it should be a way of promoting cohesion among various ethnic groups. He suggested that individuals have a natural tendency to develop bonds of affection to the ethnic group of which they are part and to which they have certain social obligations. This loyalty principle, as it operates within the context of groups, is analogous to what Henri Bergson called the morality of closed societies and its accompanying *esprit de corps.* Locke encouraged young Black artists and writers to remain loyal to and draw on the Black experience. Enriching and developing the Black community was their first and foremost task. Yet Locke did not want artists, writers, scholars, social leaders, or anyone else to be limited to their own culture.

Locke did not intend that this loyalty principle breed group bigotry; rather, he wanted it to be an antidote to such an attitude. Bigotry characterizes the larger society. Instead of pluralism, the principle of absolutism, derived from the ethos of the dominant group, prevails. People loyal to that principle express little regard for the cultural values of ethnic minorities, and minorities are pressured to reject their own values and accept those of the dominant group. The effect is usually twofold: disruption of the cultural values of ethnic minorities, and creation of perpetual conflicts between the larger society and its minorities. The pluralism-relativism principle states that the values of each cultural group are on the same footing. Locke spoke a great deal of the importance of cultural equality among groups, the recognition of which, he believed, would reduce tension among various groups. Thus, cultural reciprocity is to replace cultural domination, and cultural tolerance is the aim.

James' notion of tolerance probably influenced Locke's usage of this term. James introduced the term as a counterbalance to the "blindness in human nature," engendered by a pragmatic society whose members are bent on satisfying their own interests, often to the detriment of others. The pragmatic individual often regards his own interest and outlook as absolute and seeks to regulate or dominate the affairs of others. Such an individual is intolerant of the ways of life of others, is not open to others, does not share the world of facts and values with others, and is not available to others. Such a person is morally blind, approximating the Hobbesian type of individual, seen in the state of nature. James warned against this kind of behavior and attitude.

James did not, for the most part, extend this notion of tolerance to social groups as did Locke. James' conception of the individual and the relation of individuals in democratic society was probably derived in part from John Locke. For John Locke, as for Hobbes, the isolated individual, not social groups or associations, is the basis of what is called "natural rights," from which other civil and legal rights are derived. Civil society is an artificial construct designed to protect the natural rights of the individual. Neither John Locke nor Thomas Hobbes considered that an alternative conception of society could place social groups at the focal point, and make the rights of the social group primary and the isolated individual secondary. This is what Alain Locke and Dewey attempted to do. Dewey, however, went further than Alain Locke in his consideration of the social realm as a basis for democratic community. Dewey rebelled against the old form of individualism created by John Locke, Descartes, Hobbes, and others. His notion of the social realm is all-encompassing, nearly as broad in scope as Hegel's.

Alain Locke, in contrast, focused on the social realm as the arena in which the various ethnic cultures unfold. No American philosopher has devoted as much attention as Locke to the role of ethnic groups in creating and perpetuating communities and civilizations. Locke maintained that minorities in any society have a right to develop their own culture and to contribute to civilization generally, but in a democratic society, those rights are often questioned. They are always subject to the whims of the majority. If the minorities have grievances, they can be expressed in the form of civil dissent or protest and in accordance with due process of law. The intent of the law is to protect the rights of all citizens, a function conceived largely by John Locke and tested by Martin Luther King. Alain Locke was obviously aware that law in a democratic society should and ought to protect the rights of its ethnic minorities, and he often advocated the application of the law to produce social change for Blacks. Nevertheless, he did not place a great deal of faith in the law, recognizing that the law is often manipulated in favor of the majority.

The following section demonstrates that even if the problem of race is "solved," our society must still face the more basic problem of Dewey's eclipsed publics. Our society has not yet organized itself in ways to allow all citizens to participate in the body politic, and the reasons, as will be seen, are beyond race.

IV

Dewey, Arendt, Locke, and, to a lesser degree, James and Royce, converged on the central political problem of the eclipsed publics. Although each differed in his or her explanation of the causative factors that gave rise to the eclipsed publics, they all wanted to find ways to make democracy, its political institutions, offices, ideals, and values, accessible to all citizens. When Locke examined this problem, his focus was always on Blacks whom he wanted to incorporate into the mainstream.

As already mentioned, Locke thought the political destiny of

Blacks was linked with that of all Americans. For example: "The Negro to-day is inevitably moving forward under the control largely of his own objectives. What are these objectives? Those of his outer life are happily already well and finally formulated, for they are none other than the ideals of American institutions and democracy."[4] If the political destiny of Blacks is part of that of the larger society, and if the American political community has been eclipsed, resulting in political exclusion for most citizens, as Dewey and others maintained, Blacks have been excluded from the body politic in a twofold sense. First, racism has largely excluded Blacks from the political arena. Second, because the American body politic following the Civil War was more concerned with protecting the economic interests of big business than with the Four Freedoms, most Americans, including ethnic minorities, have been excluded from what Hannah Arendt calls the public spaces where political activities take place. Public spaces have been eclipsed by the activities of labor. Economic concerns and interests have contracted the public spaces, making Arendt's participatory democracy, which is open to all citizens who wish to participate in political affairs, virtually impossible.

Dewey, unlike Arendt, did not clearly distinguish the body politic from governmental, industrial, and commercial activities; the boundaries of these activities overlap and intersect. The way to achieve participatory democracy, in Dewey's view, was to gain control over these indirect consequences through the intelligent application of science and technology. Arendt believed that we could not effectively control these consequences because individuals were free, creative, and unpredictable. Any attempt to control such consequences, in her view, would limit human freedom; the controlling of consequences could best be achieved in a totalitarian society.

Dewey's approach to the problem of political exclusion is not adequate, for the problems of democratic societies are more profound than he recognized. His inability to recognize the fundamental problems of democracy stems partly from the fact that he attempted to find a remedy to the problem of democracy while remaining within its conceptual framework. He failed to criticize democracy from the standpoint of an altogether different and novel paradigm. True, the Great Community which he envisaged in *The Public and Its Problems* is intended to offer a new paradigm of political participation and thereby solve the problems of political exclusion, but he does not solve the problem effectively. He does not offer any concrete recommendations as to how the masses are to participate in the body politic, other than his vague prescription that they do so by "thinking scientifically" and utilizing the methods of science to handle social problems. Dewey wrote:

The prime condition of a democratically organized public is a kind of knowledge and insight which does not yet exist. . . . But some of the conditions which must be fulfilled if it is to exist can be indicated. We can borrow that much from the spirit and method of science even if we are ignorant of it as a specialized apparatus. *An obvious requirement is freedom of social inquiry and of distribution of its conclusions.* [Emphasis added.][5]

Dewey regarded the body politic as a scientific laboratory in which people, institutions, and ideas were observed, tested, and discarded if they lacked "utility." But it may be interjected here that political experience and scientific practices cannot be considered to be identical, nor did it probably ever occur to Dewey that science could be manipulated in favor of those in power and to the detriment of those not in power. In Nazi Germany, let us remember, millions of people were killed and tortured in the name of the scientific method.

Undoubtedly, Dewey uncritically assumed that the Great Community could be achieved, if existing democratic institutions, through the aid of science and technology, fulfilled their functions. They would do so to promote progress, the "ultimate value." He assumed that, in order to solve the problems of political exclusion and other social problems, existing democratic institutions did not have to be radically reorganized or destroyed. They only had to be organized to conform to the methodology of science. But science was one thing, and politics another, for one related to the realm of nature and the other to the realm of human affairs. Dewey assumed that the one was merely an offshoot of the other. As in the works of Arendt, it is evident that the above assumptions are erroneous; scientists and politicians plow different fields.

Neither Locke nor Arendt placed as much faith in science as did Dewey, and neither confused the realm of nature with the realm of human affairs. Like Dewey, Locke offered no radically new model for the body politic; nevertheless, he moved beyond Dewey, for he recognized the need to integrate minorities into American democracy. He proposed that the principles of tolerance, pluralism, relativism, and social reciprocity would solve the political exclusion problem of minorities. He believed that a society organized around the principle of pluralism would exclude no group from the democratic process. Locke failed to see that racial problems were connected to a larger problem of political democracy, namely, the problem of political exclusion of the masses in general, not just minorities. As is argued later in this book, a solution to the problem of the political exclusion of the masses requires a new concept of the state.

V

Arendt's approach to this problem has great merit and can be used to develop Locke's political thought. Much of what she said, especially in her *On Revolution*, touched on problems that concerned Locke, namely, the principles America should adopt to ensure the participation of all ethnic groups in its democratic institutions. Locke's position, it should be recalled, was that the principles of pluralism, relativism, reciprocity, among others, were needed. Arendt would probably have agreed with Locke, but she went further and offered a new concept of the state which Locke would likely have found appealing. She called this new conception of the state the council system, a system that provides spaces for exercising political freedom.

Arendt's concept of the body politic is complex, varied, and profound. Two of the most important elements in this concept, individual freedom and public space, constitute two unifying threads of her thought. Their importance emerges as she criticizes the contemporary body politic for not allowing for grassroots participatory democracy. According to Arendt, the problem of political exclusion lies largely in the party politic, which offers only limited spaces for mass participation. Under such a system of government, spaces have been reduced in size to the voting booths. Laboring and consuming activities have invaded the public political spaces. The resulting contracted spaces, she says, are not adequate for grass-roots participation. This pertains to the Russian government which relies on the one-party system, the American government which relies on the two-party system, and the European government which relies on the multiparty system. Under all of these systems, the people can participate directly in politics only through their representatives. Most of these representatives, according to Arendt, are merely function-aries and administrators whose basic interest is the next election.

In the early days of the American Republic, during the times of Thomas Jefferson, most citizens had the opportunity to par-ticipate in the body politic. The government was limited in size, and citizens had sufficient spaces to exercise their freedom. Jef-ferson encouraged this participation: he believed that a good government consisted of small elementary republics, political spaces or wards into which everyone could enter if they so chose:

Hence, according to Jefferson, it was the very principle of republican government to demand "the subdivision of the counties into wards," namely, the creation of "small republics" through which "every man in the State" could become "an acting member of the Common gov-ernment, transacting in person a great portion of its rights and duties, subordinate indeed, yet important, and entirely within his competence."[6]

Arendt continues:

It was "these little republics [that] would be the main strength of the great one"; for inasmuch as the republican government of the Union was based on the assumption that the seat of power was in the people, the very condition for its proper functioning lay in a scheme "to divide [government] among the many, distributing to everyone exactly the functions he [was] competent to." Without this, the very principle of republican government could never be actualized, and the government of the United States would be republican in name only.[7]

In comparing the American Revolution of 1776 to the French Revolution and other modern revolutions, Arendt noted a common element at least in their initial stages: they were inspired by the principle of freedom. In the initial stages of both the French and the American revolutions, the participants saw themselves as engaging in free actions. One difference between the two revolutions was that once the French Revolution began to gain momentum the participants no longer regarded themselves as free agents, but rather as men swept along by the force of history. The force of history was aiming toward the liberation of the masses from poverty and economic oppression; the French Revolution became preoccupied with social and economic issues, almost to the exclusion of political activities.

The American Revolution, Arendt said, took a different path. The American Founding Fathers concentrated their energies on creating spaces for freedom. Arendt called these spaces revolutionary councils. These councils, as distinguished from the party system, "were always organs of order as much as organs of actions."[8] In the council system the masses could participate directly in politics, whereas in the party system participation was limited mainly to elected officials. Moreover, the councils were the means by which democracy renewed itself, keeping the spirit of freedom alive.

Arendt calls the council members "the Elite." By this term, she had in mind individuals who, by virtue of their own initiative, took an active part in political activities leading others who lacked initiative, rather than in its traditional sense. She admitted that although politics was by definition the concern of all citizens, many citizens chose not to enter the political spaces. They left this responsibility to the Elite, who were self-selected, at the grass-roots level. Furthermore, members of the Elite served as deputies in the elementary republics or councils. The process of deputy selection continued on the next levels: "From these 'elementary republics,' the councilmen then chose their deputies for the next higher council, and these deputies, again, were selected by their peers, they were not subject to any pressure either from above or from below."[9] Arendt detailed how the councilors performed:

Their title rested on nothing but the confidence of their equals, and this equality was not natural but political, it was nothing they had been born with; it was the equality of those who had committed themselves to, and now were engaged in, a joint enterprise. Once elected and sent to the next higher council, the deputy found himself again among his peers, for the deputies on any given level in this system were those who had received a special trust.[10]

In providing this unique model of the body politic, Arendt offers an approach to reconciling authority and equality. Political authority emanates not from the top of the pyramid, as we are accustomed to believe, but rather from the grass-roots level. It originates within the elementary republics, among equals. It then moves upward and is vested in the selected deputies who represent their peers at the various levels of the pyramid, the hierarchical structure of the councils. Equality and authority, therefore, rest with the councilors at a given level of the pyramid, where they find themselves among equals, each of whom is vested with authority and power. Hence the reconciliation of authority and equality.

Arendt's concept of the revolutionary councils gives both form and content to democracy. In the total context of her other political writings, her new concept of the state points in the direction of a new political community in which positive freedom can be enjoyed, in which people can act freely in concert, and in which citizens can engage in what Karl Jaspers calls a loving struggle, open, honest communication.

The freedom which Locke, no less than Dewey, focused on is to be realized in a democratic society organized around what Arendt would call the principle of plurality, signifying the multiplicity, diversity, uniqueness, and equality of human beings. However, she limits her notion of plurality to individuals, especially those who participate in politics. Locke, who was more concerned with the plurality of ethnic groups, stressed this principle of plurality in order to allow for the cultural differences which each ethnic group displays and which must be preserved. The freedom of ethnic groups, he claimed, could be exercised only under the condition of cultural-political plurality. For this reason, he insisted on a democratic society in which group cultural differences and freedom could be preserved.

The notion of plurality implies cultural relativism and bars traditional absolute principles. Thinkers such as Kant, Hegel, and Royce who advocate ethical or religious absolutism usually do so in the conviction that if people conform to such absolutes, they can exercise freedom and, at the same time, approximate the ideal of morality. Locke, no less than Arendt, detected a danger in such absolutism. Rather than promoting peace, security, and freedom, it promotes unity at the expense of cultural diversity and "involves authoritarian conformity and subordination."[11] He was, of course, thinking of racial situations in America and in what we now call Third World countries, where Westerners contend that the values, ways of life, technologies, and religions are inferior to their own. Locke believed that plurality and relativism would dispel that type of absolutist dogmatism and thus allow ethnic groups, especially people of color whose culture Westerners wished to destroy, the freedom to shape their own culture and political destinies. Locke showed how value pluralism-relativism could provide the basis for democracy:

This type of understanding, it seems to me, begins in a basic recognition of value pluralism, converts itself to value relativism as its only consistent interpretation, and then passes over into a ready and willing admission of both cultural relativism and pluralism. In practice, this ideological orientation concedes reciprocity and requires mutual respect and noninterference. It pivots on the principle that the affirmation of one's own world of values does not of necessity involve the denial or depreciation of someone else's. The obvious analogy with a basic democratic viewpoint will immediately suggest itself; in fact there seems to be an affinity, historical and ideological, between pluralism and democracy, as has been frequently observed. Only this is an extension of democracy beyond individuals and individual rights to the equal recognition of the parity and inalienable rights of corporate ways of life.[12]

Unfortunately, Locke never fully developed his conception of cultural pluralism by relating it more closely to political democracy. Political democracy seemed to present a paradox for Locke. As was noted in his psychograph, he indicated how, as a Black man living in America, his life became a living paradox. On the one hand, he accepted and affirmed America's larger culture; on the other, he opposed that culture and expressed loyalty to

Black culture. This paradox pervaded his political attitude toward democracy generally. He did not want to "cross over" and become "all white" or an integrationist, nor did he want to be a complete cultural separatist, like Garvey. He sought to embrace both cultures.

Locke attempted to solve this seemingly inescapable paradox through his principle of pluralism: cultural pluralism demanded cultural reciprocity by which groups regarded one another as equals. In addition he wanted to attribute basic rights not so much to individuals but to cultural groups. He sought cultural parity instead of cultural integration, separation, or domination. He also recognized that, through the principle of cultural reciprocity, cultures within a pluralistic society could enrich one another. In that way, individual and corporate or group freedom could be exercised. But is this adequate? Can individual and corporate freedom be exercised under these conditions alone?

Without attempting to belittle the pluralistic, democratic society which Locke hoped would be realized, we may state that his model for society does not adequately speak to the problem of political exclusion. Arendt was right when she said that political democracy did not provide adequate spaces for the exercise of individual freedom. Her observation of the problem of freedom applies equally to ethnic groups. Arendt's notion of councils may be extended to ethnic groups. Such councils might be appropriate political structures through which ethnic groups could participate in democracy.

Both Arendt and Locke felt that freedom for individuals and groups could be protected only under the condition of plurality. It is not difficult to see how Arendt's council can be used to approach the paradox which democracy presented for Locke, as well as the related problem of political exclusion. Blacks and other minorities could constitute revolutionary councils. Each ethnic group could create a series of councils whose members represent a cross-section of the various communities. Although each council would ultimately be concerned with political matters, there could nevertheless be a plurality of councils representing the diverse interests of a given ethnic group. These could include cultural, educational, economic, religious, and political councils, whose members would initially be drawn from the

idiotic

utopian

grass-roots level and who would constitute what Arendt calls the elementary republics. Blacks, Jews, Chinese, Mexicans, and other ethnic groups could constitute their respective councils. These councils could in turn be organized so that political ties and open communication, involving "loving struggles" among council members, could be established among the councils. The council members would initially come from the grass-roots level of the various groups. This alternative system would thereby replace traditional local, state, and federal forms of government, which are often self-serving. Such political ties within and among councils would result in what Arendt calls a federation of councils. In this way there could be reciprocal interplay, interaction, exchange, and loving struggles among the federation of councils. Thus, each group could be loyal to its own way of life and at the same time benefit from other groups within the federation of council by sharing one another's cultural values. No ethnic group would be able to dominate the realm of human affairs, to impose absolute values on groups within the federation of councils. A group could choose whether to enter into the federation; the decision would rest entirely with the respective ethnic group, just as Arendt said it was up to the individual to decide not to enter into politics. The group that decided to enter would be self-selected; the group that decided not to enter would be self-excluded.

This federation of councils could also solve the equality-authority problem as it pertains to groups. We previously noted how Arendt solved this problem: the individuals who constitute the councils are vested with authority, and each individual on a given level of the pyramid stands among his or her peers, from whom deputies are selected to represent them at the next higher level. And so on.[13]

If we apply this model of equality and authority to ethnic groups it becomes evident that political authority would rest with no one particular group, and no longer would there be a dominant group. In the new concept of the state, the element of authority would originate among the various groups, at the various levels of the pryamid, just as it originates among individuals on each of the pyramid's layers within a particular council system. No longer would the larger, most powerful group dominate ethnic minorities, or any other minority, as is so often the case within traditional party politics. In the new state the notion of minority or majority would be limited in its application. Every individual or group would be equal, politically. No longer would big government or big business in its present form possess controlling influence, for these would have been replaced by elementary republics. And big business, if it wished to have a voice, would have to enter into the federation of councils along with other groups. Because each group would be equal, the principle of authority involved in deciding public policies and other matters would be shared equally among the groups' councilors at various levels of the pyramid.

In addition to solving the equality-authority problem, the councils could also address what Locke calls the value-conflicts problems that often arise when one group, usually the larger one, seeks to impose its absolute values on minorities, usually resulting in tensions and conflicts. In the federation of councils, such tensions and conflicts could be sharply reduced, because no group would be in the privileged position to create a monopoly of power or authority. Nor could any group create a monopoly of value because the various councilors could freely and openly communicate among themselves. In doing so, they would be able to resolve disagreements, pursue joint projects, and appreciate common values, while respecting one another's cultural differences.

VI

Du Bois shared Locke's ambivalence as to how Blacks as a group fit into American society, with its political, social, and economic institutions. Du Bois, Garvey, and Washington often agreed on the issue of segregation, but occasionally Du Bois shifted his views and insisted on a racially mixed society.

Washington, like Du Bois, encouraged the establishment of what was called economic co-operatives, organized primarily within the Black community. The co-operatives would also serve as the political base of the community, from which, both men believed, would ultimately spring the autonomy of Blacks, individually and collectively.

Du Bois outlines his concept of economic co-operatives in the *Dusk of Dawn*; he places less emphasis on labor than Washington did. Rather, Du Bois stresses consumerism. In his view, most Blacks were consumers, not producers as Washington claimed; Blacks were already segregated from the larger society and had little, if any, control over the means of production, nor did they own the means of production. Because most of the Blacks' economic power rested in the capacity to consume economic goods, not produce them, they needed to organize their consuming power, so that they could bargain with the wholesale producers to the advantage of their community. Through organized buying, Du Bois maintained that Blacks would keep the prices of the items reasonable and the quality high. He believed that as a result American society could be reorganized into a kind of democratic socialism. In proposing a socialistic economy, Du Bois was more radical than Washington, who seemed to have been a capitalist at heart.

Du Bois intended such organizations to be more than economic instruments and institutions. They would also serve as political organs through which public policies would be decided, based on the consensus of the group. When Du Bois emphasizes the political dimensions of such organizations, he is less of a segregationist; he borders on cultural pluralism. It becomes clear that Du Bois did not intend for Blacks to remain in their isolated, self-segregated communities. Like Locke and Washington, he believed that the political destiny of Blacks was inherently connected with the political destiny of the nation. These consumer organizations would unify Black and national interests. In suggesting the political nature of these economic co-operatives, Du Bois employed the term "co-operative commonwealth."

The Negro group in the United States can establish, for a large proportion of its members, a *co-operative commonwealth* [emphasis added], finding its authority in the consensus of the group and its intelligent choice of inner leadership. It can see to it that not only no action of this inner group is opposed to the real interests of the nation, but that it works for and in conjunction with the best interests of the nation.[14]

These co-operative organizations, to which Du Bois' Black Elite would provide leadership, have much in common with Arendt's councils. Du Bois' co-operative organizations may be regarded as political spaces. Arendt and Du Bois, however, differ sharply on certain issues. First, Arendt did not have a high regard for economic activities which she said were tainted with the unfree, alienated side of life, with laboring. Nor did she want to mix the two types of activities, economic and political. Both Du Bois and Washington were aware of the political potential of co-operative organizations. In most of Du Bois' other writings, especially on education, he advised Blacks to first seek political and civil rights, so as to participate in America's democratic institutions. Du Bois, no less than Locke, was concerned more with group freedom than with individual freedom. Arendt, Du Bois, and Locke agreed that the masses should look to the Elite for political leadership.

Although Du Bois recognized the need for a link between co-operative organizations and society, he never specified what sort of political structure this link would take. We may propose that Arendt's federation of councils could provide this structure, assuming that the nation's existing political and economic structures and Du Bois' co-operative organizations be reconstituted in conformity with Arendt's model of federated councils. Locke's principle of political-social reciprocity would ensure open communication among the councils. A viable, balanced political structure would give adequate consideration to labor activity. Arendt drew too sharp a line between economic and political factors. Du Bois' economic co-operatives and what may be called Locke's cultural-political councils could perhaps be an integral part of Arendt's federation of councils, within which Blacks and other minorities could participate directly in democracy.

NOTES

1. Alain Locke, "Pluralism and Ideological Peace," in *Freedom and Experience*, eds. Milton R. Konvitz and Sidney Hook. (Ithaca; New York: Cornell University Press, 1947), p. 63.

2. Alain Locke, "Values and Imperatives," in *American Philosophy, Today and Tomorrow*, eds. Sidney Hook and Horace M. Kallen (New York: Lee Furman, 1935), p. 332.

3. Alain Locke, "Pluralism and Ideological Peace," p. 64.

4. Alain Locke, *The New Negro*, (New York: Atheneum, 1968; originally published in 1925), p. 10.

5. John Dewey, *The Public and Its Problems* (Chicago: Swallow Press, 1927), p. 166.

6. Hannah Arendt, *On Revolution* (New York: Viking Press, 1965), p. 257.

7. Ibid.

8. Ibid., p. 266.

9. Ibid., p. 282.

10. Ibid.

11. Alain Locke, "Cultural Relativism and Ideological Peace," in *Approaches to World Peace* (New York: Conference on Science, Philosophy and Religion, 1944), p. 611.

12. Locke, "Pluralism and Ideological Peace," p. 65.

13. Arendt, *On Revolution*, pp. 282–283.

14. W.E.B. Du Bois, *Dusk of Dawn: An Essay Toward an Autobiography of a Race Concept* (New York: Harcourt, Brace and Company, 1940), p. 216.

THE NEED FOR GLOBAL DEMOCRACY

Although Alain Locke devoted much energy to examining the shortcomings of democracy in the United States, he did not limit his investigation to the continent of North America, nor did he think that democracy itself should be confined to North America or for that matter the Western world. In actual practice, it has been confined to the Western world, and, although democracy has existed in the United States ever since the Revolution of 1776, Blacks and other minorities have been denied the opportunity to enjoy the fruits of democracy. This is true, Locke maintained, even though the American Revolution was inspired by the principle of freedom and equality for all. This assertion of universal freedom and equality, on the one hand, and the failure to extend freedom and equality to Blacks, on the other, is a contradiction for Western democracy which will be discussed shortly. In this connection, let us discuss Locke's view on how to resolve this contradiction and other paradoxes.

The focus of this chapter is on Locke's two works "Democracy Faces a World Order" (1942) and "The Unfinished Business of Democracy" (1942). In these works Locke examined the problems of democracy within the international context, insisting that the shortcomings of democracy were directly related to what Du Bois called the color line—the segregation of people on the basis of color.

I

Locke began "The Unfinished Business of Democracy" by observing that in addition to altering the political and geographical spaces of the globe, World War II produced a revolution in "the geography of our hearts and minds."[1] Locke discussed how the war affected peoples' attitudes toward one another, how peoples of the world perceived racial and cultural differences. Whereas the forces of war have divided nations, they have paradoxically brought people closer together because these forces of the war which have "all but annihilated longitude and latitude also have foreshortened cultural and social distance."[2] Thus according to Locke, World War II had nearly erased the color line that previously divided the peoples of the world.

Because the war narrowed distances among peoples of the world, Locke stated that "we must find common human dominations of liberty, equality and fraternity for *humanity-at-large*."[3] The war, which he called a planetary civil war, called the democracies of the world into question. Western democracy, as previously noted, was forced to face its inherent contradictions, one of which was that Western democracy asked the world to assist in fighting the tyranny of totalitarianism while at the same time failing to extend freedom to people of color. Locke attempted to sharpen this contradiction by revealing that "much in the creed and practice of the totalitarian states has less obviously and less ruthlessly been part and parcel of the group belief and practice of ourselves and our allies."[4] He added,

Unfortunately they have no monopoly on power politics, imperialist militarism and economic exploitation, racist rationalizations of world rule and dominance, the harsh persecution of selected minorities, or the doctrinaire bigotries of cultural superiority. But once let such traditions and practices become overtly and widely stigmatized and a moral situation has been precipitated, with inevitable alternatives of a definite stand.[5] . . . Precisely this has happened; and I, for one, am hopeful of its reformative consequences. Confronted with the Frankensteins of our own vices, we have no choice but to repudiate them. Democracy at war must more clearly outline its position and more unequivocally avow its principles.[6]

Locke described World War II as a civil war whose theatre of battle was the world, with Japan, Italy, and Germany as the aggressors. In both World War II and the American Civil War, the conflicts could not be settled by political compromise, but rather by defeating the enemy within as well as without. The American Civil War centered on the question of whether slavery should be allowed to expand or be abolished and the issue of race was a decisive factor. The planetary civil war, World War II, centered on the question of whether totalitarian states (Japan, Italy, and Germany) should be allowed to continue to exert their imperial influence, dividing the world along the lines of dominant and subject groups, or whether their influence and power should be dismantled.

Locke suggested that Japan, Italy, and Germany be compared to the former slaveholding states of the South; European countries treated people of color much as Black slaves had been treated in the South. Locke, however, was careful to point out that the factors motivating the planetary civil war were not altogether racial: the war cut across racial lines: "In fact, its alignments of friend and foe cut diametrically across race lines. In Europe, they divide as enemies branches of the so-called 'white race.' In Asia, they divide branches of the so-called 'colored peoples'."[7] At the same time, Locke did not overlook racial elements, "for they correspond very largely to those invidious distinctions between imperial and colonial, dominant and subject status out of which has arisen the double standard of national morality."[8]

Just as World War II virtually abolished the color line, Locke said it had created the opportunity for democracy to spread worldwide. The element of color or race could help universalize the principle and practice of democracy because "color becomes the acid test of our fundamental honesty in putting into practice the democracy we preach."[9] People of the world tend to judge how well Americans are acting in conformity with their democratic ideals by observing how they treat Blacks and other minorities. Similarly, the world itself can determine how far short it falls from universal democracy by observing how it treats Third World people. This failure to extend freedom and justice to people of color highlights democracy's incompleteness. In this connection, Locke made the point that a house divided cannot stand, that the house of democracy whose business is not completed cannot stand. He evoked the words of Abraham Lincoln: "This country can no longer endure half-slave and half-free; either it will become all slave or all free."[10]

Locke conveyed an air of optimism as he drew further parallels between the planetary civil war and the American Civil War. The conclusion of the planetary war, he optimistically believed, would result in the freedom of the nations of the world; many believed that the conclusion of the American Civil War would result in the freedom of Blacks. The contradictions of colonial rule were precipitated by Italy, Japan, and Germany, just as the contradictions of America's slave economy were precipitated by the South.

Although making parallels between the two wars has some merit, Locke's equation of the planetary war with the American Civil War is not entirely viable. Sovereignty is one of the basic features that distinguishes the two wars. When the South seceded from the Union in its effort to establish its own governing body, its sovereignty conflicted with that of the previously established nation, the Union, thus making it a civil war. Similarly, in World War II the sovereignty of the Allied nations clashed with that of the Axis powers. When the American Civil War ended, the rule of the Confederacy, along with its sovereignty, was dissolved and the sovereignty of the Union was reconstituted. The conclusion of World War II, however, did not result in an international body with the element of sovereignty comparable to that of the United States or any other nation. A nation is by definition a sovereign, autonomous body with the power and authority to make and formulate its own laws and to settle international disputes through acts of war. Arendt beautifully defines it as follows: "Sovereignty means, among other things, that conflicts of an international character can ultimately be settled only by war; there is no other last resort."[11]

The United Nations (UN), created after World War II, is not a sovereign body, for it has the authority neither to precipitate a war nor to prevent one, although many believe it was established to ensure world peace. It has no standing army but often assumes authority to coordinate peacekeeping forces. If the UN were a sovereign body, with forces comparable to those of the United States or Russia, it could conceivably become an international tyrant.

Locke had much faith in the UN, as is evident by the following passage:

Significantly enough, the Phalanx of the United Nations unites an unprecedented assemblage of the races, cultures and peoples of the world. Could this war-born assemblage be welded by a constructive peace into an effective world order—one based on essential parity of peoples and a truly democratic reciprocity of cultures—world democracy would be within the reach of attainment.[12]

At the time Locke wrote these words, nuclear weapons did not pose a threat to world peace, as they presently do.

Philip H. Rhinelander, in his article "Peace: The Ultimate Challenge," notes the UN's inherent limitation in dealing with the problem of armaments:

According to its charter, the United Nations was set up "to maintain international peace and security, and to that end: to take effective collective measures for the prevention and removal of threats to the peace, and for the suppression of acts of aggression or other breaches of peace . . . ," but it [the UN] lacks power to intervene in matters lying within the domestic jurisdiction of any state and armaments fall within that category.[13]

Echoing the views of Karl Jaspers, Rhinelander does not think that the UN alone can provide the basis for a world order. Both feel that if we are to achieve such an order, we need to consider a new way of thinking about the human condition: "The task requires," Rhinelander says, "new breadth and depth of rationality capable of transcending limited cultural and ideological perspectives and of establishing a new basis of international community and understanding."[14] He adds that this new way of thinking must include the element of trust.

In his essay "The Need for a New Organon in Education,"[15] Locke also insisted that world peace required a new way of thinking. Much of this, he believed, could be accomplished through the educational process. Educators must introduce students to this new thinking process so that they would appreciate the cultural differences of the various peoples of the world. To this end, Locke said that educators must reshape student attitudes and value orientations, and encourage students to develop an attitude of openness to their own cultural values and those of others. Whereas Locke, Rhinelander, and Jaspers called for a new way of thinking, Locke said that it should include feelings as a key ingredient. Rhinelander and Jaspers placed greater emphasis on human rationality. These two positions complement each other; reason is not the slave of passion, nor is passion the slave of reason. Any considerations about world peace must allow for both of these dimensions, reason and feeling.

II

In order to clarify Locke's analysis of the weakness of democracy, let us now compare Locke's two essays "Values and Imperatives" and "The Unfinished Business of Democracy." One of the main conclusions of "Values and Imperatives" was that conflicts between the various subspecies of a given value field were inevitable because they were due to the Jungian introversion-extroversion polarity, which was rooted in human nature. In "The Unfinished Business of Democracy," he concluded that the UN, or a similar organization, could provide the basis for world order. He made similar remarks in his "Democracy Faces a World Order," although here he had in mind the Atlantic Charter: "The Atlantic Charter . . . lays down, at least in sketchy outline, the ground plan of a really democratic world order."[16] He added:

It is more than the product of the disillusionments of Versailles and Geneva; it arose from the practical necessity of countering both the creeds and the practices of our ruthless,—but mark you, consistently ruthless adversaries. Against a background of totalitarian challenge, it has been necessary to envisage a world order consistently and realistically democratic.[17]

If Locke is correct in his assertion that, because of the Jungian polarity, there will always be conflicts between individuals and groups, then it follows that the search for world order through an organization such as the Atlantic Charter or the UN will largely result in futility. Already we have called attention to the UN's limitation in dealing with the problem of armament.

Let us put aside the UN for now and briefly consider the nuclear arms race problem from the point of view of the Jungian polarity. It may well be that the problem between Russia and the United States in trying to reach some accord on nuclear weapons stems largely from this Jungian polarity. Among the Russian military and political leaders there are undoubtedly both introverted and extroverted individuals who disagree on nuclear weapons, with the introverted seeking to limit the spread of such weapons or end their production altogether and the extroverted advocating increased development of such weapons. The same can be said about American political and military leaders.

This Jungian polarity characterizes the attitude not only of political and military leaders, but also of citizens of a given country. Within the North Atlantic Treaty Organization (NATO), there is much talk about the deployment of Pershing II and cruise missiles. In Germany, there is a great deal of opposition to this proposal, and the people who constitute this opposing force may be regarded as introverts. (The extroverts are supportive of the deployment of such missiles.) How can the U.S. President, or the Russian Premier, or for that matter the UN reduce tensions between these opposing groups, introverts and extroverts?

Locke did not apply the introvert-extrovert polarity to historical-political reality as such; his "Values and Imperatives" is largely an historical and metaphilosophic description of the ways in which we undergo valuing experiences. But in "Democracy Faces a World Order" and "The Unfinished Business of Democracy," among others, he suggested that America had to become more extroverted in its effort to spread democracy worldwide; he praised America for discarding its policy of selfish isolationism of 1919, an introverted position:

We have repaired our undemocratic ways at their weakest foreign points by the timely institution of the "good neighbor policy," by statesmanlike initiative in Pan-American relations, by the practical altruisms of lend-lease aid before our formal entry into the present war.[18]. . . The universal spread of the Four Freedoms and the broad implications, however sketchy, of the Atlantic Charter have revived the original principles Alexander Hamilton must have had in mind when, in the early days of the Republic, he said: "The established rules of morality and justice apply to nations as well as to individuals."[19]

Thus, Locke wanted America to become more extroverted and aggressively involved in providing not so much military and commercial leadership, but rather moral leadership to the world, so that democracy could be extended to all nations of the world: "World leadership under the circumstances must be moral leadership in democratic concert with humanity at large."[20] Before America, or any other nation, could assume this role, it had to clean its own house by uprooting racial prejudice: "And a full share in such leadership will not accrue to any nation that cannot abandon racial and cultural prejudice."[21] Locke believed that democracy could complete its unfinished business only when America and the rest of the world began to treat Blacks and Third World people justly and fairly.

Locke was suggesting that America needed to participate in the world community on two fronts to help spread democracy: the political and the moral. From the standpoint of the political front, he held that organizations such as the Atlantic Charter and the United Nations were important; from the standpoint of the moral, he said that America could and needed to set a moral example for the world. It could assume this role only by treating Blacks at home fairly, and in so doing it would encourage the rest of the world to treat Third World people fairly.

III

Let us now consider whether America can provide this moral leadership. Human rights leaders such as Martin Luther King Jr., and Aimé Césaire would have questioned Locke's view that America could provide such moral leadership. Admittedly, King envisaged a racially integrated world, modeled on the Christian community and comparable to Royce's community, but King had doubts about whether white America could inspire the world to seek higher moral ideals. He suggested that there were too many evil forces such as racism and capitalism that prevented America from being a moral example to the world. King, in fact, assigned this moral leadership role to American minorities, Blacks in particular:

Let us, therefore, not think of our movement as one that seeks to integrate the Negro into all the existing values of American society. Let

us be these creative dissenters who will call our beloved nation to a
higher destiny, to a new plateau of compassion, to a more noble expression of humanness.[22]. . . This is the challenge. If we dare to meet it
honestly, historians in the future years will have to say there lived a
great people—a black people—who bore the burdens of oppression in
the heat of many days and who, through tenacity and creative commitment, injected new meanings into the veins of American life.[23]

One cannot read these lines without being reminded of Bergson's moral hero whose mission it is to transform closed, ethnocentric societies into open societies. The morality of the closed
society is duty-bound, static, bent on group preservation; the
morality of the open society is aspiring, dynamic, seeking to
raise humanity to the highest moral order, and pervaded with
unselfish, universal love.

Césaire, who was just as forceful as King in his critique of
American moral practices, insisted that Europeans and their
American counterparts were morally too corrupt to inspire international leadership. He observed that both civilizations, European and American, had reduced themselves to modern
barbarism, the manifestation of which destroyed Third World
nations:

And now I ask: what else has bourgeois Europe done? It has under-
mined civilizations, destroyed countries, ruined nationalities, extir-
pated "the root of diversity." No more dikes, no more bulwarks. The
hour of barbarian is at hand. The modern barbarian. The American
hour. Violence, excess, waste, mercantilism, bluff, gregariousness, stu-
pidity, vulgarity, disorder.[24]

Whereas King looked to Black Americans to interject transforming values into America and the world, Césaire turned to
Africans and their Third World brothers, just as Marx turned to
the European working class. In the following stanza Césaire
called on Africans and their brothers to assume this liberating
mission, a mission which Europeans and Americans were incapable of performing:

You are waiting for the next call
the inevitable mobilization

for that war which is yours has known only truces
for there is no land where your blood has not flowed
no language in which your color has not been insulted
You smile, Black Boy,
you sing
you dance
you cradle generations
which go out at all hours to the
fronts of work and pain
which tomorrow will assault bastilles
onward toward the bastions of the future
in order to write in all languages
on the clear pages of all skies
the declaration of your rights unrecognized
for more than five centuries.[25]

In this *Discourse on Colonialism*, Césaire suggested the need to reaffirm the values that existed in Africa's old, precolonial societies:

They were communal societies, never societies of the many for the few.
They were societies that were not only ante-capitalist, as has been said, but also *anti-capitalist*.
They were democratic societies, always.
They were cooperative societies, fraternal societies.
I make a systematic defense of the societies destroyed by imperialism.[26]

Had Locke lived until the 1960s and early 1970s, when America was dropping bombs in North and South Vietnam and during the Watergate era, he would not have been so optimistic about America's potential mission as a moral leader. Within the past forty years how much have Americans improved race relations here at home? America's present involvement in the nuclear arms race is further evidence in support of King and Césaire's contention that its moral authority had all but evaporated.

IV

In addition to the political and moral approaches, Locke affirmed that we needed to consider the problem of world order from the standpoint of culture and art. He considered this subject in a number of works, including "Internationalism—Friend or Foe of Art?" and "Understanding World Cultures." In "Internationalism," he speculated that world culture, if allowed to develop, could provide the basis for a world order. "And yet in forecast," he wrote, "one can scarcely think of a more promising or reliable touchstone of the new social order than just this very achievement—the internationalization of culture."[27] But the inter-nationalization of culture involves a paradox which complicates matters, making the world order more difficult to achieve. The paradox is that our modern world "started out with the dream of cultural cosmopolitanism to have culminated in theory and practice in intense and unprecedented nationalism."[28] If we revert to Locke's psychograph, we will be reminded that he himself suffered this paradox: "Finally [I am] a cultural cosmopolitan, but perforce an advocate of cultural racialism as a defensive counter-move for the American Negro, and accordingly more of a philosophic mid-wife to a generation of younger Negro poets, writers, artists than a professional philosopher."

Locke did not encourage the resolution of this paradox. In fact, he suggested that the cultural tensions between internationalism and nationalism were perhaps due to the Jungian polarity and therefore unavoidable. As in the views of Santayana, Locke said that "civilization and culture had to come to a parting of the ways, when the development of the one must proceed in the direction of an ever-spreading unity and uniformity, and of the other in the opposite and non-competitive direction of an increased and enriched diversity."[29]

Our modern culture is torn between internationalism and nationalism, the one leading to an encompassing unity at the expense of cultural diversity and the other to an enriching diversity at the expense of cultural union. Locke saw certain benefits for civilizations arising out of this modern cultural union and diversification, motivated largely by the new form of nationalism and racialism which he distinguished from the nationalism of the old order. The old form of nationalism contributed to conflicts among cultural groups of the world, for it was motivated by the illusion of the old political sectarianism and ethnic chauvinism on the part of certain groups of the world. Yet there was a ray of hope:

Purged of chauvinistic motives and ideals, national and racial expression, as cultural individualities, will have scope and incentive to develop more freely and with sounder values. The internationalization of culture seems to me more practical and feasible on this basis of the transformation of the significance of nationality in art than upon the alternative of its elimination.[30]

Locke thought that this new form of cultural nationalism, once divorced from its chauvinistic tendencies, should be allowed to develop for the sake of the desired internationalism. Locke did not think nationalism in culture to be abhorrent; on the contrary: "It is contemporary criticism, not contemporary art, which is at fault through obscuring the progressive cultural nationalisms of the future with reactionary political nationalisms of the past."[31]

In the new order, Locke wanted cultural and racial elements to be allowed to develop at the local level, within the soil of the various ethnic groups, from which art and cultures draw their inspiration. He also wanted art and culture to be appreciated at the universal level. In this context Royce's principle of loyalty to loyalty comes to mind: in creating the items of cultures, artists need to remain loyal to their particular localisms; in enjoying culture, people need to be loyal to civilization generally—they need to be loyal to loyalty, through which the principle of cultural reciprocity can function.

In Locke's writings on culture and art, he looked not so much to the statesman or the politician to create the new world order, but to the artists whose job it was to change our perceptions of ourselves and of others, to inspire people of the world to become more open to one another's cultural values, thus producing world solidarity. But he rejected what is meant by solidarity in the old political sense of the term: "The solidarity they [the artists] can and will achieve is not to be a doctrinal one of common interests and universalized traditions, but an integrating psychology of reciprocal exchange and mutual esteem."[32]

V

Hannah Arendt also desired world "solidarity," but she thought this ideal could be achieved not so much through culture but through a political solution. She differed from Locke in another respect. Whereas Locke indicated that the United Nations could serve as a basis for the world order, Arendt opposed this notion on the grounds that the element of sovereignty, which a body such as the United Nations would have to have if it were to be a basis for world order, was itself problematic inasmuch as any sovereign nation lacks the ability to handle international conflicts except through the act of war. In the past, sovereign states turned to war as a last resort. Today nuclear weapons have made war as the last resort obsolete: "Today, however, war—quite apart from all pacifist considerations—among the great powers has become impossible owing to the monstrous development of the means of violence. And so the question arises: What is to take the place of this last resort?"[33] To which she replied that the answer lays in an entirely new concept of the state, one that did not rest on the element of sovereignty as did the old concept of the state which had its origin in the fifteenth and sixteenth centuries.

This new concept of the state, to be sure, will not result from the founding of a new international court that would function better than the one at The Hague, or a New League of Nations, since the same conflicts between sovereign or ostensibly sovereign governments can only be played out there all over again—on the level of discourse, to be sure, which is more important than is usually thought.[34]

In the previous chapter we considered Arendt's concept of the council system, which she outlined in *On Revolution*. There she limited this concept largely to a given nation such as the United States; she did not extend it to the international community, as she did in her *Crises of the Republic*. Because the old concept of the state, which rested on sovereignty, is largely outdated and the source of conflicts among nations, she sought a new concept of the state, the council system which did not transfer international authority or sovereignty to a particular body such as the United Nations, Locke's view to the contrary notwithstanding. According to Arendt, such an authority could become the most tyrannical form of government the world has known.

Arendt gave only the slightest hint as to how her new concept of the state could be applied to the international community: "The mere rudiments I see for a new state concept can be found in the federal system, whose advantage it is that power moves neither from above nor from below but is horizontally directed so that the federated units mutually check and control their powers."[35]

As indicated in chapter 3, if Arendt's council system were adopted, Blacks and other ethnic groups could more readily participate in the body politic. If her council system were adopted by the international community, the same would be true for Third World nations, for they would have a better chance of enjoying the Four Freedoms on which Locke insists. In addition, this new concept of the state would provide an alternative to war as the last resort for handling international disputes. (How this could be done is discussed in chapter 5.)

If the council system were extended globally, a system established along the following lines would have to be implemented. The U.S. party system of government at every level—county, city, state, and federal—would have to be replaced by the council system. Similarly, other countries around the world that wished to participate in the new order would have to discard their old forms of government and adopt the council system. Within the respective federated council system of each nation, the councilors or deputies who stand at the top layer of the pyramids would constitute the grass-roots layers of the Global Council system. The grass-roots councilors of this international body would in turn elect deputies, vested with authority and power, to represent them. That is, the respective nations would select deputies to represent them at the next level of the pyramid of the Global Council, and so on. In this way, each nation, including previously ignored Third World nations, could participate in the international arena, on an equal basis because the councilors at every level of the Global System would be among their peers. Neither the United States, Russia, nor any other major superpower would be in a position, as often happens in the United Nations today, to dominate the political scene. No nation would have veto power either.

That the new Global Council System would allow for the effective integration of the Third World nations into the world political community would probably have been agreeable to Locke. This new system of government, moreover, would achieve integration without destroying the cultural differences of the various people of the world. The preservation of cultural differences, as suggested by Locke's "Internationalism—Friend or Foe of Art?" and most of his other writings, is imperative. He wanted a political organ that would make world peace possible and at the same time allow for the cultural and racial integration of the various groups. That is why he said cultures needed to conform to the principles of both internationalism and nationalism, although by nationalism, as noted, he did not mean that which characterized the old order, motivated by the illusion of national sovereignty.

In their search for world order, Arendt and Locke agreed on the notion of sovereignty. We have already pointed out why Arendt found it objectionable. For similar reasons Locke wrote:

There is, first of all, . . . that ancient political idol of the sovereign, essentially irresponsible nation. Politically sacred though it be, if we really mean to renounce force as an instrument of national policy, we must repudiate it. The totalitarian spectre has put another cast on this ancient tradition of the self-arbiter nation, or rather, torn the legal mask from its face, so that we can see the real barbarity of its character.[36]

Although Locke urged the world to repudiate sovereignty, unlike Arendt, he offered no effective political organ in its place, except to point out, among other things, that countries needed to subscribe to the principle of cultural reciprocity. At the same time, Locke almost contradicted himself when he insisted that the United Nations or the Atlantic Charter was a likely candidate for replacing the old political order. If the UN were assigned the role of establishing world peace, what would, as Arendt suggested, prevent the old form of sovereignty, this time associated with the UN, from reasserting itself? Arendt wanted to avoid the reassertion of sovereignty by introducing this new concept of the state, which complements Locke's considerations. It might also reduce the threat of nuclear war because the Global Council System would provide a way of balancing powers among nations and an organ for political discourse and concerted action, even among Third World nations.

NOTES

1. Alain Locke, "The Unfinished Business of Democracy," *Survey Graphic*. (November, 1942): 455.

2. Ibid.

3. Ibid.

4. Alain Locke, "Democracy Faces a World Order," *Harvard Education Review* 12 (March 1942): 121.

5. Ibid., pp. 121–122.

6. Ibid., p. 122.

7. Locke, "The Unfinished Business of Democracy," p. 456.

8. Ibid.

9. Ibid.

10. Ibid.

11. Hannah Arendt, *Crises of the Republic* (New York: Harcourt Brace Jovanovich, 1972), p. 229.

12. Locke, "The Unfinished Business of Democracy," p. 456.

13. Philip H. Rhinelander, "Peace: The Ultimate Challenge," *Stanford Magazine* (Winter 1982): 25.

14. Ibid., p. 29.

15. Alain Locke, "The Need for a New Organon in Education," *Goals for American Education* (New York: Conference on Science, Philosophy, and Religion, 1950.)

16. Locke, "Democracy Faces a World Order," p. 123.

17. Ibid.

18. Locke, "The Unfinished Business of Democracy," p. 458.

19. Ibid.

20. Ibid., p. 459.

21. Ibid.

22. Martin Luther King, Jr., *Where Do We Go from Here: Chaos or Community?* (New York: Harper and Row, 1967), p. 133.

23. Ibid., p. 134.

24. Aimé Césaire, *Discourse on Colonialism*, trans. Joan Pinkham (New York: Monthly Review Press, 1972), p. 59. Originally published as *Discours sur le colonialisme* (Paris: Présence Africaine, 1955).

25. C.W.E. Bigsby, ed., *The Black American Writer*, Vol. 2 Amherst: Penguin Books, 1969), p. 34.

26. Césaire, *Discourse on Colonialism*, p. 23.

27. Alain Locke, "Internationalism: Friend or Foe of Art?," *The World Tomorrow*, 8 (March 1925): 75.

28. Ibid.

29. Ibid.

30. Ibid.

31. Ibid.

32. Ibid., p. 76.

33. Arendt, *Crises of the Republic*, pp. 229–230.

34. Ibid., p. 230.

35. Ibid.

36. Locke, "Democracy Faces a World Order," p. 125.

5   MESSAGES TO THE BLACK ELITE

I

Although Black philosophers such as Booker T. Washington, Martin Luther King, Jr., Marcus Garvey, W.E.B. Du Bois, and Alain Locke were concerned with creating a just society in which Blacks and other minorities could live as citizens, each had differing ideas on what form such a society should take: racial integration, cultural pluralism, or cultural separation. They were also divided on the question of who would provide leadership in creating and sustaining this society, whatever its form. Should the masses lead themselves or should they follow an Elite, Black or white?

Garvey, who was inspired by Washington, did not believe that Blacks should look to whites for political leadership; nor did he feel that Blacks should seek racial or cultural integration. On this second point he and Washington were in agreement. But he differed from Washington in his belief that the real hope for Blacks lay in Africa, to which they should return in order to build their own civilization. There they would enjoy glory and excellence as they had done in precolonial times. Although the Back-to-Africa Movement was part of Garvey's political vision, he also sought to meet the needs of the Black masses of his times, largely the U.S. urban masses of the 1920s and 1930s. During the Great Depression, all ethnic groups suffered, but because of racial prejudice, Blacks suffered most. Garvey, largely in response to this crisis, mobilized urban Blacks and encouraged them to build their own economic, political, and cultural institutions and to do so independently of the white society whose values, practices, and institutions he considered morally corrupt. He elevated Black culture above white culture, and he instilled in the Black masses a sense of pride and dignity. Garvey's organization, the Universal Negro Improvement Association, with chapters in some thirty cities in the United States, attracted nearly half a million Blacks. His influence was also felt throughout the Third World, including Asia.

Like Washington, Garvey encouraged Blacks to advance themselves through their own efforts. Black businesses would provide the economic basis for community growth and stability. Garvey's self-effort program did not include the Elitist doctrine which was the cornerstone of Du Bois', Locke's and Arendt's political thought. Neither Du Bois nor Locke, however, clearly delineated the relationship between the Black Elite and the body politic; each merely stressed that the Elite would provide leadership to the Black community. In contrast, Arendt specifically discussed how the Elite related to the body politic. Consequently, this chapter covers Arendt's view of the Elite, together with Du Bois' and Locke's views, in order to strengthen our understanding of Locke's position on the Black Elite.

II

Black men and women, especially Black artists, writers, scholars, and social leaders, whose talents could advance the Black community constituted the Elite. Among these, for example, were Roland Hayes, Paul Robeson, Countee Cullen, Langston Hughes, James Weldon Johnson, as well as Du Bois and Locke. They were the cultural Elite because they were universally recognized as the creators and supporters of new cultural activities; some were active in political movements, though few, if any, held political office in party politics.

Du Bois wrote about the importance of the Elite's political task:

The Negro race, like all races, is going to be saved by its exceptional men. The problem of education, then, among Negroes must first of all deal with the Talented Tenth; it is the problem of developing the Best of this race that may guide the Mass away from the contamination and death of the Worst, in their own and other races.[1]. . . Now the training of men is a difficult and intricate task. Its technique is a matter for educational experts, but its object is for the vision of seers.[2]

No doubt Du Bois had Washington in mind when he wrote the following: "If we make money the object of man-training, we shall develop money-makers but not necessarily men; if we make technical skill the object of education, we may possess artisans but not, in nature, men."[3]

Both Locke and Du Bois thought that one of the purposes of the Black college was to train the Elite. Many of Washington's critics were more impressed with Du Bois' view of education than with Washington's. As early as 1930, in commenting on his disagreement with Washington, Du Bois restated his belief that he was right, by appealing to the social, technical, and economic trends that developed following the death of Washington. During Washington's time many educational institutions, particularly within the Black community, imitated Tuskegee, but after his death the Tuskegee model became less attractive, partly because the shifting American economy called for individuals with broad professional skills: lawyers, physicians, nurses, engineers, for example. Skills that would enable someone to shoe horses, make plowshares, and repair wagons, skills which the Tuskegee School provided, became outdated. Tractors soon replaced mules and wagons. As a result, Du Bois felt he was justified in stressing the importance of higher education: art, music, history, philosophy, law, medicine, literature, sociology, and economics, among other disciplines. One of the basic offshoots of this education was the development of character, which would give Black men and women the capacity to lead.

One other difference between Du Bois and Washington is important. Both felt that through education Blacks would be able to participate in democracy as complete citizens. Washington's position on the political question, however, was similar to Du Bois'; he felt that Blacks had a right to seek political equality, but he did not identify political equality with racial integration.

As noted earlier, he wanted the Black masses first to achieve a degree of economic security and only then to seek political equality, but not integration. People tend to confuse these two terms, insisting that both mean the same thing. But political equality, as Washington used the term, implied the capacity of members of the larger society to fully exercise civil rights—voting, office holding, and so on. In contrast, integration meant the social mixing of the white and Black races.

Because of the temper of his times, Washington wrote that it was expedient and wise for Blacks to accept segregation, work hard, buy land, and acquire skills. In this way, they would demonstrate to whites that they were worthy of citizenship. He felt that any effort by the Black Elite to promote the cause of political equality would do more harm than good. Washington hoped that whites would eventually and gradually bestow equality on his people. Hence, there was no need for aggressive action and agitation: "Time, patience, and constant achievement are great factors in the rise of a race."[4] But time passed too slowly or patience wore thin. It took a Martin Luther King, Jr., half a century later to persuade whites to enact laws that allowed Blacks to vote.

Locke, it will be seen, argued that whites should recognize at least the cultural achievements of the Black Elite; this would be a step in the direction of regarding them as citizens. The Black Elite might help speed up the process of cultural and political equality if the whites only recognized the achievements of the Elite.

In 1910 Du Bois organized the National Association for the Advancement of Colored People (NAACP), an Elite whose members included both Blacks and whites. Its goal was to remove or at least push back the wall of segregation, but in order to do this effectively, Du Bois felt he also had to fight the Tuskegee machine and even go beyond it. The NAACP focused on the legal side of the Black struggle. It was not enough for Blacks merely to own property and to be skillful laborers in the South. And even if they were successful in achieving these goals, there was no guarantee that whites would grant them real political participation and citizenship. According to the NAACP, the machinery of law was needed. Legal pressure had to be placed on governmental officials in order to force compliance with the Constitution, remove unjust laws, and enact new ones to protect the rights of Blacks and other minorities.

III

The concept of the Elite appears to be incompatible with the ideal of democracy. It suggests an aristocracy in which the few lead the many, like Plato's philosopher-king. Arendt, it will be recalled, was bothered by the term "Elite" which she wanted to reconcile with her notion of democracy. She tried to work around the difficulty by employing "Elite" to signify certain self-chosen members of the masses. Neither Locke nor Du Bois wanted an Elite built on wealth or power, but both believed there was an element of political and cultural distance between the Elite and the masses. In Arendt this distance was sharply reduced, as she maintained that the Elite comes from the masses.

Arendt's relation (bottom up) between the Elite and the masses is the reversal of Plato's sense of the relationship (top down) between the two. She reduced the inherent tension between the Elite and the masses, between what may be called nobility and democracy. In both Locke and Du Bois, however, an inherent tension between the notion of an Elite and the ideal of democracy, under the conditions of mass society, remained. Locke told the Elite to remove itself from the crowd in order to develop its own group consciousness; "Culture's par is always the best: one cannot be somebody with everybody's traits. If to be cultured is a duty, it is here that that element [duty] is most prominent, for it takes courage to stand out from the crowd."[5]

Both Du Bois and Locke, however, were like Arendt in that they sought to resolve the tension between the Elite and the masses. Neither regarded the Elite as totally detached from the Black masses below. Both felt that the role of the Elite was to fight for political and cultural equality and recognition, the achievement of which, it was hoped, would inevitably establish cultural equality for the Black masses. Locke and Du Bois contended that cultural equality was more accessible than any other type of equality. Locke, however, did not discourage Blacks from seeking political, social, and economic equality; in his essay "The Negro Group" he agreed with Washington that economic disparity was at the core of the Blacks' problems and that such disparity must be removed. But in the same context, he criticized Washington: "The great trouble, however, was that he [Washington] thought it possible to remedy this situation in terms of a compromise, with the acceptance of segregation—the great institution that has succeeded slavery as the *modus operandi* of the Negro's disability."[6]

If we had to place Locke in either Washington's compromise program or Du Bois' militant program, with its emphasis on political equality, Locke fits in Du Bois' camp more easily: "The compromise phase makes its characteristic gains, the militant phases make certain other gains. It is a matter of temperament as to which you interpret as the more important. I myself . . . believe that we have made more substantial gains in the militant phases than in the others."[7]

In most of Locke's writings, in contrast with Washington's and Du Bois', the focus was on what he called cultural equality. In no way, however, did he think that Blacks must duplicate the white culture in order to be accepted by them. He contended that all cultures, white or Black, were in fact and by definition equal, but with their own biases; people do not always accept this fact. People must recognize this equality.

Du Bois emphasized political equality, whereas King emphasized social equality or integration. Garvey differed from both in his insistence that Black culture was superior to white culture. All of these men were quite concerned not only with American culture, both Black and white, but also with African culture, which they felt the world needed to appreciate. Du Bois did not apparently go as far as Locke in saying that recognition of the cultural equality of Blacks was less remote than that of political equality and economic opportunity. Du Bois did agree with Washington that equal economic opportunity was important for Blacks, a contention which Locke would not deny. The point is that Locke regarded economic and political equality as secondary to cultural equality. In another sense Locke felt that the two types of equalities amounted to one and the same thing. The

Black cultural Elite first had to be recognized by whites as their equals. Once society had done so, it might eventually extend this equality to the Black masses:

Cultural recognition . . . will not be prematurely conceded; it will be granted only when it is demonstrably inevitable; but to my way of thinking, by virtue of these peculiar conditions, it is less remote than political or economic equality, because it is less dependent upon the condition of the masses. In light of the present attainment of the Negro of the younger generation, in cultural and artistic expression especially, and in the prospective social enlightment of our *talented tenth*, [emphasis added] I should say that cultural recognition of the Negro was imminent.[8]

Whether Locke was correct in saying that equality could be achieved through mere exposure will be considered below.

Locke, like Arendt, also tried to reconcile the ideal of democracy with the principle of the Elite. But unlike Arendt his model was the marketplace, with its ruthless competition. He thought this type of economic democracy could provide the norm for cultural democracy, which the Elite must seek to promote. This type of democracy, he maintained, was preferable to "the unearned philanthropic democracy of paper rights and class legislation."[9] Thus, Blacks should not sit and wait for society to give them their rights, but society needed to open itself at the top level so as to allow the Black Elite to compete among themselves and among the cultural Elite of other ethnic groups.

The marketplace model is inadequate for the Black Elite. Competition, whether economic or cultural, does not always produce the best behavior in people. As we know from the history of business in this country it can result in monopolies, where the most powerful destroy the disadvantaged. Thus, competition may stimulate creative people who are aggressive in their wish to produce, but it can discourage creativity in the less aggressive. These creative people may simply choose not to compete and may not want to deal with pressures or anticipated failures or successes.

Creativity might be nurtured in a noncompetitive environment where talented people, freed from pressures and anxiety, cooperate with and support one another. As Marx stated, competition in a capitalistic society tends to destroy people. Although Locke was trying to reconcile Elitism with democracy, he in fact reconciled Elitism with capitalism which thrives on competition.

One other problem which the marketplace model presents is that, under the conditions of mass production and consumption, its standard demands a leveling of tastes in order to reach the average. It follows that the marketplace model, if extended to the realm of culture, is incompatible with an Elite who is by definition above the average.

Locke's notion of competition can be criticized from another angle. He seemed to assume that by the very nature of our democratic society, which in principle exalts the notion of equal opportunity for all regardless of sex, religion, race, or color, the uneducated, poverty-stricken masses have the same opportunities as the Black Elite. But this assumption is not altogether valid. Within the existing political system, the aspiring Elite is, by virtue of its manifest interests or exceptional initiatives, better prepared to meet the challenge of democracy. The unemployed "street-walkers" might lack the motivation to enter into competition in order to discover their potential—what Jaspers called selfhood. Some unemployed street-walkers might have the potential to write poetry as well as Claude McKay or Langston Hughes, but unless they are allowed the opportunity, perhaps backed up by an Affirmative Action Plan to develop this potential, they will never be able to demonstrate it and thus will never be able to become part of the Elite.

As was noted, Locke said that the Elite had to play the key role in getting whites to recognize it and to appreciate Blacks generally. Locke explained what he meant by cultural recognition of the Elite and of the masses: "[It] means the removal of wholesale social proscription and, therefore, the conscious scrapping of the mood and creed of 'White Supremacy'. It means an open society instead of a closed ethnic shop."[10] As suggested earlier, this cultural and political recognition can best be achieved in an Arendt-type of community. The councils make possible the open society which Locke prized, one in which the various ethnic groups can make cultural and political contacts. Because the councils, as political organs, cut across cultural and racial boundaries, they provide spaces for open communication among individuals and groups. In addition, in Arendt's view, one need not be among the Talented Tenth in order to participate in democracy and become recognized; the only requirement is to take the initiative to enter into the political arena. Having made that entrance, one can earn the trust and respect of one's peers and to do so does not necessarily require ruthless competition. In Arendt, the community is open at the bottom from which the political Elite originates. Locke, however, desired that the community be open at the top.

IV

Arendt's concept of the political community, if adopted, could help dispel the white supremacy myth of which Locke spoke. Although this myth and its related Black inferiority myth originated in Greek antiquity, they did not become pervasive until the advent of American slavery. During the slavery era and afterwards, these myths were reinforced to provide a rationale for slavery and cheap labor; the men who controlled the political and economic institutions promoted these myths in order to maintain their positions of power and authority. Our democratic society, ostensibly dedicated to the principle of human equality, did little to challenge these errors; in fact, our so-called democratic institutions greatly supported the myths. For example, many of the Founding Fathers owned slaves.

Locke assigned to the Black Elite the task of convincing whites and Blacks that these myths had no basis in fact. This task is too great for Locke's Elite, however, if it is concerned mainly with matters of culture rather than with politics. To dispel these myths and to induce whites to develop an open attitude toward Blacks and other minorities requires a reorganization of the existing political structure of society. The party system needs to be replaced by the council system, so that the grass roots can participate directly in politics.

The council system would provide little motivation to perpetuate the inferiority/superiority myth, and anyone who wished to take part in politics could do so. The traditional institutions in which the racial myths of national sovereignty are institutionalized would be reorganized, making power, authority, freedom, and equality accessible to all, not just to select individuals.

From the era of Reconstruction to the very recent past, it was difficult for a Black political candidate, however qualified, to get elected to a major political office. First, Blacks had difficulty getting adequate financial support. Second, a Black candidate had a difficult time obtaining the votes of the larger society which was not accustomed to having Blacks as its representatives.

In Arendt's system, a minority person would have a better chance in the political arena. In the political institutions of the United States, there would be no need for expensive political campaign backing to pay for television coverage and other image-making techniques; one would merely enter into the council system. Having earned the trust of one's peers at the first level of the system, one could move to the next level, where again one would be among peers. This level, which would include representatives of the various systems of the federated councils, would be open to all: there, myths and other political propaganda devices would be replaced by facts, opinions, and open discussions that would promote trust and respect. The Black Elite would be representative of Blacks as well as other groups; in the council system, representatives of the various groups would have the opportunity to make contacts with one another—Blacks, whites, Jews, Protestants, Catholics, Chinese, Italians, among others. They would be in a position to engage in debate and to pursue joint projects.

Arendt's and Locke's positions complement each other. A genuine, open society must allow for the cultural values of each ethnic group; it must also, as Arendt suggested, be organized politically to allow for grass-roots participation and to permit the Elite members to come from the masses. Locke's Elite must, however, do more than create cultural objects, if there is to be a genuine, open society. The mere exposure of the Elite's activities and achievements is not sufficient to achieve political equality, for white Americans will not automatically appreciate the cultural achievements of Black Americans. Materialistic Americans, bent on satisfying pragmatic, individualistic interests, tend not to pay much attention to their own culture, let alone the cultures of minorities. This is true even though America's own culture is heavily indebted to its ethnic minorities and to women.

Africans and their descendants have been making history since time immemorial, but it was not until the time of Carter G. Woodson that America began to "set aside" one week each year to recognize Black historical and cultural achievements. Only recently did the U.S. Congress designate the month of February as Black History Month. In contrast, in most educational institutions, European history is studied all year. Locke thought that the makers of history and culture, the Elite, would create a positive image of Blacks in the minds of whites. One may ask whether this is the most effective way of solving the problems Blacks suffer. Race is only part of the problem; other deep-seated political problems are associated with the fact that Blacks have not had access to political power. Historically, they have been kept out of party politics. This is why we need a new concept of the state, if the Elite is to be politically effective.

V

In Locke's essay "The Ethics of Culture," which is directed mainly to Black students, he wrote that students have a duty to acquire education in the area of culture; they are morally obligated to become educated, to become members of the culture-producing Elite. What does Locke mean by culture as it pertains to education in this context? He counterposed his own definition of culture with Matthew Arnold's who wrote: "Culture is the best that has been thought and known in the world."[11] But the trouble with Arnold's definition, according to Locke, is that it stresses external rather than internal factors. Locke explained: "Rather is it the capacity for understanding the best and most representative forms of human expression, and of expressing oneself, if not in similar creativeness, at least in appreciative reactions and in progressively responsive refinement of tastes and interests."[12]

The connection between duty and culture is as follows: one has a duty to actualize one's potential, to develop oneself to the highest capacity, to become cultured. Education is normally construed as imposing the duty to develop intellect, the rational faculty. To this end, Washington felt that Blacks had a duty to acquire specific technical skills. Locke did not stress this type of knowledge; he insisted that each individual had a duty to develop his or her own character and tastes.

In traditional moral theories there is much talk about duty to others: always act in such a way as to respect the humanity in others (Kant); love thy neighbor as well as thy enemies (Jesus); it is better to suffer wrongdoing than to commit an act of wrongdoing (Socrates). Locke's view of duty, at least in this context, was directed more toward the self than others. One first has to develop one's self, after which one can be in a position to help others to develop themselves. One does have duties to help others develop in order to fulfill one's ethical and social obligations, but when the concept of duty is extended to education, one's foremost duty is to develop one's self, to acquire culture. It is a self-imposed duty: "No one can make you cultured, few will care whether you are or are not, for I admit that the world of today primarily demands efficiency."[13] Although here Locke's views on the relationship between duty and culture is directed mainly to Black students, they apply equally to any audience.

As has been noted, Locke's conception of culture was somewhat at odds with the ideal of democracy. Because a democracy that is controlled by the standards of the marketplace operates to standardized tastes, there is little incentive to enlarge the intellectual culture of the masses. Therefore, Locke told the Elite that, if it wished to develop itself, it must move beyond the crowd: "In the pursuit of culture one must detach himself from the crowd."[14] One senses what seems to be a Nietzschean influence here: "Your chief handicap in this matter as young people of today is the psychology and 'pull' of the crowd."[15] This is where the duty to be cultured becomes important. Locke added, "Dare to be different—stand out!"[16] The Elite has a duty to lead the masses; in turn, he suggested that the masses have a duty to follow the Elite, who points the way.

Although Locke, no less than Du Bois, echoed the Nietzschean mass-Elite distinction, there is a sharp difference between Nietzsche's concept of the Elite and Locke's. Nietzsche makes the master-slave distinction. The values of the masters are entirely different from those of the slaves who constitute "the herd." The values of the masters flow from the principle of domination and are expressed as: "Might is right"; the values of slaves flow from the principle of submission and are expressed as: "Turn the other cheek." Not only do the masters and the slaves oppose one another's values, but also the masters despise the slaves and their way of life. By dominating the slaves, the masters keep them "in their place" and maintain the elevation of their own position. Nietzsche noted the distinction between the two types of moralities:

There is *master morality* and *slave morality*. . . . The moral value-distinctions have arisen either among a ruling order which was pleasurably conscious of its distinction from the ruled—or among the ruled, the slaves and the dependants [sic] of every degree. In the former case, when it is rulers who determine the concept "good", it is the exalted, proud states of soul which are considered distinguishing and determine the order or rank. The noble human being separates from himself those natures in which the opposite of such exalted proud states finds expression: he despises them. It should be noted at once that in this first type of morality the antithesis "good" and "bad" means the same thing as "noble" and "despicable."[17]

In contrast, in Locke as in Du Bois, the relation between the Elite and the masses is not outright hostility, although an element of tension exists between the two. Indeed, Locke maintained that the Elite has a duty to elevate itself above the masses, but it achieves and holds this elevated position in order to uplift the masses, not to keep them in their place. Cultural and psychological distance is required between the Elite and the many, but this does not suggest in any way that the Elitists may despise those in the masses. On the contrary, the Elite remains loyal to the Black masses and vice versa. Without the principle of loyalty and the element of distance, there would undoubtedly be explosive tension between the masses and the Elite. Locke's Elite stands to inspire the masses to embrace higher standards of tastes, to move beyond what Nietzsche would call the slave morality. The effort of the Elite will enable the masses to overcome this slave morality, for the good of the Black community and the Republic. By doing so, Locke believed that the cultured Blacks would benefit the community: "Strive to overcome this [the psychology of the herd] for your own sake and, as Cicero would say, 'for the welfare of the Republic.' "[18]

How is this cultured way to be attained? Should Black institutions of learning put more emphasis on the fine arts and music? Should Black students be required to take a certain number of courses in the humanities? These, according to Locke, are important questions, and he suggested that students should be encouraged to take such courses. But the path to high intellectual culture involves something more personal. "I content myself," Locke wrote, "with the defense of [high] culture in general, and with the opportunity it gives of explaining its two most basic aspects—the great amateur arts of personal expression—conversation and manners."[19] Yes, the fine arts are important, but equally important are what he called the personal arts: "they are their foundation."[20]

Many people equate a superficial knowledge of the fine arts with possession of high culture. Some people even believe that the objects of the fine arts—paintings, sculptures, rare books, and so on—are consumer items primarily to be bought and sold at a profit. To become cultured, according to Locke, it does not suffice merely to possess the products of culture, nor is it enough to have "inert" knowledge of the fine arts or other elements of culture. The knowledge of culture has to be translated back into "personal refinement and cultivated sensibilities."[21] One becomes cultured by engaging intensively in the products of the fine arts to the extent that these affect not only the intellect but the emotions as well, resulting in a refined sensibility. Transformed in this way, the cultivated personality will have a greater power responding to people and things. His or her refined speech and manners will reflect what Whitehead called a certain "style" from which springs the power of one's personality, where the fine arts are firmly assimilated and interwoven, transforming art into life and life into art: "Whoever would achieve this must recognize that life itself is an art, perhaps the finest of the fine arts—because it is the composite blend of them all."[22]

One need not study the fine arts exclusively in order to become cultured. Scientists, too, can become cultured. Under certain circumstances, Locke claimed that studying science can be culturally more enriching than studying the humanities: "Science, penetratingly studied, can yield as much and more culture than the humanities mechanically studied."[23] Therefore, the point of view and the degree of intrinsic interest one brings to bear on that content is of greater importance. Locke encouraged college students to concentrate on at least one course in the humanities to increase their chances of becoming cultured.

As the educated person becomes cultured, he or she will be in a greater position to join the ranks of the producers of culture. Locke was well aware that not every educated person would become a great artist or writer. Yet, each person in the process of becoming cultured probably possesses a latent artistic temperament, "if it only expresses itself in love and daydreaming."[24] If a person cannot become a great producer of culture, he or she can at least develop an appreciation of certain cultural items. Thus, each educated person has the duty to keep his or her standards of tastes above those that govern the masses. When Locke spoke of the masses in this context, he meant both the Black and white masses: "And as Americans," Locke wrote, "we all share this handicap of the low average of cultural tastes."[25] He added: "A brilliant Englishman once characterized America as a place where everything had a price, but nothing a value, referring to the typical preference for practical and utilitarian points of view."[26] For Locke, then, the Black Elite had a mission to uplift the standards of tastes of *both* whites and Blacks.

Locke regarded conversation as a key element in personal culture. He suggested that the art of genuine conversation in mass society was slowly being destroyed. He warned the Elite about the dangers of mass society, and he insisted that the Elite had to persist in developing and preserving the personal arts: manners and conversation. Let us take Locke's notion of conversation a little further by considering it in the context of our contemporary world.

There are certain parallels between Locke's view of conversation and James W. Carey's view of communication in a technological world. In a recent article, "High-Speed Communication in an Unstable World," Carey describes how technological communication—cable, computer, and satellite—is a double-edged sword: it can bring people of the globe closer together, or it can pull them farther apart. For example, millions of bits of information can be processed in a matter of minutes on one side of the globe and shared by people thousands of miles away. That technological communication can drive people further apart is explained by Carey who sees such a mode of communication as involving a contradiction:

The simultaneous growth, then, of a worldwide, integrated system of technological communication has as its dark underside the spread of division and revolt and disharmony. . . .

Wherein lies the contradiction? It seems as if the ability to convert knowledge into forms that can be transmitted and utilized by highly technological systems dries up the interpretive capacity to understand other people. When knowledge is bleached into information, it becomes less reliably informing. The technical system, for all its power, is in many ways superficial and creates problems with mutual understanding: the ability to grasp an argument, listen to people who speak with foreign accents, and interpret complex cultures that are not one's own.[27]

When Locke died in 1954, our technology had hardly reached its current stage. But Locke foresaw its consequences, its advantages and disadvantages. He wanted to use technology to strengthen ties among people of the world, but in order to be effective, the usage of such technology required that it also relate to the social and personal aspects of human existence. For example, in our mode of communication we have to be concerned with more than what he called mere informational knowledge, the kind of knowledge that today's computers manipulate. Carey and Locke are in agreement here.

Locke, in his "Coming of Age," anticipated Carey by about fifty years. In this essay, which is concerned with the education of the masses, Locke suggested what type of education was needed to balance technological communication and to promote international understanding:

By radio, motion picture, visual materials of all sorts, the adult education radius of teaching and propaganda must be extended to the dimensions of an international age. That means more than mere lengthened scope of operations; it means, more critically, the discovery of fresh common denominators of human interests and values, fresh emphasis on the social aspects and implications of knowledge and deeper concern with personal and group attitudes than with mere informational knowledge or individual skills.[28]

Although Locke regarded the art of conversation as an antidote to the corroding influence of mass society, if he were writing today, he would probably apply his view of conversation to the negative effects of technological communication. For evidence see the above passage in which he regarded "mere informational knowledge or individual skills" as something to be fought against. Today he would agree with Carey regarding the activities involved in genuine personal communication, namely, understanding, questioning, struggling, and interrogating. These basic activities are needed as a counterbalance to high-speed technological communication, for if such counterbalance is not cultivated, a greater disunity among people of the world will result. Carey says that this counterbalance might be achieved if people developed a deeper appreciation for such disciplines as history and literature which nurture the art of interpretation, a view with which Locke would be in agreement.

VI

Although both Locke and Arendt thought culture and politics were closely linked, Arendt went further than Locke in providing justifications for this relationship. In doing so, she relied heavily on Kant's theory of the aesthetic as formulated in his *Critique of Judgement*. The connection between politics and aesthetics can be appreciated if we review Arendt's interpretation of Kant's *Critique of Judgement* which she found compatible with her conception of the body politic. In her view, the political realm owed its existence to what she called the condition of plurality, the condition under which people appear as distinct, unique individuals. Whereas individuals are unique, they also have something in common, that is, the capacity to understand one another through language. Her notion of plurality is used in contradistinction to the traditional notion of human nature, which signifies that human beings possess the element of rationality which distinguishes them from the lower animals.

Kant's theory of aesthetics has no place for an absolute principle which demands self-consistency as in his views on morals, which are based on the notion that all people possess reason. Arendt found that his aesthetics allowed a kind of openness in judgment that forbade absolute thinking, and also permitted a plurality of perspectives. Furthermore, she maintained that such judgments owed their validity largely to the presence of other judging persons. This is one reason why she thought the political community was so important.

In the *Critique of Judgement* Kant shifted from stressing the need to be in agreement with one's self, the need for self-consistency as his moral theory enjoined, to the need to be in agreement with others. The presence of others with whom we might reach some accord provides the basis for the validity of aesthetic judgment. Moreover, aesthetic judgments involve what is called an "enlarged mentality." Arendt interpreted Kant's enlarged mentality as follows:

In the *Critique of Judgement*, however, Kant insisted upon a different way of thinking, for which it would not be enough to be in agreement with one's own self, but which consisted of being able to "think in the place of everybody else" and which he therefore called an "enlarged mentality" (*eine erweiterte Denkungsart*).[29] . . . The power of judgment rests on a potential agreement with others, and the thinking process which is active in judging something is not, like the thought process of pure reasoning, a dialogue between me and myself, but finds itself always and primarily, even if I am quite alone in making up my mind, in an anticipated communication with others with whom I know I must finally come to some agreement. From this potential agreement judgment derives its specific validity.[30]

This notion of an "enlarged mentality" enabled Arendt to make the connection between politics and culture. She thought that by assuming this enlarged mentality one engaged in political thought or judgment. For to think politically, one had to have the capacity to reach agreement with others and at times think in the place of those whom the judging person represented. Judgments, she said, referred to the public aspect of the world and were therefore political. The judging person, like the statesman, considered diverse perspectives and the opinions of others; one had to move beyond one's private feelings. One had to

achieve impartiality, generality, and objectivity. Aesthetic judgments could not be made in isolation, just as political actions—
in Arendt's sense of the term—could not be enjoyed in isolation:
"it [aesthetic judgment] needs the presence of others in whose
place it must think, whose perspectives it must take into consideration, and without whom it never has the opportunity to
operate at all."[31] She agreed with Aristotle that, in the political
realm, persuasion rather than force or violence ruled intercourse
among citizens. Physical force or violence was harmful to the
body politic because of its coercive or domineering nature.

The same can be said of philosophic truth, which Aristotle
distinguished from political discourse. Philosophic knowledge
involves a process of compelling truth, whereby conclusions
follow logically from premises; this process is coercive. Aesthetic
judgments, on the other hand, involve freedom because they
rely on persuasion. Genuine political discourse allows the judging person to think and act with autonomy, without being com-
pelled by any sort of absolutes.

Arendt's Elite, who constitute the council system, can be seen
as engaging in political judgments:

Political thought is representative. I form an opinion by considering a
given issue from different viewpoints, by making present to my mind
the standpoints of those who are absent; that is, I represent them. This
process of representation does not blindly adopt the actual views of
those who stand somewhere else, and hence look upon the world from
a different perspective; this is a question neither of empathy . . . nor
of counting noses and joining a majority but of being and thinking in
my own identity where actually I am not.[32]

Thus, the Black Elite, and for that matter any other political Elite,
must assume this enlarged mentality in order to make effective,
valid judgments applicable not only to the Black community,
but also to the entire political arena.

This type of political thinking is applicable to the problem of
the nuclear arms race. Jaspers and Rhinelander, as noted earlier,
are right when they say that a new way of thinking is needed
in order to meet the ultimate challenge posed by the threat of
nuclear war. They do not believe that the problem is altogether

a matter of technology. Nor do they believe that when the superpowers reach an agreement as to what constitutes a balance of technological might, so that the two are checked by mutual fear, we will have achieved a solution to the arms race.

Although Locke did not use the term "enlarged mentality" and his focus with regard to world peace was on culture and education, his notion of the need for global thinking (see chapter 6) closely approximated Arendt's notion of the enlarged mentality. According to Locke, education should introduce us to global thinking and thereby prepare people to acquire this enlarged mentality. Through mutual understanding, people will be able to share the world together, without the threat of war. A number of authorities in the United States have recently said that the solution to the nuclear arms problem lies in education. Even Dewey would have agreed with this statement. Locke, however, would have criticized him for placing too much stress on technological education. Locke demanded that education should emphasize the study of cultural values.

Arendt's notions of the political Elite and the council system are formulated, respectively, in her *On Revolution* and *Between Past and Future*. But she never combined these two notions as we are attempting to do here; she did not show how the political Elite exercised political thinking as described above. These two notions are compatible and reinforce each other, and in combination they strengthen Arendt's own political thought, rendering it more coherent. The same is true for Locke's view. Locke needed to broaden his notion of the Elite so as to include a political Elite in Arendt's sense of the term, one that originates from the masses and is politically representative of the masses.

Of course, in order for this type of representation to be effective, people would need to adopt a structure similar to Arendt's council system, wherein power and authority would be shared among equals. In a federated council system, the Black Elite would not be isolated from the Elites of other ethnic groups. Rather, the councils would provide spaces for the councilors to act in concert at the various levels of the pyramid structure of the system. If the councilors were to adopt the enlarged mentality, the atmosphere of openness could pervade the entire political community. This would counteract the self-interest that dominates party politics today. In the new political order, the Elite who engaged in genuine political thinking as opposed to ideological mudslinging would, by virtue of this enlarged mentality, cut across all ideological, cultural, ethnic, and racial boundaries. Those who assume the task of true statesmanship would cut across national boundaries and shoulder the political burdens of the world. Witness King, Du Bois, and others.

The council system would probably not end all "power struggles" and value conflicts that pervade politics. As Locke maintained, people will always have value differences and conflicts. But in the new system in which everyone would have access to power and authority, at least at the grass-roots level, and in which power and authority would be shared among peers, power struggles and value conflicts could be sharply curtailed.

Locke repeatedly stated that most of the value conflicts in human affairs spring from dogmatic, absolutist thinking. This type of thinking, he maintained, inhibits open communication among people, resulting in a group imposing its "absolute" values on others who often resist such imposition. Arendt's notion of political thinking would discourage such dogmatic thinking because her concept involves persuasion, through which people give and take in face-to-face dialogue.

Thus, the Black Elite must approach the problems people face on many fronts, two of which are the cultural and the political. In addition, the cultural Elite and the political Elite need to combine their efforts. The Black Elite must continue to produce culture, as Locke insisted. But a cultural Elite by itself is not sufficient. The community should also develop a political Elite who will be more directly involved in politics. Both the cultural and the political Elites should be representative of the community, an ideal that can best be achieved in a council system in which the Black Elite can establish political ties with the Elites of other groups. Such a system provides a relatively permanent, yet flexible, organ for performing the business of politics, in ways that are fair, open, and accessible to all.

NOTES

1. W.E.B. Du Bois, "The Talented Tenth," in *The Negro Problem: A Series of Articles by Representative Negroes of To-Day*, Booker T. Washington and others, eds. (New York: A.M.S. Press, 1903), p. 33.

2. Ibid.

3. Ibid.

4. August Meier, Elliott Rudwick, and Francis L. Broderick, eds., *Black Protest Thought in the Twentieth Century*, 2d ed. (Indianapolis: Bobbs-Merrill Company, 1976), p. 16.

5. Alain Locke, "The Ethics of Culture," *Howard University Record* 18 (January 1923): 182.

6. Alain Locke, "The Negro Group," in *Group Relations and Group Antagonisms*, ed. R. M. MacIver (New York: Harper and Bros., 1944), p. 50.

7. Ibid., p. 47.

8. Alain Locke, "The High Cost of Prejudice," *The Forum* 78 (December 1927): 502–503.

9. Ibid., p. 504.

10. Ibid.

11. Locke, "The Ethics of Culture," p. 179.

12. Ibid.

13. Ibid., p. 178.

14. Ibid., p. 181.

15. Ibid.

16. Ibid., p. 182.

17. Friedrich Nietzsche, *A Nietzsche Reader*, trans. R. J. Hollingdale (New York: Penguin Books, 1977), p. 106.

18. Locke, "The Ethics of Culture," p. 182.

19. Ibid.

20. Ibid.

21. Ibid.

22. Ibid.

23. Ibid., p. 183.

24. Ibid.

25. Ibid.

26. Ibid.

27. James W. Carey, "High-Speed Communication in an Unstable World," *The Chronicle of Higher Education*, July 27, 1983, p. 48.

28. Alain Locke, "Coming of Age," *Adult Education Journal* 6 (January 1947): 3.

29. Hannah Arendt, *Between Past and Future*, (New York: Viking Press, 1968), p. 220.

30. Ibid.

31. Ibid., pp. 220–221.

32. Ibid., p. 241.

6 HISTORICAL STUDIES IN EDUCATION

I

Alain Locke urged that Black colleges offer courses pertaining to Black culture, so that youth could develop a positive self-image. He also urged that strong Black men and women provide leadership in these colleges. As a cultural pluralist, Locke examined the education of Blacks within the context of American culture. However, he often examined knowledge and inquiry within an international context, insisting that by increasing our knowledge of other cultures of the world we could promote world peace.

This chapter focuses on Locke's essay, "The Need for a New Organon in Education," (1950) whose audience was the larger society and not just Black Americans. He chose this audience because he argued that educators contended that their own cultural values were superior to those of ethnic minorities. Therein lay the problem of education and other cultural problems. As the solution, he offered an outline of a new philosophy of education. He saw a close link between the crisis in education and the crisis in American culture, although he never clearly spelled out the nature of the cultural crisis. Later in this chapter it is argued that Locke's views can be incorporated into the works of the African philosopher Kwasi Wiredu who argued for decolonization of African thought.

In the first part of "The Need for a New Organon in Education," Locke identified three problems in education: the first had to do with the fact "that contemporary learning suffers from a serious and immobilizing lack of any vital and effective integration, both as a body of knowledge and as a taught curriculum"; the second, that knowledge had not been effectively brought to bear on the social-cultural realm: "and third, that unless some revitalizing integration is soon attained, not only the social impotence of our knowledge must be conceded in spite of its technological effectiveness, but a breakdown of culture itself may be anticipated."[1] But Locke also pointed to a more basic problem—dogmatic attitudes or values—which are discussed below.

Locke noted that most philosophers concurred with his understanding of the three factors. He also pointed out that most of the proposed solutions offered by philosophers and educators included the following: the need to tie education to the practical demands of living, the need to broaden the students' social visions, and the need to sharpen the students' critical faculties.

This emphasis on practical knowledge and sharpening of critical skills pervaded Dewey's view on education. Frederick Douglass and Booker T. Washington, too, insisted on the importance of practical knowledge; such an emphasis was to be expected in a pragmatic society. In the search for integrating or coordinating elements, which were also intended to make knowledge practical, people became preoccupied with orientation general education, and core-curriculum courses, among others. The "Great Books" plan was introduced in order to broaden the student's perspective and social vision and to connect the student's thinking with major interests of contemporary life, whether they were personal or social, local or global. Each of these proposals, Locke said, had the following aspect in common: "the laudable attempt to link academic learning with the practical issues of living, and thus develop critical acumen and trained aptitudes for responsible intelligent action."[2]

Locke recognized that each of these proposals had something to offer but they were inadequate in and of themselves. It is not sufficient merely to reorganize the content of the subject matter giving new emphasis by changing focus and perspective. Nor is it enough to broaden the student's social outlook. Rather,

Locke urged the adoption of a new way of thinking about the content of the reorganized subject matter and a new way of teaching this content:

Accordingly, these suggestions of a much needed supplementation are brought forward in the conviction that mere curriculum extension or revision is insufficient, and that a more fundamental methodological change both in ways of teaching and in ways of thinking is necessary, if we are to achieve the objectives of reorientation and integration so obviously required and so ardently sought.[3]

In calling for a new way of thinking about the subject matter, Locke seemed to be echoing Peirce and Dewey. Although he did not mention them, he did allude to the Logical Positivists and the semanticists. He agreed with them "to the extent that their project of 'unified knowledge' calls for a more precise and more relevant logic than the verbalist and formalistic one."[4] But he even had problems with their proposal of a new logic, because such a logic, "instead of yielding a clarifying and critical instrument, remains up to the present more recondite and abstract than the old logic it plans to supersede."[5]

What did Locke cite as the aims and objectives of education? Like Whitehead, he thought that educators should have as their goals more than those pervasive in education today: the acquisition of information, the accumulation of facts, and the "objective" analysis of facts. As noted previously, he thought that educators needed to devise plans that would introduce integrating elements into education. Like Whitehead, he, too, insisted that the broadening of the student's vision should be among the chief aims of education. The goals of broadened vision could be achieved largely through what Locke called global thinking and process understanding. The notion of process understanding, which Locke never clearly defined, supports the contention here that Locke was sympathetic to process philosophers such as Dewey and Whitehead, who also insisted that educators should aim at developing the students' capacity for evaluative criticism. Locke wrote: "We are making the assumption, of course, that global thinking, and what has been called 'process understanding,' and the capacity for evaluative criticism are compositely the prime objectives of the several general educational schemes."[6]

Locke insisted, however, that unless educators first dealt directly with the most basic problem, that is, changing the ways in which students think, educators' efforts to achieve the above objectives would be futile. Regardless of how much information the students acquired, they would still cling to the values of their own culture. Hence, there was a need for a new organon that would allow students to recast old attitudes and develop open attitudes toward others. This is what Locke required to reintroduce values in education: "If modernized contemporary education is to deal with attitudes, it must perforce grapple realistically with values and value judgments; if it is to build constructive mind-sets, or even fashion efficient critical ones, it must somehow restore the normative element in education."[7] Locke was aware of the difficulties involved in attempting to change student attitudes. The difficulties were due to a fine line between what he called remedial attitude reconstruction and political or religious indoctrination. If educators set out to change student attitudes, this already presupposed a value commitment on the part of the educators, suggesting that certain attitudes or values ought to be encouraged and others discouraged or dispelled.

II

If Locke had regarded the element of belief as the basic ingredient of knowledge and inquiry, then in a sense he would have been in less treacherous waters. He would have shared Dewey's claim that education should enable students to examine their beliefs critically in order to learn to entertain meaningful, valid, consistent, and workable beliefs and to dispel erroneous, meaningless, and unworkable ones. According to Dewey, meaningful beliefs were socially useful, and the erroneous were not. Many argue that erroneous beliefs are the prime ingredients of religious and political indoctrination.

But there is a fundamental difference between Locke's epistemological orientation and that of the Pragmatist in whose views the notion of belief, as already noted, has a central place. Rather, basic to Locke's view is the notion of attitude.

Although it may be fairly easy to distinguish between indoctrination and education proper from the standpoint of beliefs, it is not so easy from the standpoint of attitudes. There are generally acceptable criteria for distinguishing between true and false beliefs, but what meaning do criteria for distinguishing between true and false attitudes have? Pragmatists such as Dewey and James offered the principle of utility as the criterion for knowledge. In a sense an attitude is like a prayer: it is quite difficult to assign truth value to either. It does not make sense to say "Rev. Jones' prayer last Sunday was false." Yet it does make sense to say, "Hitler's attitude about the Jews was wrong and false," for in this case, the result was evil action.

Although Locke did not seek to assign truth values to attitudes, he did make a moral commitment when he talked about attitudes and their place in education. In fact, it will be remembered, he agreed with Santayana that all values derived from feelings or attitudes. From this it follows that there are right and wrong attitudes, or, stated another way, there are right and wrong values which are often shaped in youth by the educative process. This is why Locke said that educators must take a value stand and take corrective measures to reshape attitudes. He was referring especially to the larger society's dogmatic attitude that its values were superior to those of its ethnic minorities.

In "The Need for a New Organon in Education" Locke suggested corrective measures for reshaping the attitudes mainly of college students. But in "Minorities and the Social Mind," Locke offered a procedure for molding attitudes and behavior during the students' earliest school years. He thought that an effective handle on racial problems required beginning with elementary school education, during the formative stages of a youth's character and outlook. Here, Locke used language drawn from the area of medicine. In order to promote health for individuals and the community at large, it was not sufficient to treat symptoms of disease, nor was it practical to try to eliminate germs altogether. Rather, the practical approach, supplemented by other treatment, lay in preventive medicine. Similarly, educators, Locke said, must commit themselves to preventive medicine in the area of race relations, in order to uproot the emotional bases of racial conflicts: "Preventive medicine does not hope to abolish germs; it works on the principles of controlling sources of infection, of building resistance, or fighting poison with antidotes."[8]

This approach offered a key to the problem of indoctrination at least for elementary education. It speaks to the problem of indoctrination because Locke insisted that one way to educate children against racial prejudice was to make them aware of cultural differences, but such an acquaintance "should take place under controlled situations; in other words, that he [the student] be deliberately educated rather than just arbitrarily indoctrinated with regard to these things."[9] Locke meant that the classroom should serve as a clinic, a controlled environment, in which educators could help build resistance to prejudiced and biased attitudes, and not just mild palliatives and correctives.

Pushing his preventive medicine analogy further, Locke suggested that the school could provide the situation for "sterilizing the emotional beds of pride and prejudice, realizing that not all pride is healthy, and that the variety which is founded upon the depreciation of other groups and thrives at their expense is unsound and dangerous."[10] This removal of false pride and prejudice could be accomplished by teaching children the cultural histories of America's ethnic groups. Such an approach would render much group vanity and egotism intellectually impossible or ridiculous.[11] Not only did Locke want children in school to become acquainted with the traditions of various cultures, but he also thought that the school offered opportunities for "human contacts under the controlled influence of the school as a definite antitoxin to the social virus inherent in the social heredity and the uncontrolled social background."[12]

Most of Locke's suggestions, included in his preventive medicine concept, have been put into practice through bussing and other school integration programs, but these programs have met with much resistance. Does this in any way indicate a weakness in Locke's preventive medicine proposal? The answer is probably yes, for in fact, schools have been used to *promote* racism. If Locke were active today, with racial and cultural crises profound in the United States, the Middle East, Central America, and other parts of the world, rather than talk about preventive medicine he would declare the world to be in a state of emergency. He would recommend that educators worldwide work to repair the minds of youth, as physicians in intensive care units work to save the lives of patients with failing hearts.

Between the publication of "Minorities and the Social Mind" (1935) and "The Need for a New Organon in Education" approximately fifteen years passed. Yet both essays develop the same theme: the need to teach students to have open attitudes to the cultural values of others. In "The Need for a New Organon in Education," Locke did not use the preventive medicine concept; instead, he emphasized a methodology to which students and teachers should subscribe, the historical-comparative approach.

Educators are to avoid the problem of political or religious indoctrination in elementary and secondary schools by organizing school programs around scientific principles. The same could be done for college students: appeal to the methodology of science upon which the historical-comparative approach rests. Through this approach one may objectively study the values, practices, and institutions of various cultures, and make cross-cultural comparisons and contrasts. Of equal importance is that similarities, contrasts, and conflicts should be traced to their historical origins.

The historical-comparative approach could then warrantably be maintained as the only proper (in the sense of the only scientific) way of understanding values, including particularly those of one's own culture and way of life. It would be regarded as educationally mandatory to view values relativistically in time perspective, so as to comprehend value change and development, and likewise, to see them in comparative perspective, so as to understand and appreciate value diversity.[13]

Showing how this method can dispel dogmatic, absolutist thinking, Locke added: "Thus there could be derived from critical relativism a corrective discipline aimed at the undermining of dogma-forming attitudes in thinking and the elimination of the partisan hundred percentist mentality at its very psychological roots."[14]

III

To the extent that Locke wanted to reintroduce the study of values into the educative process and inquiry, he had much in common with Whitehead and Dewey. In *The Aims of Education*, Whitehead identified three patterns within the educative process: romance, specialization, and generalization. In the first stage, romance, the feeling of excitement is dominant; this is the stage of freedom, manifest in adventurous, creative activities by which learning takes place in leaps and bounds. These feelings of excitement, Whitehead stated, should also pervade the second stage, although they should not be dominant. According to Whitehead, educators usually get fixated in the second stage, specialization, and fail to allow the students' minds to develop in accordance with their rhythmic patterns to the final stage. In the stage of generalization, inert, disconnected facts are utilized, transformed into wisdom with a balance of depth and breadth. In this final stage, which is a dialectical synthesis of the two previous stages, intellectual vision is enlivened by the feelings of romance, of freedom and adventure. During the generalization stage, wisdom is exercised and students learn to make effective value judgments that result in virtuous actions. Whitehead sees a close link between virtue and global thinking, and between virtue and evaluative criticism.

Like Whitehead, Locke placed evaluative criticism over reason and analytic skill; both saw a close tie between values and feelings. The same is true of Dewey, who erased the distinction between means and ends by insisting that means and ends constituted a continuum. Although Locke did not altogether destroy this distinction, in his analysis of values he emphasized feelings, attitudes, and preferences, almost to the exclusion of ends and consequences. Neither Locke, Whitehead, nor Dewey drew a sharp distinction between facts and values. Values were relative to an individual's feelings which could be regarded as having a basis in fact. Locke was aware that, through cultural conditioning and other social pressures, one could easily develop dogmatic attitudes, biases, and prejudices, particularly toward people whose life-style differed from one's own. He blamed traditional educational practices for fostering such attitudes created by certain mind-sets engendered by our culture. Any new educational programs should effectively change such attitudes by reinstating values considerations in education so that students could develop what Locke called a constructive mind-set. By this term he meant an open, critical attitude toward all cultures.

Dewey spoke at length about critical thinking and the normative regard for values as key ingredients in education. In this way education became practical and useful in a technological society. Unlike Locke and Whitehead, Dewey made beliefs the centerpiece of his value and education theories. The educators' task was to encourage the student to critically examine his or her beliefs, sorting out the inconsistent ideas and reinforcing those that promoted social growth and harmony.

Dewey did not have a high regard for historical studies, focusing rather on present and future conditions. As his model of education and enquiry he used the methodology of the physical sciences and technology. They would be instrumental in controlling the fluxes and transformations that push present conditions into the future. Dewey insisted that students develop skills in these areas in order to transform present social and physical realities and envision future possibilities.

Whitehead, on the other hand, placed a greater emphasis on historical knowledge, but as a process philosopher, like Dewey, he kept his focus on the experiences of the present and on future possibilities. Locke would have criticized both Whitehead and Dewey for placing too much emphasis on the present and the future, and not enough on the past.

Dewey and Whitehead were interested in what Locke called cultural values—the artistic, intellectual, and spiritual products of civilizations. All three wrote extensively on art and aesthetics. Whitehead's models of civilization were ancient Greece and modern England, whereas Dewey had technological America as his model. Locke criticized both men, and other educators as well, for limiting their interest to a particular culture, usually their own. Obviously, there were other civilizations besides Greece, England, and America. What about the ancient civilizations of Confuscius' China, the Queen of Sheba's Ethiopia, or Askia the Great's Timbuktu (West Africa)? In view of what Locke said about the importance of the historical-comparative approach, it might be very educational to compare and contrast, for example, classical Greece with classical Egypt, ancient India with ancient Germany. Analyzing such cultures in this way, Locke would have suggested, might help to overcome the cultural biases rooted in the American educational process. He would have encouraged this type of historical-comparative study because it would provide a balanced account of history by which value considerations get re-introduced into education, without resorting to dogmatism.

Among the scholars whom Locke pointed to as having provided scientific models for the historical study of cultural values were Arnold J. Toynbee, F.S.C. Northrop, Charles Morris, Margaret Mead, and Geoffrey Gorer. Each attempted to bridge the gap between fact and value by scientifically tracing their historical developments. Hegel's grand historical methodology, no less than Marx's, attempted to offer an historical account of all facts and values, with its emphasis as understanding the conflicts out of which these arose. Locke undoubtedly opposed the methodology of Hegel, Marx, and other dialecticians, and he also opposed their insistence on a "preconceived logic" of history. Locke was interested in methodologies which "try to make history reveal its own process logic, by following on a comparative historical basis the operational connection between an age and its beliefs, a culture and its system of values, a society and its ideological rationale."[15]

Toynbee and Northrop, in whose theories of history dialectical principles linger, seem to have forced Locke into the dialectical camp, but Locke said that he accepted their views with "limiting reservations." Toynbee also made certain metaphysical assumptions about history and God's place in it; Locke tried to avoid making metaphysical commitments, because such commitments presuppose absolutes, which Locke abhorred. He found absolutes objectionable because he felt they provided the basis for a totalitarian society.

Locke did not successfully discard metaphysics altogether. His own value theory rested on certain metaphysical presuppositions regarding the nature of human beings and society. It is unclear how one can develop views of education without making certain metaphysical assumptions about human nature. If one assumes that the basic feature of human nature is reason or rationality, one's view of education takes a certain form which will undoubtedly emphasize the need to develop our rational faculty, as in the view of Plato. If one's view of human nature, by contrast, places weight on the feeling or emotional dimension, one's view of education takes another form which will undoubtedly emphasize the need to develop our faculty of feeling, as in the view of Whitehead. Locke seemed to be closer to Whitehead than to Plato. He also shared in part Jung's views of human nature and education. Witness the important role he assigned to the introversion-extroversion distinction.

Locke maneuvered himself into an equally difficult position when he opposed the dialectical interpretation of the historical nature of cultural values, conflicts, and harmonies. One need not attribute dialectical principles as rigid as Hegel's or Marx's; however, there is some truth in their views of history, as will be explained shortly. Although Locke himself accepted a theory that allowed history "to reveal its own process logic," this process logic was in essence dialectical. It is an internal dialectic which unfolds in accord with the passions and preferences of individuals and groups. In this regard, Hegel would agree, for he placed great emphasis on world heroes.

A study of history reveals that change occurs dialectically out of the clashing and the converging of the diverse ideas of individuals and groups. If Locke wanted to understand the roots of cultural values, and historically the nature of conflicts among various cultures, it is not altogether clear how he could not have considered this dialectical nature of history, as well as the powerful individuals and groups who directly alter the course of history.

Although in his "Values and Imperatives" Locke offered a novel way of explaining the nature of value conflicts and convergings, his explanations were largely ahistorical. Nevertheless, he seemed to allow for a sort of dialectical interplay among the categories of feelings: exaltation, tension, acceptance or agreement, and equilibrium or repose. He also suggested that there were dialectical interplays and tensions between values of Jungian introverted and extroverted types: within the field of religion, the introverted mystic and his or her followers withdrew from the world; the extroverted reformer confronted the world. Individuals within the religious community were divided between these two types of leaders, giving rise to a basic source of religious conflict that often resulted in social change.

A dialectical view might suggest that there are individuals who are neither fully introverted nor fully extroverted, but who represent a synthesis of both types, or who attempt to resolve the conflicts between both types. Such a view, if further developed and applied to history, may be useful in explaining the value conflicts that have historically arisen among various societies and civilizations. Wherever there are value conflicts, whether in a given field such as religion or between different fields, for example, religion and politics, the resolution of such conflicts results in the synthesis of the opposing elements.

Consider the conflicts that occurred as the Muslims in the Middle Ages invaded Egypt and parts of the Middle East where Greek and Christian cultures had been established. Beyond the political and military struggles and conflicts, there were brutal clashes of ideas and ideologies. Out of these, Islamic philosophy emerged which was a synthesis of the cultural values of Arabic and African cultures and the Greek and Christian West. Thinkers such as Avicenna and Averroes contributed to this dialectical synthesis, and they at once represent it. They stand, ideologically and philosophically, somewhere between the Jungian extrovert and introvert value polarities. Averroes appealed to Muslims, Christians, and Jews alike, and he was also a dialectical thinker who attempted to reconcile the opposing views of Plato and Aristotle. If one is to grasp the historical nature of value conflicts and harmonies, as Locke insisted, it is imperative that one allow for a dialectical interpretation of history.

Is this dialectical interpretation of history compatible with the methodology of science, particularly the social sciences? Locke did not seem to think so. Toynbee, on the other hand, seemed to have done an adequate job of incorporating the dialectical principle into his own view of history. Is not the study of history a social science? Bergson, too, with his scientific outlook, gave a dialectical interpretation of biological evolution. He insisted that the forces of growth and stagnation, which are rooted in the process of life itself and which are diametrically opposed, are dialectical in character. We do not know what reactions Locke had to Bergson, with whom he studied in France.

In *The Two Sources of Morality and Religion*, (1932) Bergson sought to take an historical-comparative approach to the study of values, tracing their conflicts and developments. He modeled his studies on the methodology of the biological sciences, and he sought to investigate living reality, out of which, in his view, morality, religion, science, and mysticism emerged. Like Locke, White-head, and Dewey, Bergson thought that science could not suc-cessfully discard values, and that to appreciate the interconnections between facts and values, we must move be-yond science to mysticism which is also dialectical. Bergson also claimed that the teachings of the great mystics, such as Socrates, Buddha, and Jesus, illuminated the world by the beacon of love; furthermore, the teachings of the mystics are incorporated into the educative processes, customs, and world outlooks. By set-ting examples, the mystic inspires one to repudiate one's dog-matic, ethnocentric value creeds, replacing them with love and the attitude of openness. Although Bergson used the scientific method to study religion, morality, and mysticism, he under-stood the limits of the scientific method, which were that it cannot offer genuine values: Human beings can rely only on the great mystic for genuine values.

Locke had an ambivalent attitude toward the methodology of science. On the one hand, he criticized American philosophy for rigidly embracing the methodology of science, which stressed objectivity almost to the exclusion of values and attitudes. As he wrote:

Because of this logico-experimental slant, we again have made common cause with the current scientific attitude; making truth too exclusively a matter of the correct anticipation of experience, of the confirmation of fact. Yet truth may also sometimes be the sustaining of an attitude, the satisfaction of a way of feeling, the corroboration of a value. To the poet, beauty is truth; to the religious devotee, God is truth; to the enthused moralist, what ought-to-be overtops factual reality.[16]

On the other hand, he urged that the methodology of the sci-ences was essential for the new organon by which genuine values could be incorporated into education and inquiry. By combining the scientific method with the historical-comparative method, cultural values could be examined objectively and humanistically. Locke called this scientific humanism: "We face, accordingly, a type of scientific humanism, with an essentially critical and relativistic basis. Its normative potential can issue only from the more objective understanding of difference and the laying down of a scientific rather than a sentimental kind of tolerance and understanding."[17]

Locke's ambivalence toward science was directed primarily toward the traditional employment of the scientific methodology. Until recently, most scientists ignored value consideration and sought to keep their investigation "objective" or "value neutral." Locke's contention was that neither scientists, educators, nor philosophers could remain neutral. They had to take a normative stand on value issues and teach students to do the same if a remedy was to be provided for our cultural crises.

Locke's ambivalent attitude toward science might be explained away if we look closely at his notion of scientific humanism. Locke maintained that philosophy must become not only scientific, but science must become also philosophic in order to effectively consider value issues. Thus, on the one hand, science permits an objective approach to the study of values; on the other, it will force science to become open to the study of values—it will humanize science. "The gains," Locke said, "would thus be mutual, to value analysis on the one hand, and to the scientific method, on the other."[18] Thus, he attempted to close the traditional gap between science and the humanities, and to dispel dogmatic thinking which tended to dominate both fields. He wanted to replace dogmatic thinking with evaluative criticism, the type of thinking which should dominate the educative process and inquiry.

IV

As noted earlier, Locke insisted that a new apparatus of education should be concerned with broadening the students' mind, dispelling dogmatic thinking, reshaping attitudes and values, encouraging critical thinking, and introducing integrating elements into the overall educative process. Although most of what he said has been aimed at liberal arts education, his view has great implications for the scientific and professional curricula. No longer should scientists and professionals boast of the importance of value neutrality. Whereas the study of facts is of primary importance, a related concern is to appreciate the interconnections between facts and values, including their historical aspects. It follows that, to achieve the objectives mentioned above, individuals in the scientific and professional fields must also come to recognize the importance of the histories of the various cultures of the world. An American engineer who goes to Egypt to build an irrigation canal should be knowledgeable about Egypt's cultural history and about the influence of the ancient Egyptians and Ethiopians on the science, art, and philosophy of the ancient Greeks. An American nurse practicing medicine in Baghdad should know something about the history of Islam and its political conflicts there. In that way, the engineer or nurse might not automatically attempt to impose American values on the Egyptians or Baghdadians and might come to respect cultural differences. Industrialized Western nations that export their technological goods, as well as specialists and advisors, to non-Western nations send people trained mostly in America and Europe who have little knowledge of the history and cultural values of non-Western nations and often impose their values on these nations. Hence, conflicts arise.

According to Locke, the historical-comparative approach, when applied to scientific-professional areas, was another way of narrowing the gap between science and the humanities, between facts and values. Because of the emphasis on formal analysis and specialization, most American students in scientific and professional areas have little opportunity to learn in a systematic way about cultural values, and many feel that the values of others are inferior. The Whiteheadian schema may be applicable here. If educational institutions allow students to move beyond the second stage of specialization to the final stage of generalization and wisdom, the students might come to have a higher regard for cultural values.

Although this historical-comparative methodology possesses great merit, one must guard against a danger: the distortion of historical facts. Often when teachers attempt the historical-comparative approach, owing to certain "mind-sets," they tend to uphold their own culture as the ideal standard against which other cultures are to be measured.

In American educational institutions, students are often taught that the classical Greeks achieved intellectual and cultural perfection and that the ancient Africans fell far short of their standards. Certain Western educators often ignore the fact that Homer, Thales, Euclid, and Plato among others were educated in Egypt where they learned art, mathematics, science, and philosophy and took this knowledge back to Greece. Furthermore, many Western educators instill in their students the belief that the ancient Egyptians were white people, set apart from the rest of Africa. According to a certain myth, whites created the cultures of ancient Egypt; a related myth is that the Black people of Africa have no history and made little or no contribution to world civilization. A historical-comparative investigation into these cultures will reveal that such ideas have no basis in fact.

Investigators may guard against this distortion of history by not limiting themselves to a single standard on the subject matter. Rather, investigators should identify a plurality of standards, particularly the standards inherent in the cultures under investigation. As Locke suggested, one must allow each culture to reveal its own process logic and standards in order to appreciate the diversities and similarities among cultures and in order to see how the various cultural values of the world might have inhibited or enriched each other. In that way, Locke hoped, one could advance understanding of the cultural differences of the people of the world.

As Locke suggested, cultures need to be rigorously investigated in order to understand them and to eliminate dogmatic thinking about them. There is also the need to dispel certain erroneous ideas. African history, for example, is riddled with many myths that have no basis in fact. In order to justify slavery and colonial rule, some Westerners engaged in dogmatic thinking. Accordingly, there arose the myth that Africans and their descendants were inferior, a myth deeply engrained in the minds of people throughout the world. In order to dispel this myth and to provide a balanced account of African history, educational institutions throughout the world, particularly in the Americas, should integrate the study of African history into the curriculum along the lines suggested above.

Moreover, there are certain traditional values in African history, as in other cultures of the world, that need to be studied, preserved, and incorporated into American society. These values go beyond those that have been exploited and synthesized by Western culture. Through antiquity, the Middle Ages, colonial times, and the present, Europeans have taken more than their share of Africa's resources: spiritual, material, intellectual, and human. Nevertheless, Westerners can benefit from studying Africa's cultural past, by identifying and subscribing to certain traditional models that might help to direct the course of the Western world. Some of these are the African sense of community and cooperation as opposed to the Western values of individualism and competition (Hobbes); the African sense of family, respect for elders and for the dead; the African notion of communal property and respect for nature—rocks, trees, rivers, deserts, plants, animals and human beings. Environmentalists in this country, especially, might learn much.

Certain African societies are still concerned about preserving elements of the old way of life. Within Black communities in the Americas, remnants of traditional African values may be found; these values have played key roles in shaping these communities, as reflected in folklore, song, and music. These values have also contributed to the larger American culture.

V

In their concern about the educational process, American educators invariably turn to the ancient Greeks—Socrates, Plato, and Aristotle, whom they regard as the ideal educators. Many Western educational practices have been influenced by Plato's views as expressed in the *Republic*. But there are other models of learning and scholarship, many of which are provided by African history—for example, the illustrious learning centers of ancient Egypt and Ethiopia, and medieval Timbuktu, where Greeks and other scholars of the world came to study.

Let us consider medieval Timbuktu. In the Middle Ages this

was one of the most renowned learning centers of the world situated in the heart of Black Africa, founded and run by Black Africans. A West African king, Mansa Musa (1312–1337) built learning centers throughout the Sudan, Gao, Jenne, and Timbuktu, and attracted the best scholars of the Muslim world. Felix Du Bois described the scholars of the University of Sankoré as follows:

The scholars of Timbuctoo yielded in nothing to the saints and their miracles. During their sojourns in the foreign universities of Fez, Tunis, and Cairo, "they astounded the most learned men of Islam by their erudition." That these negroes were on a level with the Arabian savants is proved by the fact that they were installed as professors in Morocco and Egypt. In contrast to this we find that Arabs were not always equal to the requirements of Sankoré.[19]

Among the great scholars of the University of Sankoré was Ahmed Baba (1556–1627) who is credited with having written over twenty books in the areas of astronomy, law, science, religion, and philosophy. Among his books are the *Miraz*, which is a history of the Sudanese people, and *El Ibtihadj*, which is a biographical dictionary of Muslim scholars. His personal library, the largest of any single scholar at that time, consisted of more than 1,600 volumes.

Scholars such as Baba conducted classes mostly in the form of lectures and open discussions. In comparison with today's educational institutions, the Sankoré curriculum was less specialized, and the professors possessed a wide range of intellectual interests which they shared with their students. Many of these scholars were also active in the political arena; some were Socratic gadflies and midwives. Inasmuch as many people believe that our educational process places too much emphasis on analytical skills and specialized knowledge, the educational practices of Timbuktu might serve as models for reorganizing elements of our own system. Indeed, scholars such as Baba could serve as educational role models and be an inspiration to many students and scholars, particularly Africans and their descendants.

VI

Contemporary African scholars, educators, and philosophers are increasingly recognizing the need to reorganize Africa's educational process. This might begin by discarding most European values and by reintroducing into the curriculum Africa's own values derived from precolonial and present experiences. The Ghanian philosopher Kwasi E. Wiredu, among others, is concerned with the specific problem of decolonizing Africa's philosophic thinking. In his "Philosophical Research and Teaching in Africa: Some Suggestions Towards Conceptual Decolonisation," he writes:

To decolonise our philosophical thinking means divesting our thought of all undue influences from the modes of thought of our erstwhile colonisers. The linguistic, or more specifically the conceptual, liberation just mentioned is perhaps the most fundamental form of decolonisation. It does not, of course, consist in rejecting all doctrines originally conceived and formulated in a foreign language: that would be unspeakably absurd. What it means is that one takes care that one's acceptance of any such doctrine is not conditioned by the peculiarities of the given language or culture.[20]

Wiredu suggests that philosophy classes in Africa should study the history of traditional African philosophy. Such classes would also be concerned with the history of both Western and non-Western philosophies (for example, Indian, Chinese). Thus, Wiredu is suggesting that, in order to effectively decolonize African philosophic thought and scholarship, the plurality of philosophic traditions must be considered.

In this regard, Wiredu's position parallels Locke's view of the historical-comparative methodology. Locke's position is generally applicable to Wiredu's educative processes which require that African educators pay more attention to the traditions and histories of African cultures and make comparative studies, tracing their conflicts and harmonies. The African philosopher H. Odera Oruka holds that the world will benefit by studying the wisdom of African sages who were also philosophers. This will allow Africans to reexamine and reaffirm certain traditional cultural values, to integrate them into the present way of life, and thereby to envision future possibilities.

One of the weaknesses of Locke's position is that he over-emphasized the importance of analyzing the cultural values of past civilizations. Although we need to focus our telescope on the past in order to understand the present, we must also focus on the present and future. Foresight is stressed by process philosophers such as Dewey and Whitehead. A combination of foresight and hindsight methodologies will strengthen Locke's scientific humanism and help overhaul education in both America and Africa.

NOTES

1. Alain Locke, "The Need for a New Organon in Education," *Goals for American Education* (New York: Conference On Science, Philosophy, and Religion, 1950), p. 201.

2. Ibid., 202.

3. Ibid.

4. Ibid., p. 203.

5. Ibid.

6. Ibid., p. 204.

7. Ibid., p. 205.

8. Alain Locke, "Minorities and the Social Mind," *Progressive Education* 12 (March 1935): 142–143.

9. Ibid., p. 143.

10. Ibid.

11. Ibid.

12. Ibid.

13. Locke, "The Need for a New Organon in Education," p. 209.

14. Ibid.

15. Ibid., p. 207.

16. Locke, "Values and Imperatives," in *American Philosophy,Today and Tomorrow*, eds. Sidney Hook and Horace M. Kallen (New York: Lee Furman, 1935), p. 317.

17. Locke, "The Need for a New Organon in Education," p. 208.

18. Ibid., pp. 210–211.

19. Felix DuBois, *Timbuctoo: The Mysterious*, trans. Diana White (New York: Negro University Press, 1969, originally published in 1896), p. 285.

20. This paper was presented at the First Africana Philosophy Conference, Haverford, Pennsylvania, July 1982.

7 PARITY FOR BLACKS IN EDUCATION

As our society undergoes rapid technological innovations, especially in the computer industry, there is a growing concern that unless educational programs are reorganized, a decade from now most of the American population will have become technologically illiterate, incapable of understanding and using these new technologies. There is a fear among assembly-line workers that they will someday be replaced by robots. Such fear is not without justification.

In addition to the social, cultural, economic, and political crises plaguing our society, the rapid development of high technologies has begun to create crises in the area of education. Scholars, philosophers, officials in government and industry, and educators especially are reconsidering the aims and nature of education. Their anxiety and concerns are often reflected in such questions as: What is the role of the university? What is the meaning of the liberal arts? What is the place of science and technology in the educative process? Are scientific inquiry and education value neutral? Should education prepare people merely to make a living in the robotic society of the future? Should education aim to develop character? These questions are not new, many dating back to the time of Socrates. The ancient Egyptians and Ethiopians, whose civilizations influenced the ancient Greeks, undoubtedly raised similar questions. The same is true of Black American educators from the time of Frederick Douglass and Booker T. Washington, W.E.B. Du Bois, and Alain Locke to the present.

Although American Blacks have experienced integration, separation, and segregation, at the level of both ideology and practice, Black educators generally share this country's ideals. Many of the questions raised by Black educators are identical to those raised by educators in general. In addition, because of racial oppression, after the era of Reconstruction Black educators had to consider different, yet equally important, issues. Among the questions on their agenda were the following:

Should education have as its aim the training of the Black masses in vocational and agricultural skills?

Should higher education seek to develop an Elite?

What is the role of the Black college?

What can be done to desegregate America's educational institutions?

What is the role of the privately funded Black educational institutions?

What is the role of the publicly funded Black educational institutions?

What can be done to raise funds to support Black educational institutions?

What can be done to standardize[1] American education?

Many whites who thought they knew "the solution to the Negro problem" offered answers to a number of these questions. As will be seen, Locke found their solutions largely unacceptable.

In his essay "Negro Education Bids for Par,"[2] as well as in other essays, Locke asked what could be done to standardize Black education. He also sought to define the role of the Black college. This chapter considers this essay and also discusses the views Du Bois expressed in his book, *The Education of Black People*.[3]

In "Negro Education Bids for Par," Locke focuses on two themes: the social and political impediments that originated largely in the era of missionarism and philanthropy preventing Black youths from receiving quality education comparable to whites, and the steps required to overcome these impediments. Locke called attention to the need for strong educational leadership, by Blacks and for Blacks. He argued not only that Black educational institutions must be run by strong Black leaders, but also that a basic function of these institutions must be to train future leaders. These themes are discussed below.

Later in this chapter, Locke's notion of leadership which the Black college is to nurture and exercise is criticized on the grounds that it provides no effective organization for institutionalizing power and authority in the community. History demonstrates that once a leader as powerful as Booker T. Washington or Martin Luther King, Jr., has passed away, the political power and influence arising out of the Black community and associated with such powerful individuals have invariably declined. As a possible remedy it is argued that a new concept of the state is needed, one modeled on Arendt's council system. The new state will be run not by party politicians, but by councilors in whom power, authority, and leadership, shared among equals, will be vested, and by whom the traditional gap between "town" and "gown" will be closed.

I

Locke began his essay by observing that since Reconstruction, when many Black educational institutions were being founded, the educational facilities and resources of Blacks have been below those of whites. Much of this gap can be traced to the practice of segregation whereby "separate race education prevails over more than two-thirds the total potential school population of Negro children."[4] Blacks did not generally choose this segregated education; in 90 percent of instances, discriminatory separation was involuntary, forced on Blacks by the larger society.[5] Hence, the separate education of Blacks is a public concern. The public must assume the moral responsibility of upgrading the separate education of Blacks. Locke suggested that a system of separate education should not exist in democratic societies, but inasmuch as such a system did arise and became well entrenched, the society should adjust to it by establishing parity between Black and white education.

Locke noted that efforts to provide funds in support of Black education from the days of Reconstruction to the time he wrote "Negro Education Bids for Par" in 1925 relied on religious missionary contributions, other philanthropy, and private endeavors. Private support endeavors, except the Jeannes and Slater funds and the Rosenwald grants, which extended aid to support

the improvement of public school facilities, have done a dis-
service to Black education. The main reason is that, in aiding
Black education, the private sector tends to regard the task as a
moral burden; the motive for giving was one of charity, not
parity. Locke said that such motives and attitudes must be
changed to motives of justice and "square-deal" if Black education was to achieve the same standards as white education.

If the public sector were to assume responsibility for Black
education, as it does for white, Blacks would benefit, the philanthropists would benefit, and so would other taxpayers generally. Under the system of separate education, Blacks, as
taxpayers, are supporting the education of whites, whereas their
own educational standards and facilities are far below those of
whites: "Negro education costs double and yields half."[6]

While writing this article, Locke observed that the public was
becoming increasingly aware of its social responsibility in supporting the education of Blacks. Yet, he realized that much had
to be done to increase this awareness. The real indication of this
limited awareness, he said, lay in the commitment of certain
states to their fundamental duty and their reawakening to the
principle of local responsibility in matters of education.

As illustrations of this renewed sense of public responsibility,
Locke called attention to the North Carolina state program,
"which by special appropriations invested five millions in permanent school equipment for Negro schools in the four-year
period 1921–1925, and practically doubled its maintenance ex-
penditures for the same period."[7] Other states which made similar investments included Georgia, Kentucky, Texas, and
Delaware. These were signs of progress, the initiative for which
came from the public sector, but Locke warned that "we must
not consider such progress any more than the *plain duty and
common obligation* [emphasis added] of every community."[8] He
said *repeatedly* that the public had an obligation and a duty to
support Black education, and he added, "never for any reason
of temporary advantage or special appeal must it be allowed to
assume in the public mind the aspect of a special responsibility,
a private enterprise, or a philanthropic burden."[9]

By stressing that the public had an obligation to bring Black
education up to par, Locke was suggesting that the public—

public officials, agencies, and institutions—needed to make a commitment to what we now call Affirmative Action. Generally, Affirmative Action means that society must make extra efforts in awarding grants and contracts to women and minorities and in recruiting "qualified" women and minorities in the areas of employment and education. These extra efforts will give them "fair play" in these areas, which may eventually offset prior years of oppression and discrimination. Defenders of Affirmative Action say that society has a moral responsibility to make a commitment to Affirmative Action and to see that its policies are practiced and observed. Opponents of Affirmative Action regard it as a burden, and some say that it is illegal and immoral; some even say that Affirmative Action is a kind of reverse discrimination. Still others contend that an Affirmative Action plan is unconstitutional because it appeals to the rights of certain groups, whereas the Constitution is intended to protect the rights of individuals. Against this latter protest, the point may be made that the Constitution also recognizes that within a democracy ruled by the majority, minorities can easily be oppressed and rights can be ignored. The Constitution allows for certain measures to protect the rights of minorities, but whether these measures are adequate is debatable. Locke, of course, would have defended Affirmative Action as it pertains to education and the rights of minorities generally. His view of what was required to bring Black education up to par clearly anticipated Affirmative Action plans, which are as urgently needed today as they were when Locke was writing.

With regard to establishing what Locke calls "standardization" in American education many people today suggest that integration and bussing, at least at the elementary and secondary school levels, will solve the problems. This proposal, which has been tried and practiced in various parts of the country, has met much resistance, even from some liberals. At the college level, much opposition exists to integration and Affirmative Action. George Wallace, it will be remembered, stood in the doorway at the University of Alabama in 1963 in the symbolic attempt to block integration. Within recent years there have been many racial struggles over bussing in South Boston and elsewhere.

With regard to college education, Locke did not call for complete integration, nor did he want a forced separate education for Blacks. During his lifetime the practice of forced separate education for Blacks prevailed throughout the South and in certain Northern communities. With forced separate education Blacks fail to get a fair deal and whites get more than their share, as they exploit the taxpayers including Blacks who, like other poor people, often pay more than their share of taxes. Because separate education had become the "norm," Locke said that Blacks needed to make the best of it; this they could do by maintaining separate education, provided the public assumed responsibility for standardizing Black education. Locke, as we have seen, blamed the failures of Black education largely on missionary enterprises and other philanthropic efforts, notwithstanding the fact that a few private funding agencies, acting with good intentions, have benefited Black education.

In order to establish standardization in Black education, Locke recommended what may be regarded as a threefold approach. First, there must be a reduction of philanthropic support to unworthy Black institutions, such as those controlled by missionary forces and other outside influences that are not in the best interests of Blacks. Second, competing private Black institutions, especially in the Southern states where the largest number of Black educational institutions are located, should concentrate their resources, efforts, and facilities. Third, public Black educational institutions must expand. If Black educational institutions, such as the one now in the Atlanta University complex, were to combine their resources, efforts, and facilities, they could help standardize Black education. Locke said that such educational centers should be a standardizing influence in every important region of the Negro population.

Locke focused on the harm which shortsighted philanthropy and other missionary enterprises had done to Black education. At the same time, he did not want to completely discourage private agencies from supporting Black education. They, too, could help to standardize education, if their policies were based on sound, scientific pedagogy and the right motives (that is, fair play or justice). Locke wanted the private agencies to be more selective in providing support; he suggested that these agencies continue to support the worthy institutions and discontinue supporting the unworthy ones, although he neglected to identify which institutions were worthy.

More important, Locke wanted private funding agencies to assist in standardizing education by supporting private Black educational institutions so that they could become concentrated and, once they had done so, to continue to support them. The public could help to standardize education by assuming increased responsibilities in founding new educational institutions for Blacks and by providing additional support for those that already existed. Thus, if Black education were to achieve standardization, two related needs had to be fulfilled: concentration of private educational institutions on the one hand and expansion of public educational institutions on the other. Both sectors, private and public, have important roles to play: "As the public education of the Negro expands the private schools concerned with his education must concentrate, which is their one great opportunity to lift themselves to modern standards of efficiency."[10]

Some people within the larger society today are talking about the need to concentrate educational resources, institutions, and facilities. In addition, because of our lagging economy and other socioeconomic problems, certain educational institutions with strong technological, scientific, and professional programs have combined with industry and government. Among the educational institutions that have taken this route are the Massachusetts Institute of Technology (MIT), Rensselaer Polytechnic Institute (RPI), and Stanford University. A few years ago Tuskegee Institute discussed making a similar move; the proposal never came to fruition, however, partly because it had difficulty in attracting industry to the area. It might be to Tuskegee Institute's advantage to persist in this effort, if it can successfully combine with government and industry, without giving up its institutional autonomy. This might solve the funding problems of some Black educational institutions and might stimulate research that would benefit the community.

Of course, the motives of these institutions for concentrating are quite different from the motive Locke had in mind: he wanted to bring Black education up to par with education in the larger society. MIT, RPI, and Stanford, which have established what are called "Industrial Parks" and "Incubator Spaces," are not so much interested in achieving standardization; that was achieved much earlier in the histories of their respective institutions. Most of these institutions are interested in advancing science. Then there is the question of the economy. Many of these institutions have been motivated to concentrate and combine in order to help stimulate our economy. Funded partly by government, partly by industry, and partly by private sources, the supporters of this trend concur that, in addition to advancing science and technology, industry will benefit by utilizing the scientific and technological resources created by the scholars and researchers at these institutions. New technological items can be created and introduced to the marketplace. Once put to commercial use, they can stimulate our economy and thereby provide a competitive edge against foreign economies. Within a prospering economy, where unemployment is reduced, where, stimulated by the new technologies, the interest rates are reduced and the American people are spending more, there will be more money available for industry to expand, resulting in a greater supply of money and a stronger government and economy.

Many people, however, warn against this type of concentration of government, industry, and education. One major danger is that the laboring, leveling-off standards of the marketplace and government, geared to mass society, will infect the standards of excellence in the university. The standards of the marketplace will become the controlling norm for every quarter of society, including the university. Furthermore, there is the deep fear that industry and government, which provide much support to private and public educational institutions, already have too much control over research and scholarship. It is argued that the standards for research and scholarship are largely set by industry and government, without whose support very few universities could keep their doors open. Locke wanted standardization, but he certainly did not want this type, whose validity and motivation derived in part from the marketplace. Much of his writing, no less than Du Bois', was aimed at liberating education, Black and white, from such control. Both were what the military calls "Pointmen," the infantrymen who in jungle warfare move ahead of a body of troops, cutting a path with a machete, so that the rest of the troops can follow. As Point-men, Locke and Du Bois cut paths for academic excellence and autonomy for Black education, the lack of which, according to Locke, was due largely to the old missionary impulse.

II

Nearly sixty years have passed since Locke urged that Black education be raised to the standards of the larger society. It may be questioned whether he would still insist on this goal today when American education as a whole is generally considered to be mediocre in comparison with education in countries such as Japan. Many high school graduates in America read at fifth grade level and can barely do simple arithmetic.

With Blacks almost always trailing behind whites, then, one may conclude that the standards for Black education are far below the unacceptable mark. If Locke were writing today, he would have to ask what could be done to standardize education in America so that *all* students could approximate the standard of excellence. Many say that, with regard to elementary and secondary schools, the fault lies with the teachers and that the fault could be corrected if they were given merit raises. Will that solve the problems? The problems in elementary and secondary education are probably related to the problems in college education. Each educational level is hampered by an incomplete conception of education, a conception which states that education should prepare students merely for "making a living." Education should have a higher aim, however, to awaken in students their own mental and spiritual powers, so that they can cut their own paths through the jungle of life. In the classroom, the teacher's primary role should be to call attention to the particulars of experience, to the facts, and to stir the students' imagination so that the particulars can be appreciated and examined in a larger context and point the way to the path of wisdom. Ultimately, wisdom should find its application in the affairs of the community.

Although Locke sometimes opposed Booker T. Washington's program, in his essay, "Negro Education Bids for Par" Locke spoke approvingly of Washington's educational program. He said that the conflict between the Hampton-Tuskegee program and the so-called higher education or liberal arts program, which Du Bois advocated, was beginning to be resolved. Consequently, there was "the growing realization that the Tuskegee-Hampton program and that of the traditional Negro college are supplementary rather than antagonistic."[11] Because Locke regarded both types of programs as equally valuable, he urged public and private funding agencies to support both types.

Many of Washington's critics claimed that the shortcomings of the liberal arts Black colleges were largely due to his domineering personality. He was so dominant a figure that he was able to persuade funding sources to donate to the Tuskegee-Hampton program rather than to the traditional Black colleges. Here Locke defended Washington: "It was not the fault of the Hampton-Tuskegee idea that the so-called higher education of the Negro could not for a generation compete with it in dramatizing its own values."[12] Although Washington did indeed possess a domineering personality, Locke also suggested that his mind could produce original ideas, as was evident by his unique educational program. His program with its practical orientation contributed not only to Black education, but also to American education in general. Locke wrote, "The conception of education back of that idea [that is, the Hampton-Tuskegee program] was original; indeed in its day it was in advance of American educational reform."[13]

The public is usually slow to accept a new idea, practice, or technology. But the American public was willing to accept the new educational program which Hampton and Tuskegee offered. In the first place, the program spoke to the practical mind of the American people. At the turn of the century, when Washington emerged, the industrializing processes were gaining momentum. Second, it appealed to the American people because it exerted, as it still does

a strong, sentimental appeal through its race and community service, and through making all institutions and agencies that come under its influence missioners of the masses, galvanizers of "the man farthest down," and exponents of a naturally popular doctrine of economic independence and self-help.[14]

Although some of Washington's critics claimed that he was successful with his program because he "compromised" the rights of Blacks to whites, Locke did not agree: "But for every adherent this program has won through what its critics have called its 'concessions' to the popular American way of thinking, including the characteristic conciliatory optimism of its philosophy of race contacts, it has, I think, won ten by its concrete appeal and demonstration of results."[15]

According to Locke, one of the greatest factors in the success of the Hampton-Tuskegee program was Washington's leadership which the popular American mind came to appreciate. In contrast, higher education programs within the Black community did not enjoy such powerful leadership, nor were they able to prepare their students to assume such leadership after graduation.

In Washington's day, Black higher education was in the hands of weak administrators, many of whom were white and were serving the interests of whites. Moreover, although Washington designed his educational program to meet the needs of the Black community and the American society generally, Black higher education had an entirely different orientation, appealing to the isolated individual, and "trying to justify itself either by depreciating the rival program or merely by abstract self-appraisal of its own values."[16] Black educational policy, practice, and orientation were quite compatible with the missionary activity out of which it arose. This activity was incompatible with the leadership of which Washington was representative,[17] a leadership that encouraged racial pride, self-help, and social reform. In contrast with the Hampton-Tuskegee program, the traditional Black college failed in two ways: (1) it had no strong leaders, and (2) it had not produced effective leaders to justify its social values. Locke admitted that the traditional Black educational institutions had turned out well-educated men and women, but he emphasized that they had failed to produce strong leaders. Hence, these institutions needed more reform than mere theoretical defense or renewed public support, if they were to achieve standardization.

Locke did not belittle the ample role some traditional Black colleges had played in education. Among these he included such institutions as Howard, Fisk, Morehouse, Atlanta, Wilberforce, Virginia Union, Johnson Smith, and Lincoln. He noted that, since the war,[18] each of those colleges had grown with respect to student body, faculty, and equipment, "and most of them have attained standard scholastic rating."[19] The fact remained, however, that in spite of growth, "there has persisted a reactionary conservatism of spirit and atmosphere."[20] The old missionary, paternalistic principle still prevailed, and the administrators functioned in an autocratic manner and atmosphere that inhibited the institutional, individual, and group development of racial spirituality, self-direction, and autonomy. Locke noted, however, that the students began to rebel against this type of control. They wanted autonomy and racial control and sought to develop racial interests. Because Black colleges existed under forced separation, Blacks were in a position to gain control of these institutions. The leadership would rest with Blacks, not with white executive boards and presidents. Locke contended that under Black leadership, the missionary impulse would have little, if any, effect on Black education. But he also observed that many of the separate Black educational institutions were in fact under white executive control and even when they were not, the principle of missionary paternalism still held. Hence, no autonomy and no self-leadership existed. Racial separation was regarded as a curse rather than a blessing, as a negative rather than a positive factor: "This type of education constantly reminds Negro youth, in the midst of a sensitive personal and racial adolescence, of the unpleasant side of the race problem, instead of utilizing it as a positive factor in his education."[21]

At this point, Locke stated what he thought should be one of the main purposes and justifications of Black university education: "The highest aim and real justification of the Negro college should be the development of a racially inspired and devoted professional class with group service as their integrating ideal."[22] The Black college should train the Black Elite. Speaking especially of the separate Black college, he added:

Certainly the least that can be expected and demanded of separately organized Negro college education is that in the formative period of life the prevailing contacts should be with the positive rather than negative aspects of race, and that race feelings of a constructive sort should be the stimulating and compensating element in the system of education.[23]

But Locke maintained that most Black educational institutions did not nurture this positive attitude toward the Black race, an attitude that should manifest itself in community service. It will be recalled that Locke suggested that Washington was successful because his institution helped promote such an attitude, which suggests that Washington's educational ideal was largely valid. This was evident by his success in promoting racial loyalty and community service.

In "Negro Education Bids for Par," Locke suggested that Washington's educational program, at least during the first quarter of the century, was guided by the right ideal. In much of Locke's other writings however, his own view of education seems to be closer to Du Bois'. Both Locke and Du Bois emphasized art and culture over vocational skills in training the Black Elite. Thus all three educators—Washington, Du Bois, and Locke—agreed that education should prepare Black youth to assume social leadership of the Black community, but they differed on the means of training. Both Locke and Du Bois encouraged Black youth to reject materialistic individualism, an attitude that was so prevalent among Americans and that Washington, some say, encouraged. Washington shared the American economic dream and at the same time encouraged group service. This was one of Washington's paradoxes.

Locke suggested that most of the Black colleges, controlled by the ideals and values of the larger society, were misdirecting the energies of Black youth by urging them to acquire a materialistic, individualistic attitude. This attitude, together with the negative factor of race which was nurtured in most Black colleges, provided the background for a problem with which Locke was struggling: What could be done to restore the *social values* of higher education for Blacks? If the Black college created an atmosphere in which Blackness was regarded as objectionable and the controlling materialistic values were to be pursued, then it was clear why the Black college had lost its social values. In attempting to solve the problem of making the Black college serve the Black community, he proposed the following:

The lapsing social values of higher education for the Negro can, I think, be recovered only under race leadership, for they must be tactfully coaxed back in an atmosphere of unembarrassed racial councils, charged with almost a family degree of intimacy and confidence. To provide such a positive-toned community ought to be one of the first aims and justifications of the Negro college.[24]

In most of Locke's other writings, he urged social interaction among the races to reduce racial tensions and to advance human understanding. In his essay "Negro Education Bids for Par," however, he gave little attention to the principle of social reciprocity.[25] He instead emphasized that Black education was one of forced separation and that Blacks ought to make the best of this situation by gaining control of their own educational institutions. As leaders and directors, Blacks would provide models for Black youth, and both present and future leaders would serve the community. Under these conditions, if Black educational institutions were to fulfill their potential, Black youth would discard the attitude of materialistic individualism and pursue an attitude of benefit to the community.

In most discussions of Black colleges today, the most pressing problem is said to be that of acquiring adequate funding to keep the doors open. Although Locke recognized that funding was a problem for Blacks, he did not regard it as the paramount difficulty: "Whatever the needs for more adequate financial backing and support of the Negro college, the need for liberalizing its management and ideals is greater."[26]

Since Locke wrote these words, the management and ideals of the Black college have become somewhat more liberalized. Most of the Black colleges and universities are directed by Black administrators and managers, and most of these institutions offer Black Studies programs although since the latter part of the 1970s funding for many of these programs has been reduced. Black educational institutions still have a long way to go before they achieve the goals Locke outlined.

Although most Black educational institutions have Blacks in

high administrative positions, in many of these institutions the boards of trustees have a sizable number of whites who are also officers in major corporations. Du Bois warned that the interests of people from industry who sit on the governing boards of Black institutions may not always coincide with the interests of the Black community. Locke would have agreed. He insisted that Blacks be in control; he would probably have allowed for a mixed governing board, only if Blacks remained in control. As a solution to the problem of educational autonomy, Du Bois suggested that Black colleges become financially independent by relying almost exclusively on the support of their Black alumni. These colleges would be fully autonomous[27] and not be beholden to either governmental or corporate officials. One practical problem involved in Du Bois' solution is that today's high cost of living requires enormous finances to keep educational doors open. Another consideration is that most Black alumni have not become financially independent or amassed a great deal of wealth and so are not yet in a position to give generously. Many Blacks can barely pay for their own children's education, let alone donate large sums to Black educational institutions.

Although since the 1960s there has been a renewed interest in studying African and Afro-American history and culture, materialist values still dominate the aspirations of many Black youth and educators. This is understandable, for most Black educational institutions, like the institutions in the larger society, have as their mission the preparation of youth to make a living. Upon completing their college education, Black youth are expected to seek employment in major firms and institutions. Unfortunately, Black educators do not aggressively encourage educated college youth to return to the Black community and provide the community's leadership and skills needed.

Other difficult questions which Locke considered which are presently being debated in the courts are the following:

What should be the policy of American colleges and universities with respect to the recruitment of students?

Should Black educational institutions teach mainly Black students?

Should white educational institutions teach mainly white students?

In a predominantly white institution such as Auburn University in Alabama, how many Black students should be allowed to participate in its program?

Or, in a predominantly Black institution such as Tuskegee Institute in Alabama, just sixteen miles from Auburn University, how many white students should be allowed?

Neither the courts nor educators, Black or white, have settled this issue. Du Bois felt that Black colleges should be concerned almost exclusively with the education of Black youth, which meant, among other things, allowing the students to acquire knowledge of Black culture and social problems. First, they must acquire knowledge in these areas; second, they must acquire knowledge of science so they will be prepared to handle the affairs of the world generally and of the Black community specifically. In the passage that follows, Du Bois stresses what he considered the basic principle upon which the Black college should rest:

The American Negro problem is and must be the center of the Negro university. It has got to be. You are teaching Negroes. . . . Upon these foundations, therefore, your university must start and build. Nor is the thing so entirely unusual or unheard of as it sounds. A university in Spain is not simply a university.[28]

Du Bois considered in broader terms what the educational program should consist of: "The curriculum of a college of this sort would be comparatively simple: The idea of acquainting growing youth with what the world has known in science and art and what it is doing today; and in making that acquaintanceship as complete and thoroughly as time allows."[29]

In response to the question of who should be allowed to attend Black colleges, Du Bois wrote:

Negro communities, Negro private schools, Negro colleges will and must be organized and supported. This racial organization will be voluntary and not compulsory. It will not be discriminatory. It will be carried on according to a definite object and ideal, and will be open to all who share this ideal. And of course that ideal must always be in accord with the greater ideals of mankind. But what American Negroes must remember is that voluntary organization for great ends is far different from compulsory segregation for evil purposes.[30]

Locke was in partial agreement with Du Bois on these basic issues: forced segregation for evil purpose is an evil, Black educators should have as one of their basic goals the introduction of students to Black culture and problems, Blacks should have control of their own educational institutions, and Black colleges should have as their primary concern the education of Black youth.

Locke was not a cultural separatist, however; he was a pluralist. America, with its plurality of ethnic groups, could benefit greatly by allowing contacts and social reciprocity among racial groups in its educational institutions. Locke contended that such contacts and social reciprocity were required if Black education were to achieve par and parity.

Although Locke held that Blacks should take over the administration and management of Black education, he suggested that learning institutions should be open to white youths, just as white institutions of higher learning should be open to Black youths. The key principle here was open, balanced competition; Black educational institutions must compete "for race patronage with other institutions of higher learning accessible to Negro students."[31]

It was previously pointed out that Locke thought that the Black college should train Black youth for leadership. If Black educational institutions were to be open to white youth, would this aim apply to them also? Locke suggested that this aim would apply: "Developed in modern ways to its full possibilities, however, the Negro college ought to become the prime agency in recruiting from the talented tenth the social leadership which is an urgent need, both racial and national, in the difficult race situation in America."[32] In this passage, the phrase "recruiting from the talented tenth" is ambiguous. It could mean the Talented Tenth within the Black community, or it could mean the Talented Tenth within the larger, white community, or both. Locke probably intended the last meaning because it is consistent with his support of contacts and social reciprocity among leaders of all ethnic groups in order for democracy to work in America.

If we assume that this interpretation is correct, then what formula, with race as a basis, should be used to decide how many students should attend which institutions? And what should be the Black-white ratio?

Locke suggested the proper ratio of Black youths attending white colleges operating under the system of open, balanced competition:

The ratio of the total enrollment of Negro college students in mixed as compared with separate institutions, allowing for a strictly collegiate grade of instruction in the latter, is clearly one to three, and the ratio of degree graduates, according to the careful yearly statistics of the education number of The Crisis, is roughly one to two; that is, for every two degree graduates from standard Negro institutions for the last few years, there has been one from the private and state universities of the country at large.[33]

Suggesting that this ratio should be the norm, because of its educational and social benefits, Locke added:

These facts re-enforce two important principles. First, the inter-racial contact that is lost at the bottom of the educational ladder is somewhat compensated for at the top. It is of the most vital importance to race relations and the progress of democracy in America that contact be maintained between the representative leaders of the white and Black masses.[34]

Here Locke was dealing with a twofold issue: white educational institutions should be open to Black students, and Black educational institutions should be open to white students. Locke went into much detail about the ratio of Black youths in white institutions, but he was vague about the ratio of white youth in Black institutions.

Some related questions come to mind. Should the ratio of Black to white students in private, white educational institutions be the same as the ratio of Black to white students in public, white institutions? Similarly, should the ratio of Black to white students in private, Black institutions be the same as the ratio of Black to white students in public, white institutions? Are white educational institutions—private or public—morally obligated to recruit Black youths, and are Black educational institutions morally obligated to recruit white youths? What should be the ratio of Black to white instructors at white institutions, and what should this ratio be at Black institutions? Had Locke lived when Affirmative Action became an issue, as it presently is, what would his attitude have been on such controversial issues? Should Black colleges apply Affirmative Action in an effort to recruit white youth? Should white colleges apply Affirmative Action in an effort to recruit Black youth?

Locke would likely have favored Affirmative Action, if doing so would help achieve parity in American education. Because white educational institutions have greater resources and facilities than their Black counterparts, and because whites have a moral and social obligation to bring Black education up to par, Locke would have said that white institutions, private and public, had a greater obligation to recruit Black youths and instructors than Black institutions to recruit white youths and instructors.

In this connection another question arises: inasmuch as Locke believed that Black education should train youth for social leadership, especially in the Black community, does this aim apply to white youths educated in the Black college? Are white youths, so educated, to provide leadership to the Black community, or are they to return to their own community? Locke would probably have said that they should return to their own community but keep contacts with Black leaders in the Black community. This inference is based on Locke's insistence that Blacks must gain control over their academic community and by implication also gain access to the power of the larger political and social community, which, in the past, has been controlled by whites.

Although Locke wrote at length about how education should prepare Black youths for social leadership, he never spelled out what form this leadership should take. Should Black youth, while attending Howard, Fisk, Tuskegee Institute, Spelman, or Stanford, devote much energy in areas such as political science, law, government, and international affairs, courses that might, as some believe, prepare them for social leadership roles? Should Black youths, upon graduating from college, run for political office? If so, to whom should they turn for financial backing, and in which areas of government—county, city, state, or federal—would it be most desirable for Blacks to be seated in order to uplift the Black community and America generally?

Locke did not talk much about party politics. The social and political realities of his times discouraged most Blacks from seeking political office, and so he did not look to party politics as models of social leadership for the college-going Black Elite. Locke turned to other areas for models, one of the most important of which was the one offered by Washington. In his leadership role, Washington knew how to dramatize the social values of education. Although he never held public office, Washington knew how to combine a vocational educational program and party politics into an effective, unified program in order to better the Black community and America generally.

III

Some of his critics considered Washington's style of social leadership a "one-man-show." He nearly dominated the theater of action in the Black community, allowing little room for concerted action on the part of other Blacks. This type of domineering influence was not altogether healthy for the Black community. True, he got results, but in the realm of human affairs, should results be the ultimate value? Is there anything to be said about the importance of a community of peers, where no one asserts his or her opinions as absolutely valid for all times and all places?

Washington went a long way in bridging the gap between the academic community and the broader socio-political community, but this bridge seemed to have collapsed after his death. Why did no one trained at Tuskegee Institute assume Washington's mantle following his death? Nearly half a century would elapse before anyone demonstrated leadership qualities comparable to or surpassing Washington: Martin Luther King, Jr., educated at Morehouse College. Since King's death, the Black college and community have not produced anyone who has approximated his greatness. Nor has the larger society for that matter.

Black colleges can create leaders when a serious effort is made to allow for a new political organ, based on neither party politics nor a particular personality. This new political organ will remove the traditional wall between the educational community and the body politic. This organ, of course, is Arendt's council system.

The council system, although intended for the wider political community, could be incorporated into the academic community, thereby providing an antidote to autocratic leadership which many institutions, Black and white, have experienced. The council system could replace the committee system and other structures.

One of the objectives in this chapter has been to suggest a solution to a problem Locke posed, that of developing and exercising leadership, power, and authority in the Black community. The whole United States should adopt what may be called the federated council system. In such a system, political connections between Black colleges and other institutions, businesses, churches, labor organizations, and farmers' associations could be made. No longer would the Black community have to rely on a Washington, a King, or for that matter the elected President. Power and authority would have been vested in the councilors. Under this new system black educational institutions would have to train councilors who, in addition to performing their political tasks, would educate the community in science, technology, government, and so on. Individuals in Black colleges and in the political community with demonstrated effective leadership skills would serve as models for Black youth, many of whom would become councilors or statesmen.

Developing genuine leaders is a difficult task. It is not like training youth to become engineers, nurses, or social workers, which requires learning specialized skills. Karl Jaspers was aware of the difficulties involved in training genuine leaders (what he called statesmen):

Politics in this sense—the thoughts and actions that bring all-encompassing order into the human community—is not a profession to be learned. Statesmen are not produced by schools of political science. They are not professionals or specialists. They represent the ethos of a people, something that everyone should and could understand. They are not working at a trade but are called to serve the common cause.[35]

Difficult as it may be to train statesmen, the spirit of statesmenship, like wisdom, can be imparted:

But statesmen, if they are great, are not isolated phenomena. They attract men of similar stature, let them come to the fore, let them learn by taking part in the business of government. If we want to speak about a school for statesmen, it means personal apprenticeship in the spirit of a community where political thinking is practiced as a kind of universal thinking that cannot be directly taught.[36]

Frederick Douglass, Booker T. Washington, Mary Bethune, W.E.B. Du Bois, Marcus Garvey, Martin Luther King, Jr., Malcolm X—each of these individuals was a statesman in Jaspers' sense of the term. So were Washington, Lincoln, Roosevelt, and Churchill. Of course, not every councilor whom the Black colleges set out to nurture will satisfy this model of statesmanship, but the model can still serve as an inspiring guide.

When Locke, Du Bois, and others talked about training youth for leadership, they were speaking primarily of leadership in the Black community. Owing to computer technologies and other forms of communication, the world has gotten smaller, and the consequences of statesmen's actions affect the entire planet. We have formed a planetary network. In addressing a given issue, political leaders have to think beyond their particular community, even beyond the Western world. Not all councilors can become statesmen, yet Americans, Black Americans especially, must develop statesmen capable of handling the affairs of this planetary network. If the council system were adopted as an international order, it could offer a forum in which Blacks, women, and other minorities, and even Third world countries, could participate effectively in the realm of human affairs. Black education must prepare youth for that task.

NOTES

1. Alain Locke used the term "standardized," but by this he meant parity or equality rather than uniformity or regimentation.

2. Alain Locke, "Negro Education Bids for Par," *Survey* 54 (September 1, 1925).

3. W.E.B. Du Bois, *The Education of Black People*, ed. Herbert Aptheker (Amherst: University of Massachusetts, 1973).

4. Locke, "Negro Education Bids for Par," p. 567.

5. Ibid.

6. Ibid.

7. Ibid.

8. Ibid., p. 568.

9. Ibid.

10. Ibid.

11. Ibid.

12. Ibid., p. 569.

13. Ibid.

14. Ibid.

15. Ibid.

16. Ibid.

17. Ibid.

18. Ibid. Locke never said which war he had in mind; I presume he is talking about World War I.

19. Locke, "Negro Education Bids for Par," p. 569.

20. Ibid.

21. Ibid, p. 570.

22. Ibid.

23. Ibid.

24. Ibid.

25. In many of his other works he exalted the principle of social reciprocity, insisting that cultural values among diverse groups must be shared: appreciated, enjoyed.

26. Locke, "Negro Education Bids for Par," p. 570.

27. Du Bois, *The Education of Black People*, pp. 139–148.

28. Ibid., pp. 92–93.

29. Ibid., pp. 146–147.

30. Ibid., p. 152.

31. Locke, "Negro Education Bids for Par," p. 593.

32. Ibid.

33. Ibid.

34. Ibid.

35. Karl Jaspers, *The Future of Mankind*, trans. E. B. Ashton (Chicago: University of Chicago Press, 1961), p. 239.

36. Ibid., pp. 239–240.

8   EDUCATING THE MASSES

I

Clearly, Alain Locke like W.E.B. Du Bois, argued strongly for the need to educate the Black Elite, but there is another side to Locke's thought. In the 1930s and 1940s he turned his attention to the problem of adult mass education. He claimed that in order to improve the conditions of Blacks and promote the spread of democracy generally, society must educate the masses, especially Blacks who for centuries had been denied adequate education.

In his writings on mass education, Locke said little about educating the Black Elite. Did this shift in emphasis indicate a contradiction in Locke's thought? Did it represent a complete reversal of his thought? Du Bois's views on Black education reveal an apparently contradictory position comparable to Locke's. In his works on the education of the Black Elite, Du Bois claimed that such education should take priority over all other types, as Locke argued. Herein lies the core of the controversy between Du Bois and Washington, who obviously opposed such an educational program. Although Du Bois remained steadfast in the conviction that the Black Elite should receive the best training possible, he was also concerned with the training of the masses. As John J. Ansbro in his *Martin Luther King, Jr.*, observes, "Although Du Bois did emphasize the mission of the Talented Tenth, it would be inaccurate to conclude that he did not have a concern for the educational development of other

Black students."[1] Du Bois was not altogether unconcerned with the education of the Black masses, but he was not as interested in mass education as Locke and Washington. With regard to Black education, Locke entertained both positions—an Elitist education and a non-Elitist, folk and mass education. Seen in a broader perspective, his views represented the effort to synthesize the opposing ideals of Du Bois and Washington.

Did Locke successfully achieve such a synthesis? Was Locke toying here with another paradox? His position appears to be paradoxical, or at least ambiguous. As seen in the two previous chapters, Locke's position on an Elite education was somewhat at odds with Washington's. Washington argued that an educated Elite was not needed to lead the masses; if the masses were properly trained in laboring skills, they would be able to lead themselves. If Locke wanted to educate the masses, as Washington insisted, what role would the educated Elite play? Would an educated Elite still be needed to lead the educated masses? Here Locke was bordering on a paradox. If not, it is safe to say that he had difficulties deciding this issue: which type of education should be given priority—Elite or mass education?

This chapter examines Locke's views of adult mass education and shows how his ideas compare with those of Washington. The latter part of the chapter relates Locke's concepts to certain modern developments in technology and suggests ways in which knowledge about high technology and culture can be disseminated to the Black masses.

Before Washington, Americans gave little attention to adult education of any type: as already noted, he was original in establishing a program of vocational education, the social value of which he dramatized. Although Southern whites recognized the social value of Washington's educational program, in the early stages of its development they were reluctant to adopt it in their own communities. Had they adopted Washington's program, Locke believed that segregated education in the South would have ended. Segregation and racism permitted Southern whites to feel that Washington's program of vocational education was best suited for the Black community, not their own. If whites had accepted such a program during its pioneering phase, "an educational reconstruction that has yet to be accomplished would have been successfully inaugurated."[2]

In his "Reciprocity Instead of Regimentation" (1934), Locke noted that the vocational program which Frederick Douglass had initiated as early as 1880 and which Washington popularized, underwent a number of phases in its development. In the first phase, when Washington was giving the program its inspiration, Southern whites accepted it in theory but, as noted, were reluctant to adopt it themselves. In the second phase, whites gained a greater appreciation of the program's practical value and adopted it, although under a different name: "Vocational education when given to Negroes became known as industrial education; it was called technical or vocational education when it was offered to whites."[3] This distinction produced several consequences which affected both whites and Blacks. Because whites did not want to identify with an educational program initiated and designed by Blacks, "although it was just as definitely adapted to the situation of the 'poor whites' as to that of Negro peasantry,"[4] they failed to reap the economic benefits which the program offered. Although Blacks were the first to implement a program of vocational education, whose economic advantages they shared from the start, "when the program took its full stride it became, on the Negro side, a truncated thing, a blind-alley side shift, so that the major economic effects of this type of education were lost to the South that had in theory accepted it."[5]

At the same time that support of the white vocational program was increasing the support of the Black educational program was decreasing. Because of racism, whites were not motivated to support Black educational institutions. Owing to this lack of support, Blacks had to start anew to enjoy any standard type of technical education. They had to get "a painful second start through the land grant colleges and their programs, imitating feebly such slight programs of technical and vocational education as were worked out for white youth."[6]

Locke blamed whites for creating a segregated educational system within which both races were adversely affected, although the greatest hardship fell on Blacks. Locke sought to lay part of the blame on Booker T. Washington for failing to attack segregation vigorously. It is generally believed that Washington subscribed to the conservative attitude shared by most whites at the time, that because of the Blacks' handicaps and disabilities segregation was desirable. Moreover, because of the Blacks' blighted economic situation they needed a special type of education. Locke realized the importance of this issue, but was ambivalent on the matter: "There is no more controversial question than this very one, whether because of his handicaps and disabilities the Negro stands in need of a special variety or program of education, just as there is no more reactionary and dangerous position than the offhand assumption that he does."[7] In this passage Locke opposed the notion that Blacks needed a special type of education. In the next quoted passage however, Locke admitted that the Blacks' situation was special, but only in the sense that it was "a special instance of a general problem requiring special attention and effort, perhaps, because of its acute degree but in its significance and bearing upon educational problems and methods considered generally diagnostic and universally applicable."[8]

Nevertheless, Locke did not want to equate the Blacks' special situation with segregation, as Washington presumably did. Rather, he wanted to equate it with the special situation that characterized any minority group anywhere in the world. In any event, Locke thought that any educational program for Blacks or a similarly oppressed group must incorporate the group's cultural-racial history and problems, and not focus exclusively on practical subjects.

The study of cultural subjects in mass education is important not only because of their intellectual value, but also because such subjects inspire learners to acquire knowledge. Locke maintained that this element of inspiration was especially important for Blacks who had been damaged psychologically and spiritually by the conditions of oppression. If the Black masses were not inspired to acquire education through the study of cultural subjects, their education would be a failure. As evidence for his claim about the importance of inspiration, Locke drew on a number of cases from around the world, noting that "from the earliest days of educational work with culturally disadvantaged groups, from Toynbee Hall and Ruskin College down to the Hull House and Reedsville, from the Cheapside Cockney and the Ghetto Jew to the emancipated Southern Negro to the Sovietized Russian peasant,"[9] the success of these programs lay in the study of cultural subjects.

Among the cultural subjects Locke wanted to integrate into the education of the Black masses were those that appealed to the imagination and feeling such as art, history, music, and literature. Both adults and children are more open to learning when the subject matter excites the emotions. As an example, Locke considered the era of Reconstruction when, for the first time, Blacks as free people were given some educational opportunities. At that time, many learned how to read by reading the Bible. The Bible is an effective text for teaching Christian oppressed people reading skills, as well as for providing general knowledge about the human condition. Blacks could identify with Jesus who struggled with evil, suffered, and expressed compassion for those who suffered. The Bible represents Jesus, Moses, and other religious figures through vivid images and symbols, which excite the intellect, imagination, heart, and soul. Would not Whitehead regard such religious literature as a useful tool for keeping the pattern of romance alive in education?

Although Locke never used the term "romance" in this context, he evoked a similar idea when he discussed the ways in which the Bible inspired Blacks to read. He said that those who began by reading the Bible learned to do so "with a momentum that got ahead by leaps and jumps rather than by inches."[10] With this observation, he generalized that mass education for any oppressed group "must have a dynamic and enthusiasm-compelling drive."[11]

Locke did not want to say, however, that mass education must be dominated by religious studies. He urged groups to study their own racial and cultural history, as well as the cultural history of others. If Blacks were given the opportunity to study the cultural history of others, they could overcome a segregated education and increase understanding among all ethnic groups of the world.

To the degree that Washington's educational program did not stress cultural subjects, his program involved intellectual segregation. Washington went no further than Whitehead's stage of specialization. Locke, like Whitehead, began with romance, allowed for specialization, and moved on to the stage of generalization. Locke wanted to allow for the Whiteheadian sense of romance. His exaltation of specialized or practical knowledge is also evident in his agreement with Washington that Blacks needed to acquire skills. Whitehead's sense of generalization was encouraged when Locke said that Blacks had to become acquainted with the widest possible number of cultures and seek to discover the universal principles that underlay these cultures. In "The Need for a New Organon in Education," it will be recalled, Locke spoke of the importance of evaluative criticism, a notion comparable to the Whiteheadian notion of wisdom.

During Washington's times, racially separate education was common; perhaps this helps to explain why he limited his program to Blacks. The prevailing attitude of that era was that Blacks were intellectually inferior to whites, and so needed a separate program. The larger society also believed that for Blacks cultural subjects were "beyond their reach." Obviously, Washington accepted segregation, but it is not altogether clear whether he shared the attitude about the Blacks' so-called cultural inferiority. It is clear, however, that Washington did not aggressively challenge this attitude, as Locke did. Locke was aware that the disparity between Black and white education would grow if it were not linked with the concerns of the larger society. Yet, he wanted to establish this link without destroying the racial and cultural integrity of Blacks and other ethnic groups. He agreed with Washington that adult education should include the "man farthest down," but he also included economically, politically, and culturally deprived individuals of the larger society. In this regard, adult education should be based not so much on race or culture, but on "the common bond of condition":

How much further along, for example, the program addressed to the tenant farmer and his improvement would be if this *common bond of condition* [emphasis added] had been intelligently faced even a half generation ago! The Tuskegee program of practical farmer education would have swept through the South with full local and state support and with a single eye to the economic improvement of the standard of production and of living.[12]

By calling attention to economics, Locke seemed to share Washington's concerns. Had Locke overlooked the fact that he had begun his analysis by suggesting that cultural and racial elements were more important than the economic? Was he being contradictory here? Or was this simply another of his paradoxes? To remain consistent with his position on adult education, which, as Washington maintained, "must not only include the man farthest down but must begin with him,"[13] Locke had to pay more attention to economic issues. "The man farthest down" has a greater interest in feeding himself and his family than in reading poetry or history, regardless of its aesthetic appeal. Locke was aware how difficult it was to spread cultural subjects to the deprived masses: "The second generation does add something to the adult education movement. In doing so they have to do a very difficult job. They have to actually root these new taste [sic] for them [i.e., cultural subjects] in the mind of the masses."[14] To whom did Locke assign the difficult job of rooting cultural taste in the masses? He never identified who should carry out this task, but he may have meant the Black Elite. Who else would be capable? Can the masses lead the masses? He also thought that the mass media could play an important educational role in this area.

Today, the mass media, especially those controlled by the larger commercial networks, devote most of their time to entertainment and sales. There are a few TV programs for children, but overall the educational value of most adult programs is almost negligible.

Locke had an ambivalent attitude toward the mass media as they pertained to adult education. On the one hand, he thought that they could further cultural and social literacy among the masses. On the other hand, in his "Education for Adulthood," he criticized the mass media for frustrating the efforts of adult education, being more concerned with low-level entertainment than with educational programs.

II

In the 1930s and 1940s, when Locke was writing about educating the masses, America received a large influx of European immigrants who had to be Americanized. Community colleges began to be established in major cities. Later, the community college program was extended to include people other than immigrants, people who sought education beyond high school. Today most of the community colleges offer courses to prepare students for vocational and technological careers or to enter the four-year college. The community college, however, like the four-year college and university on which it is modeled, has not effectively integrated what Locke called cultural subjects into its program. In many programs, more than 90 percent of all courses are practical, focusing on technological and vocational materials; only a small portion of the programs are concerned with liberal arts courses. It would seem that a balanced curriculum would be one that incorporates cultural values into every subject matter, including the practical.

Locke rightly insisted on the importance of adult education. Although technology has increased the condition of dependence, the need for mass education, both Black and white, is as urgent today as it was when Locke wrote.

Until recently, Black youths were virtually not allowed to attend engineering schools, and many technological firms would not hire Blacks as salespersons or managers, positions in which they would be exposed to high technology. As a result, the Black community is now unprepared to reap the benefits which the technological industries offer. The benefits include: (1) employment at a professional level in major firms; (2) establishment of technologically related firms involving telecommunications, computer softwares, and computer programming, within the Black community; and (3) application of recent technological developments to social problems in the Black community, as in the areas of health care, crime prevention, and teenage pregnancy.

Black educational institutions and organizations can play a major role in preparing Blacks, including the masses, to meet the challenges of technology. Although a few of the Black colleges, Tuskegee and Howard, for example, offer degrees in an area such as engineering, how much effort are these institutions expending to reach the masses? In addition, if the community college is not altogether successful in reaching the masses, what can be expected of the four-year college or university?

Most institutions of higher learning, Black and white, are not organized in ways to reach the masses, but they can be restructured to do more than they are presently doing. Tuskegee Institute, for example, offers both liberal arts and technological subjects. In the area of the technological, it places a heavy emphasis on engineering, veterinary medicine, and agricultural science. How knowledge about these areas can be made available to the Black community generally is an important question. As it is a difficult question to answer, the response here will be suggestive and brief.

A reasonable approach to this problem lies in what Locke called the concentration of resources.[15] Let us, however, extend Locke's phrase to include industry and government. As suggested in the previous chapter, this would require creating at Tuskegee Institute or a similar Black college an Industrial Park. These new resources and facilities would coordinate and perform research for industry and government, from which funding would be derived and by which knowledge would be disseminated to the masses.

As a result of this government-industry-university alliance, Black colleges could assist industry in developing and manufacturing useful products for the Black community and the nation generally. Second, Black businesses could establish an economic base for the community, reducing unemployment and thus stimulating the economy. Third, the Black masses could be taught the basic skills of computer programming, word processing, telecommunications, among others, as well as cultural subjects that need to be integrated into practical subjects in order to provide the masses with a more balanced education.[16] Located within the community, the Industrial Parks could make knowledge about high technology and culture readily accessible to the masses who, like the students in the university, could come to grasp the underlying principles and the interrelations among the subjects. If Locke were writing today, he would recognize the need to establish Industrial Parks and cultural centers within which the above-mentioned skills could be integrated.

Today many university administrators whose institutions have created Industrial Parks are attempting to establish guidelines for the problem of conflict of interest that often arises, for example, when members of the faculty devote too much time consulting for industry. Although this problem merits attention, an equally important problem which administrators, both Black and white, ought to address is as follows: What can be done to introduce the study of cultural values into the Industrial Parks? Humanities and social science centers must be effectively incorporated into such parks, just as they should be incorporated into the university's core courses. In that way, industrial employees as well as university students who participate in the program can benefit from an experience in which practical knowledge and normative issues are placed in perspective.

In most institutions with Industrial Parks, cultural subjects are not emphasized, although administrators claim that the parks are designed to give the students a balanced education. In fact, the purpose of the parks is apparently satisfactory to the interests of industry and government. However, the parks have not yet fulfilled their potential: efforts could be made to establish cultural centers that integrate theory and practice, values and facts into these parks. If such centers could be effectively established in the parks, they would provide the intellectual atmosphere for the Whiteheadian and the Lockean models of education described above.

The masses might be reached in yet another way. Many community organizations and institutions, such as PUSH, NAACP, SCLC, and the National Urban League, in conjunction with the Industrial Park programs, could become more aggressively involved in the education of the masses. For example, they could offer community-based tutorial programs aimed at high school and college dropouts to prepare them for reentry into the educational process.

Arendt's political council system could also be a useful organ for adult education. Educational councils could be established, through which the self-selected masses at the grass-roots level could take the initiative to educate the masses. Educational councilors would inform the masses about public policy issues, recent scientific and technological findings, and the cultural activities of Blacks and other groups. In this way democracy could be made practical.

Locke would not have had any difficulties with this council system proposal, as it pertains to adult education. As will be recalled, he did not want Black education to be separated from the adult education program of the larger society. Because the federated council system would permit a racially mixed political community, the adoption of this system would help overcome the separated system which Locke abhorred. Furthermore, this interracial contact in the area of adult education especially would be a primary way of promoting understanding among ethnic groups.

NOTES

1. John J. Ansbro, *Martin Luther King, Jr.: The Making of a Mind* (Maryknoll, New York: Orbis Books, 1983), p. 202.

2. Alain Locke, "Negro Needs as Adult Educational Opportunities," *Findings of the First Annual Conference on Adult Education and the Negro*, 1938, p. 6.

3. Alain Locke, "Reciprocity Instead of Regimentation: Lessons of Negro Adult Education," *Journal of Adult Education* 6 (October 1934): 418.

4. Ibid.

5. Ibid.

6. Ibid., p. 419.

7. Locke, "Negro Needs as Adult Educational Opportunities," p. 5.

8. Ibid., p. 6.

9. Ibid.

10. Ibid., p. 7.

11. Ibid.

12. Ibid., p. 9.

13. Ibid.

14. Alain Locke, "Popularized Literature," in *Findings of the Second Annual Conference on Adult Education and the Negro*, 1940, p. 49.

15. In his essay "Negro Education Bids for Par," *The Survey* 54 (September 1, 1925), Locke explains "concentration of resources." By this he meant that most of the rival private Black colleges should combine and concentrate their resources to form one standard and resourceful college and university center thereby "pooling their plants, faculties,

students and resources" (p. 568). Here he had particular reference to the Atlanta college complex.

16. In "Negro Needs as Adult Educational Opportunities," Locke suggested the following courses which could be used to organize education for the Black masses: (1) the field of health and hygiene, (2) vocational training with the modern frontage of vocational guidance and job-placement, (3) agricultural extension with emphasis on the important new aspects of cooperative management, marketing, and buying, (4) training in the community aspects of social and economic problems, and (5) practical cultural education through amateur production in the craft and the applied arts (p. 9).

9   THE NEED TO DESEGREGATE SCHOOLS

Alain Locke spent most of his adult career decrying the evils of a racially segregated school system. His works undoubtedly exerted influence on the American mind. On May 17, 1954, a little over a generation following the death of Booker T. Washington, the U.S. Supreme Court faced one of its most important decisions (Brown vs. Board of Education) of the twentieth century; it decided that the practice of compulsory racial segregation in public schools was unlawful. Although Locke's health was worsening and he died less than a month later, he presumably died knowing that his life-long efforts were not in vain.

I

The decade of the 1950s indeed marks a turning point in the history of the Black American struggle for equality. Beginning in 1955 Martin Luther King, Jr., initiated a bus boycott in Montgomery, Alabama, which resulted in the desegregation of the city's busses and subsequently other public facilities throughout the country.

Locke, no less than Du Bois, as a Socratic gadfly, was among the earliest Black leaders to call for school desegregation. As early as 1925, in "Negro Education Bids for Par," Locke had advocated an end to segregated education because it was detrimental for Blacks. That essay focused mainly on the Black college. In 1935, some two decades before the Court's decision,

Locke, in "The Dilemma of Segregation" considered the problem of segregated public schools in detail.

This chapter is divided into two parts, the first of which centers on Locke's "The Dilemma of Segregation": the second part considers the tradition of natural law, as formulated by H.L.A. Hart, and shows how that tradition was compatible with Locke's own view about how law could be applied to desegregate public schools.

As a beginning point to our discussion, it would be beneficial to return to Locke's position on this problem as he dealt with it in "Negro Education Bids for Par," bearing in mind that here Locke was talking primarily about higher education. Like Du Bois, he recognized that missionary activities, philanthropy, and other private endeavors had led to racial segregation of the Black college. Because the segregated educational system had become institutionalized, Blacks should make the best of it by gaining administrative control of these institutions and by teaching courses that emphasized Black culture and history, so that students would develop a sense of self-worth. In this way graduating Black students would be able to exercise effective leadership within the Black community.

At the time Locke wrote, it appeared that he was committed to the view that they should remain segregated. But he reversed his outlook when he considered elementary and secondary education. In some of his works he talked about the need to desegregate the educational system, and in others, he denied the need. For example, he argued that Black colleges, especially the private ones, did not have to push for integration or desegregation. Paradoxically, the Black segregated college, as mentioned in Chapter 7, has certain advantages which could be increased manyfold if the larger society provided additional support. On the question of integration he mentioned that a proportional number of Black youths should be allowed to attend white educational institutions, but he never, as we observed earlier, specified what the Black-white ratio should be at Black colleges. Throughout most of his writings, Locke claimed that education at all levels—elementary, secondary, college, and adult—should be organized on the principle of cultural and ethnic reciprocity in order to further understanding among the world's diverse ethnic groups. This is one of the chief aims of education, Black and white. "The Dilemma of Segregation" went beyond this principle of reciprocity. Here he placed greater emphasis on the need to integrate public educational institutions.

Locke began the essay with reasons justifying why segregation of public schools became a practice during the first generation of Reconstruction. The reason was that segregated education was forced upon Blacks by the larger society. Locke did not think segregation was a problem for the first generation of Blacks; in fact, he said it was both necessary and favorable for them. Segregation became problematic following the first generation: "In the second generation, these special provisions and auspices, initially favorable and necessary, became anachronisms and handicaps."[1] Thus, he assigned to the second generation, which included his contemporaries, the task of making the public aware of its duty to support Black education. When Locke discussed the problem of the Black college, he said that the private Black college needed to concentrate its resources and the public-supported Black college needed to expand its resources. "Personally, I can see the time when it will be necessary for many private schools for Negroes to discontinue voluntarily upon due notice in order to force upon the community the assumption of their proper duty and burden."[2]

Locke advocated discontinuing special separate schools for Blacks because they no longer served a purpose and were "now invidious as buffers of a system of educational segregation."[3] In most of Locke's other writings on this subject, he usually accused missionaries and other private agents of establishing and maintaining segregation in education. In "The Dilemma of Segregation," however, Locke suggested that Blacks themselves were to be blamed for perpetuating segregated education. Because of their limited social vision, among other things, Black educators kept the Black schools racially separated. It was advantageous because it provided them job security:

These temporary and short-sighted gains are usually motivated by the same desire for careers for Negro teachers and educational administrators and such pressure of public sentiments as lacks patience to see a mixed teaching staff slowly evolve out of the seasoned adjustment and progressive education of social feeling in a system with mixed students.[4]

If Black educators and the public at large had repudiated this short-term view and had instead considered the long-term consequences for Black education, a major factor preventing desegregation of public schools would have been removed. The dilemma, for which Blacks were partly responsible, thus lay in the conflict between these two sets of views. In most of Locke's other writings on the race question, he regarded whites as the source of the dilemma. But here we see a complete reversal: "I think the basic dilemma of educational segregation arises from the inevitable conflict between the short-term and the long-term point of view [which Blacks held] on this question."[5] He advised Black leaders to discard this short-term view: "My opinion is that the Negro community under intelligent leadership must be taught to see and regard as paramount the long-term interests,— which is another way of saying that principles rather than expediency must dictate if constructive progress is to be made."[6] Again he noted the negative effect of the Black leaders' narrow view and the need for the courts to intervene in the question of segregation: "The main difficulty right here is the narrowing of view forced upon the very class that should give this leadership by the self-interested ambition for professional openings and livelihood."[7] Here the courts could play a viable role:

In the fact of this natural short circuit in the process of progress, I find the chief justification for legal procedure,—the appeal to the courts, to outflank this unwitting betrayal of the mass interests by the few and the equally lethargic and often over-estimated prejudice and group resistance of the white community toward the admission of Negroes to the public school system on the basis of equality.[8]

Thus the Blacks' short-term view may have been a major stumbling block in efforts to desegregate the schools. But following the Supreme Court's decision in 1954 up to the present, whites have been the chief opponents of desegregation; within the past few decades we have witnessed a reversal of the source of the problem. It was the Black community which took the initiative to integrate the schools in Little Rock, an initiative which whites tried to block. Similar opposition was expressed when Blacks sought to desegregate higher education.

When the Supreme Court demanded that the public schools be desegregated, almost every state in the Deep South resisted. Although the Court said that desegregation should take place "with deliberate speed," most states responded by enacting laws that would enable them to abandon or close down the public schools altogether. Consider the ways in which Georgia, Louisiana, and Mississippi reacted:

Georgia. In November of 1954, by a vote of 210,488 to 181,148, Georgians approved a constitutional amendment permitting the operation of a "private school" system, supported by tuition grants of public funds, in the event the General Assembly saw fit to shut down the public schools.

Louisiana. In November of 1954, by a vote of 217,992 to 46,929, Louisianans endorsed a constitutional amendment to permit the state to use its police powers to maintain segregated schools.

Mississippi. In December of 1954, by a vote of 106,832 to 46,095, Mississippians voted to give the legislature authority to close the schools rather than submit to their desegregation.[9]

When Blacks persisted in their efforts to desegregate the schools, most whites did in fact react by abandoning public schools and establishing "private schools" that barred Blacks. If we consider the historical context of the private schools as they pertain to desegregation, an interesting irony presents itself. Locke opposed the private schools which Blacks were maintaining because he felt they prevented integration. Most of these schools were discontinued; yet in their absence integration did not follow, as Locke thought it would. Thus, private Black schools did not prevent desegregation; it was the other way around— the private *white* schools prevented desegregation. By depending so heavily on public funds for support, they also channeled funds away from the public schools which most Blacks attended.

Private white schools have perpetuated segregation in elementary and secondary education, and private white colleges have played a similar role in higher education. Until 1975 Bob Jones University, a private institution in South Carolina, would not allow unmarried Blacks to attend because it believed that interracial dating was wrong. Other white institutions, both public and private, perpetuate segregation by claiming that, in spite of their commitment to Affirmative Action, they "have a difficult time recruiting Black faculty and students." Although a number of institutions have established Affirmative Action Plans which technically conform with Executive Order 11246, in practice they often fail to comply with the Executive Order when it comes to hiring, promoting, and recruiting Blacks by resorting to loopholes in the law.

II

Since an Affirmative Action Plan can be—and often is—easily manipulated by institutions to keep out Blacks, Affirmative Action can be regarded as a weak weapon against segregation. A much stronger weapon is the more direct use of the law itself. Locke advocated the legal approach. Even before the Court ruled segregated public schools unconstitutional, Locke was saying that the segregated school system was morally and legally wrong and that the law should be used to amend the wrong.

When the NAACP under the leadership of Du Bois encouraged the use of the courts and legal measures to desegregate public facilities, it intended mainly that the approach be applied to whites who were regarded as the source of the problem. Locke also intended that the law be applied to whites to make them do right. If we closely examine how he felt that law should be used, another irony becomes evident. The law was also to be brought to bear on the Black educators who hampered desegregation, who short-circuited the process.

The irony is that the law can—and usually does—work both ways. It can be used to encourage desegregation, which is what the Supreme Court intended, or, it can be used to prevent desegregation, which is what the legislators, with the support of the masses, of most Southern states achieved. The same is true of Affirmative Action. It can be manipulated so that an institution can give the impression of compliance with the law in its efforts to do justice to Blacks. Having an Affirmative Action Plan is one thing: aggressively implementing it is quite another.

Prior to the 1954 Court order, the country accepted the separate but equal policy, a policy which never worked in practice largely because "separation and a parity of standards and facilities are naturally antagonistic and rarely if ever co-exist."[10] This was why Locke said the law was needed to overcome the separation and establish parity.

Let us return to Locke's "The High Cost of Prejudice" in which he said the job of the Elite was largely to convince whites that members of the Black Elite were culturally equal to whites. There is an important contrast between that essay and "The Dilemma of Segregation." In the former, he did not mention how the law could be used to establish equality for Blacks. In the latter essay, he offered law as the only hope: "The law seems to me, then, to be one of the only resorts possible,—if not the only one."[11]

Around the time Locke was writing this essay, he was also developing his Jungian introversion-extroversion distinction, as formulated in "Values and Imperatives." However, he did not apply this distinction in his analysis of the dilemma of segregation. It may well be that the source of the problem of desegregation lies partly in this Jungian polarity. Members of the community, both Black and white, who seek to maintain segregated schools are dominated by introverted values; those who want to desegregate are dominated by extroverted values. One is conservative and the other progressive. If this Jungian polarity is applicable here, then the law has little, if any, use at all because the source of conflict is largely in human nature. Also applicable here is the Arendtian "enlarged mentality" which might help to overcome the narrow-mindedness which Locke thought objectionable. Once that has been overcome, once people acquire an open attitude toward one another, then the application of law may be more effective in desegregating the schools.

Locke recognized that the law, though a powerful tool, could not produce immediate change or change without temporary setbacks. Nevertheless, Blacks and whites must not be discouraged, he said. They must "risk the odds of variation in the decisions because of local conditioning circumstances in the courts, face the difficulties of practical enforcement even after favorable decisions, and count upon retributive community sentiment and behavior in some instances."[12]

Locke offered the following as a tactic: "Favorable decisions or pending appeals should be used by public-spirited and sanely balanced citizens' committees as bargaining points for progressive adjustment toward the equalitarian goal."[13] This position obviously contrasts with Martin Luther King's who understood the limitations of court actions in promoting desegregation. At any rate, in Locke's day the courts were constituted largely by racists who opposed racial mixing.

King objected to the gradual process of social changes which the law necessitates. King did not rely very much on positive law, that is, human-made law; instead, he appealed to what he called the higher law of conscience. Moreover, he argued, that the system of segregation had to be attacked directly, but nonviolently. He introduced this direct-action, nonviolent method as an alternative to both legal and political tactics. In contrast, Locke regarded the political route as the only alternative to legal methods. Yet he preferred the machinery of law because it could reach a larger body of people; political pressures were local. He wrote: "The legal system has through the machinery of appeal more reliable access to a wider circle of public opinion beyond the local community and a firmer tradition of impartiality."[14]

The history of desegregation efforts demonstrates that the "tradition of impartiality" is largely false. In most instances, the law was not impartial; rather, it was used to resist desegregation. King and his followers were jailed a number of times, and in most instances the whites who committed crimes against civil rights workers were given light sentences. They were often released without penalty. Of the political method, Locke wrote:

The political channels of effective pressure are purely local or primarily so in the American political system, and what little potentiality of appeal they have from the counter-pressure of biased local tradition and sentiment is itself legal. So the political pressure attack is in the second instance a legal resort and the choice between that and the straight legal approach is then not a matter of principle but of expediency.[15]

Because the political method is basically the legal method, Locke did not regard the two as being in conflict with each other.

In fact, he held that both methods were complementary. King would have agreed, but he obviously preferred the political. Both methods, however, complemented King's nonviolent, direct-action movement to which he assigned the highest value.

When Locke outlined the strategy for legal recourse, he spoke in concrete terms, called attention to the difficulties, and anticipated setbacks. One such difficulty was the law itself, which directly supported the segregated system. Locke argued that this type of difficulty could be overcome: "Discriminatory legal decision and precedent are decidedly more difficult to maintain and more embarrassing both because of the machinery of appeal and the operation of the principle of precedent."[16] People seeking to desegregate the schools should rely on certain key tools, including (1) the ramifications of the principle of precedent, rather than the sentimental concern of an aroused community; (2) competent Black lawyers rather than the amateurish and superficially trained lawyers; and (3) use of the court of appeals, if a case is defeated in the lower courts (in the initial stages, one should be prepared to suffer defeat).[17]

Although Locke praised the NAACP's persistence in attempting to get the courts to end racial discrimination, in most instances when legal battles were fought cases would often be lost by default because public support weakened after the initial defeat. Locke, however, urged Blacks not to admit defeat so quickly. They should persist in the legal struggle, even if they had to struggle with their backs against the wall, as it were: "It is worth the protest in the enhancement of self-respect alone, even if no practical results were to be obtained; and the latter outcome is scarcely conceivable if instead of a few isolated cases scores were instituted."[18]

Locke's entire argument against segregation, as has been noted, centered on the concept of law. Although he contended that society had an obligation to bring Black education up to par through desegregation, he also suggested that there was a legal and moral correlation between society's *obligations* to provide Blacks quality education and Blacks' *rights* to such an education. He did not, however, offer a sufficient justification in showing the connection between such obligations and rights.

It is difficult to determine which tradition of law Locke was accepting; on closer inspection the evidence suggests that he accepted the natural law tradition as represented by such thinkers as John Locke upon whose view the American Constitution rests. Although John Locke assigned an important role to the social contract, he nevertheless felt that the social contract, together with natural rights, ultimately rested on natural law which is discovered by reason. It is difficult to render a precise definition of natural law. Natural law originated in Greco-Roman antiquity, and in that society natural law was regarded as "that part of the code of any particular society that is common to all other legal codes as well."[19] In the Middle Ages natural law came to mean an ideal norm applicable to all human beings.

III

H.L.A. Hart is representative of a more recent variation of the natural law tradition. His position differs from John Locke's in the following way: Where John Locke held that our natural rights included life, liberty and property, Hart is not as interested in defending such rights, which he finds acceptable. Rather, he gives a new twist to the natural law tradition when he claims that if people possess any moral rights at all, "it follows that there is at least one natural right, the equal right of all men to be free."[20] Thus, the right that all people possess to be free is a natural right, a right that need not be created by society but is given by nature.

In the area of U.S. education, this natural right of which Hart speaks has come to mean that everyone, including children, should have equal opportunity in education. Here we are construing the notion of equal opportunity to be synonymous with Hart's notion of natural freedom. This natural right has been denied Blacks. Despite the separate-but-equal policy which our country enacted, society has continued to force most Blacks to educate their youth in separate and unequal facilities, the Supreme Court ruling of 1954 notwithstanding.

Hart is of interest in this context because, in addition to his natural law views which seem to be compatible with Locke's own, he makes a distinction between general and special rights. He describes the distinction as follows: "The assertion of general rights directly invokes the principle that all men equally have the right to be free; the assertion of special right . . . invokes it indirectly."[21]

One way of clarifying these two types of rights is to consider the notion of interference. General rights bar another person from unjustifiably interfering with one's right to freedom as long as one does not interfere with the freedom of another or harm another when exercising the right to freedom. When one exercises one's general rights, there is a moral justification to determine how another is to act. That is, one is in a moral position to say to others: I have a right to do what I am doing—don't unjustifiably interfere with me.

The relationship between special rights and the notion of interference is a bit different. Special rights, says Hart, unlike general rights, arise out of a special relationship which individuals or groups establish with one another. A promise or contract is an obvious example out of which special rights arise: "By promising to do or not to do something," Hart writes,

we voluntarily incur obligations and create or confer rights on those to whom we promise; we alter the existing moral independence of the parties' freedom of choice in relation to some action and create a new moral relationship between them, so that it becomes morally legitimate for the person to whom the promise is given to determine how the promisor shall act. The promisee has a temporary authority or sovereignty in relation to some specific matter over the other's will which we express by saying that the promisor is under an obligation *to* the promisee to do what he has promised.[22]

If the promisor fails to keep the promise, then the one on whom the right is conferred is morally justified in interfering with the freedom of the promisee and is morally justified in curtailing the freedom of the promisee.

When one applies Hart's notion of special rights to the issue of Black education, one has a way of justifying the correlation between moral rights and duties. As an application of general rights, society promised all citizens, including Blacks, an equal opportunity in education, but society failed to keep its promise as it pertains to Blacks. Then, in an effort to correct this injustice, in the "interest of Blacks," society enacted the separate-but-equal law, which grew largely out of the special conditions forced on Blacks. This separate-but-equal practice and law satisfied Hart's special circumstance, under which special rights were created.

Having made that promise to Blacks, however, society failed to fulfill one element in that promise: while keeping Blacks segregated, society failed to give them parity in education. According to Hart it then follows that, having failed in its promise, society is not free to carry on "business as usual" in the area of education. Segregationists claim that as free citizens they have a right to send their youth to any schools they choose and to organize the educational institutions in any way they see fit, even if this means maintaining a dual school system. If Hart's considerations are applied here, Blacks and other desegregationists have special rights to diminish or interfere with the freedom of the segregationists and to push for desegregation if this is how they wish to exercise such interference. Locke was seeking a legal basis for achieving parity in education. Drawing on Hart's conception of special rights is a deeper moral basis, which can provide the grounds for legal action. In addition to general rights, Blacks have special rights in the area of education, which society should recognize. Deriving from these special rights, Blacks have the authority in matters of education and other social institutions to morally force society to recognize these rights. Accordingly, society is morally and legally obligated to recognize such rights, and Blacks have a right to quality education. A similar claim can be made for Blacks in South Africa who also live under a segregated system created by Europeans.

NOTES

1. Alain Locke, "The Dilemma of Segregation," *Journal of Negro Education* 4 (July 1935), 406.

2. Ibid.

3. Ibid.

4. Ibid.

5. Ibid.

6. Ibid.

7. Ibid.

8. Ibid., pp. 406–407.

9. W. D. Workman, Jr., and Patrick E. McCauley, "Reinforcement of School Segregation" in *Crucial Issues in Education*, rev. ed., eds. Henry Ehlers and Gordon C. Lee (New York: Holt, Rinehart and Winston, 1959), pp. 201–202.

10. Locke, "The Dilemma of Segregation," p. 407.

11. Ibid.

12. Ibid.

13. Ibid.

14. Ibid., p. 408.

15. Ibid.

16. Ibid., p. 409.

17. Ibid., pp. 409–410.

18. Ibid., p. 410.

19. Frederick A. Olafson, *Society, Law, and Morality: Readings in Social Philosophy* (Englewood Cliffs, N.J.: Prentice-Hall, 1961), p. 9.

20. Ibid., p. 173.

21. Ibid., p. 183.

22. Ibid., pp. 179–180.

10 THE NEW NEGRO'S CONTRIBUTIONS TO AMERICAN CULTURE

I

If Alain Locke felt it was the responsibility of the Black Elite to refine and uplift the tastes of the masses through adult mass education and cultural leadership, then by implication he thought that the Black masses lacked the capacity for creative activity. This attitude toward the masses is evident in his "The Ethics of Culture" which contrasts sharply with his writings on adult mass education. Yet Locke did not consistently state that the creative capacity of the Black masses was limited. His attitude on this subject was as paradoxical as his attitude toward Booker T. Washington's educational program and adult education in general. On the one hand, he maintained that the aesthetic tastes of the Black masses lacked refinement and, on the other, he insisted that the Black masses were the repository of cultural and spiritual energy, from which the artist must draw in order to produce culture. Locke documented the artistic capacity and achievements of the Black masses in a number of works, including his celebrated *The New Negro*, an anthology of works of Harlem Renaissance artists and writers which Locke edited. The anthology includes four of his own works, "The New Negro," "Negro Youth Speaks," "Negro Spirituals," and "The Legacy of the Ancestral Arts."

This chapter considers the first two essays, as well as the "Foreword" to *The New Negro* and a number of other essays, including Locke's "Negro Contributions to America" (1929), "The

Contribution of Race and Culture" (1930), and "The Negro's Contribution to American Art and Literature" (1928).

In the "Foreword," Locke stated the aim of his book as follows: "This volume aims to document the New Negro culturally and socially,—to register the transformations of the inner and outer life of the Negro in America that have so significantly taken place in the last few years."[1] Although Locke was well aware that the Blacks' objective social conditions were being transformed in the 1920s, his main goal here was to call attention to the inner spiritual transformations of Blacks at that time.

There is ample evidence of a New Negro in the latest phases of social change and progress, but still more in the internal world of the Negro mind and spirit. Here in the very heart of the folk-spirit are the essential forces, and folk interpretation is truly vital and representative only in terms of these.[2]

In the past, Locke observed, people interested in understanding Blacks erred by focusing almost exclusively on their external conditions. The sociological analyses of these conditions were often biased because the investigators were conditioned to approach the subject of Blacks through stereotyped attitudes. Whites perceived Blacks as a problem, a perception which whites forced Blacks to accept. Whites who created this image of Blacks did so by focusing on their social-economic conditions, and thus ignoring or discrediting their cultural contributions and spiritual resources. It is this inner subjective soil of Black life on which Locke wanted to concentrate, so that both Blacks and whites could achieve a deeper understanding of Blacks. To the degree that whites focused on the objective side of Black life, they were looking in the wrong place. Consequently, their commentary was "*about* the Negro rather than of him, so that it is the Negro problem rather than the Negro that is known and mooted in the general mind."[3] Moreover, in the past, many whites had assumed the task of speaking for Blacks. This led to unhappy results. Locke wanted Blacks to speak for themselves: "Whoever wishes to see the Negro in his essential traits, in the full perspective of his achievement and possibilities, must seek the enlightenment of that self-portraiture which the present developments of Negro culture are offering."[4]

If, by 1925, Locke's New Negro was making an appearance on the American scene, from whence did he or she come? Which cultural factors contributed to his or her origin? What were the sources of this new identity? There are no simple answers to such questions because change did not occur suddenly in an historical vacuum. Locke's "Negro Education Bids for Par," published the same year as *The New Negro*, may shed some light on the atmosphere under which the Old Negro was beginning to be transformed into the New Negro.

"Negro Education Bids for Par," it will be recalled, attributed the Blacks' poor education in part to the harmful role played by philanthropists, missionaries, and the race leaders-educators, who were responding to the "problems" of the Old Negro. Because society regarded the Old Negro as a social burden, the whites designed educational institutions of higher learning to solve such a problem. But such institutions added to the problem largely because they were in the hands of weak leaders, most of whom were white.

Although most of the college-going Black youths during the mid-1920s were conditioned to accept the myth that they were a problem to themselves and society, a myth created by philanthropists, missionaries, and others, a number of Negro youth began to rebel against the education they were receiving. Locke reportedly sided with the student rebellion that took place at Howard University in 1925, and as a consequence he was fired (but reinstated in 1927). Students wanted self-control and autonomy: "The widespread student and alumni unrest of the last eighteen months in one Negro college after another—Tallahassee, Lincoln University in Missouri, Fisk, and Howard, . . . — is significant evidence of this rising demand for liberal reform, educational self-direction and autonomy."[5]

Given a more detailed analysis of this phenomenon of unrest, Locke wrote: "For while these breaks occur nominally over questions of alumni control and student discipline, they all come to a head in a feeling of racial repression and the need for more positive and favorable conditions for the expression and cultivation of the developing race spirit."[6]

Noting the incompatibility between the psychology of the Old Negro and the psychology of the New Negro, Locke wrote:

So obviously there is a set to Negro collegiate education that does not conform to the psychology of the young Negro. Partly as a negative reaction to conservative management, partly as a response to developing race consciousness, Negro student bodies are developing the temper of mind and mood that has produced the nationalist universities and the workers' colleges.[7]

Although Locke was concerned mainly with describing the new spirit among Black college youth who began to rebel against the old order, this new spirit was not limited to the college setting. It was national and even international in scope: "Although there are few centers that can be pointed out approximating Harlem's significance, the full significance of that [the outburst of creativity in the Black community] even is a racial awakening on a national and perhaps even a world scale."[8] In this country, the center for the atmosphere of this new spirit was Harlem, New York.

Consideration of Harlem's role in the creative movement of Blacks in the 1920s and 1930s will throw further light on the question of the cultural factors that contributed to the origin of the New Negro.

Following World War I, the mass migration of Blacks from the South to the Northern cities, and to Harlem especially, played a major role in the emergence of the New Negro. Locke observed that Harlem became a galvanizing force which distinguished it from other urban centers, but he did not specify the nature of this force. Harlem attracted not only Southern Blacks, but also Blacks from the West Indies, Africa, and other Third World countries:

It has attracted the African, the West Indian, the Negro American; has brought together the Negro of the North and the Negro of the South; the man from the city and the man from the town and village; the peasant, the student, the business man, the professional man, artist, poet, musician, adventurer and worker, preacher and criminal, exploiter and social outcast.[9]

As diverse as these individuals and groups were, in Harlem they discovered and shared common ground. Prior to the Harlem migration, Blacks around the world were not cognizant of the racial bonds that united them: "The chief bond between them has been that of a common condition rather than a common consciousness; a problem in common rather than a life in common."[10] Harlem changed this; "Negro life is seizing upon its first chances for group expression and self-determination."[11]

When sociologists attempt to explain the development of social movements or trends, they frequently identify specific individuals who were "responsible" for such developments. Because Locke placed such a high value on the Black Elite, one would expect him to have credited the Black Elite for inspiring the Harlem migration and Renaissance. Instead, he named a different source, the masses themselves: "It is the 'man farthest down' who is most active in getting up."[12] During the 1920s, the masses were leading the Elite. "One of the most characteristic symptoms of this is the professional man himself migrating to recapture his constituency after a vain effort to maintain in some Southern corner what for years back seemed an established living and clientele."[13]

In this Harlem experience, the old leader-follower relationship was reversed: "The clergyman following his errant flock, the physician or lawyer trailing his clients, supply the true clues. In a real sense it is the rank and file who are leading, and the leaders who are following. A transformed and transforming psychology permeates the masses."[14]

Did this reversal in relationship between leaders and followers contradict Locke's view that the masses needed leaders, without whom the masses would be incapable of advancing? Did the Harlem experience support Washington's view that the masses could lead themselves? It was precisely at this point in the history of America that the Black masses became gadflies and midwives, stimulating social reform.

With regard to the creation of the New Negro, Locke, as already noted, suggested that the Harlem experience was largely responsible for the emergence of the New Negro, who, upon arriving in Harlem, rejected his old "Uncle Tom" identity. Many of the old race-leaders failed to grasp the realities and ramifications of the experiences of the New Negro, although they sensed that the Black masses were assuming a new identity. Nevertheless, they thought that such an identity was a "passing phase," an attack of "race nerves" so to speak, an aftermath of the war. Locke warned the larger society that it must reckon with the New Negro whose arrival on the sociological battlefield was permanent. The larger society must seek to fully understand this New Negro and must take him seriously. Locke had a similar message for Blacks themselves: "For this he [the Negro] must know himself and be known for precisely what he is, and for that reason he welcomes the new scientific rather than the old sentimental interest."[15]

Whites, as well as Blacks, must seek a deeper understanding of the new Negro by replacing sentiment with science. If such an understanding were to be achieved, Locke maintained, this might promote racial harmony. Locke spoke of the importance of an "intelligent representative element," among both Blacks and whites, which would benefit from this understanding. Although Locke did not use the term "Elite" in this content, the notion of the intelligent representative seems to be the same as his notion of the Elite.

The effort toward this [cooperation among the races] will at least have the effect of remedying in large part what has been the most unsatisfactory feature of our present stage of race relationships in America, namely the fact that the more intelligent and representative elements of the two race groups have at so many points got quite out of vital touch with one another.[16]

Locke was suggesting that, although the masses played a primary role in the initial stage of the Harlem Renaissance, the Elite of both groups, Black and white, had an important role to play. They had to work together to ensure racial harmony. Locke wanted this type of contact between both Elites to supplant what he called long-distance philanthropy: "that the only safeguard for mass relations in the future must be provided in the carefully maintained contacts of the enlightened minorities of both race groups."[17] Locke also sought other changes, "less charity but more justice; less help, but infinitely closer understanding."[18] All of this, and more, he suggested was needed to reduce antagonism between the races.

Long-distance philanthropy and charity, Locke suggested, were incompatible with the New Negro, who was discovering his power of self-determination. The New Negro was moving forward toward his own outer objectives which Locke described as being identical with the ideals of American institutions and democracy; his inner objectives were still in the process of formation. These outer objectives were manifest in public programs, whereas inner objectives were more a manifestation of a consensus of feeling than opinion, of attitude than of program. Claude McKay reflected an aspect of the inner attitude and objective of the New Negro:

> Mine is the future grinding down to-day
> Like a great landslip moving to the sea,
> Bearing its freight of debris far away
> Where the green hungry waters restlessly
> Heave mammoth pyramids, and break and roar
> That eerie challenge to the crumbling shore.[19]

Locke contrasted McKay's defiant poem with James Weldon Johnson's poem which expressed "an attitude of sober query and stoical challenge."[20] Locke had in mind Johnson's "To America."[21]

Locke warned that this new attitude of the Blacks should not express itself in a defiant, superior feeling as was suggested in some of McKay's poems.[22] Locke spoke more approvingly of the attitude reflected in James Weldon Johnson's works; he indicated that most people felt as he did: "We wish our race pride to be a healthier, more positive achievement that a feeling based upon a realization of the shortcomings of others."[23]

In any event, racial oppression had frustrated the expression of the creative energies of most Black Americans. Nevertheless, Locke saw the opening of constructive channels into which the balked social feelings of the American Negro could flow.

Which channels did Locke have in mind? With which movements should Blacks in America identify in order to express their creative feelings? Locke considered the Harlem experience within an international context, and he identified two movements Black Americans should promote: one was that of acting as "the advance-guard of the African peoples in their contact with Twentieth Century civilization; the other, the sense of a mission of rehabilitating the race in world esteem from that loss of prestige for which the fate and conditions of slavery have been so largely responsible."[24] Blacks were to be gadflies and midwives on both the national and international front in order to rehabilitate both Africans and Black Americans in world esteem.

Locke seemed to be drawing on his Black Elite views here, although he did not use the term "Black Elite." in most of his works, he used "Black Elite" to refer to the Talented Tenth. Here also he seemed to be suggesting that the American Black masses were to be the Elite in an international context and point the way for Africa and other Third World nations. On this point, Locke seemed to be in agreement with Garvey: "Garveyism may be a transient, if spectacular, phenomenon, but the possible rôle of the American Negro in the future development of Africa is one of the most constructive and universally helpful missions that any modern people can lay claim to."[25] When Locke discussed African art and culture, he made a claim that conflicted with this passage, in which he told Black Americans to help move Africa to the forefront of world civilization. We will return to this paradox in Chapter 11.

If Blacks, Locke maintained, would participate in such international causes, they would help promote the prestige of Blacks around the world as well as at home. Yet Locke suggested that Blacks should not get involved in such international movements to the extent that they failed to develop adequate attention to the most immediate, pressing tasks here at home. This latter task was the reevaluation by whites and Blacks alike of the Negroes in terms of their artistic endowments and cultural contributions, past and prospective.

II

In most of his works Locke observed that there was a close relationship between the Blacks' racial experiences and their cultural contributions. As noted earlier in his essay "The Contribution of Race to Culture," Locke struggled with what he called a terrific dilemma: nationalism versus internationalism.[26] It is important that culture originate from within the soil of a given nation or ethnic group; at the same time, culture must be enjoyed at the international level in order to promote peace. Locke touched on this paradox when he argued that the Blacks' creative movement in the 1920s should join with the international struggle and advance the cause of Blacks around the world. At the same time, he cautioned Blacks not to get too involved on the international level, indicating that their greatest hope lay in changing the attitude of both whites and Blacks locally and nationally to produce a more open attitude among the races. Already he was torn between nationalism and internationalism.

Both Du Bois and Garvey and, in the 1960s, Malcolm X and King, struggled with this paradox. The Pan-African Movement in which Du Bois and Locke played key roles enabled them to link the Black struggle with the Third World struggle. Locke, more than Du Bois, had a greater interest in the cultural component of Pan-Africanism. Locke's interest in this cultural component coincided wtih a number of French-speaking African intellectuals who subscribed to the policy of racial assimilation. Locke and other Harlem Renaissance writers exerted much influence on the French-speaking assimilationists. These African intellectuals, inspired by people such as Richard Wright and Claude McKay, came to gain a greater appreciation of their cultural heritage. As Joseph E. Harris observed,

The greatest of French-speaking Africans, therefore, came from the Harlem Renaissance of the 1920s. Writers like Alain Locke, Countee Cullen, Langston Hughes, Du Bois, and others from the United States, Claude McKay from Jamaica, Eric Walrond from Guyana, Nicolas Guillen of Cuba, Jean Price-Mars from Haiti, and others represented the international group of Black writers who had a particular influence on their French-speaking brothers, especially on Leopold Senghor.[27]

Aimé Césaire, whose views we have already considered, was also inspired by the Harlem Ranaissance writers.

At no time did Garvey change his mind about the need for a racially separate society. But as Locke recognized, Garvey stimulated the sense of internationalsim and race consciousness among Blacks and other people of color. The younger Malcolm X also endorsed race consciousness and separatism, but, later in his career, after having made his trip to Mecca, he began to talk as an internationalist, insisting that unity among all people of the world was needed, regardless of race or nationality. King was consistent in advocating the principle of integration. Although much of his civil rights activities focused on the problems Blacks faced in America, he understood that the problems Black Americans suffered were in part worldwide. King was among the first Americans to oppose the Vietnam War; this war, as King insisted, was in part a racial war, fought for the purpose of protecting white America's economic interests and subjugating the Vietnamese. He believed that the Christian community, founded on the universal principle of love, would speak to the nationalism-internationalism paradox.

Locke relied on his principle of reciprocity to solve this paradox. Each racial group, in keeping with the principle of cultural autonomy and self-determination, should seek to develop its own culture and by so doing would conform to the principle of nationalism. But racial tension would continue to erupt among nationalities and racial groups if each acted as though the cultural products of a particular nation belonged exclusively to that nation or race. The problem lay in the old notions of proprietorship and vested interest, notions which Locke rejected because they produced conflicts among groups. Although each group has a right to develop its own cultural products, no group owns the cultural products, once they have been developed. They belong to the international community, to world civilization generally. What Locke wanted to do, therefore, was to replace the notion of cultural proprietorship with the principle of cultural reciprocity, of free trade in culture.

> But do away with the idea of proprietorship and vested interest,—and face the natural fact of the limitless interchangeableness of culture goods, and the more significant historical facts of their more or less constant exchange, and we have, I think, a solution reconciling nationalism with internationalism, racialism with universalism.[28]

Locke understood that race loyalty often created tension among people, yet he did not want to abandon the factor of race altogether: "It is not the facts of the existence of race which are wrong, but our attitudes toward those facts."[29] In the past the factors of race created problems among people largely because "the various creeds of race have been falsely predicated."[30] In the past certain groups had used race as a political tool to their own advantage and to the detriment of others; in addition, "in many instances the cultural virtues of race are falsely appropriated by nationalities."[31] The element of race is bad when it is used to promote a political ideology—Hitler's super race, for example. If freed from its political ideology and practices, "the cult of race is free to blossom almost indefinitely to the enrichment and stimulation of human culture."[32]

If the racial element were allowed to blossom, so that self-determination could be enjoyed and if the principle of reciprocity were allowed to prevail, unity among people at both the international and national level could be approximated. A world that seeks unity by allowing its minorities to determine their own destiny, and at the same time allows the various groups to share one another's cultural values, stands a better chance of achieving its goal of world unity than a world that seeks unity by imposing uniformity at the expense of the cultural integrity of its minorities. This kind of uniformity is at most undesirable because it rests on the old, erroneous assumption, especially characteristic of the Western world, that universal unity requires that we all be alike. The old type of unity is objectionable because it harbors the belief that certain groups are superior, others inferior; certain groups progressive, others backward; certain groups illegitimate, others normal, and so on. Thus, the old form of unity must be replaced by cultural reciprocity. In that way, a new type of thinking about politics may be achieved, a manner of thinking which "may be styled free-trade in culture." Free-trade in culture is just the opposite of cultural proprietorship: one seeks domination, the other sharing and exchange. By "free-trade in culture," Locke did not mean to suggest that cultural goods could be manufactured, bought, and sold in the same way one manufactures, buys, and sells material goods. Rather, "culture has root and grows in that social soil which, for want of a better term, we call 'race'."[33] Hence the importance of race consciousness and the sharing of goods, in the international community, which grows out of race consciousness.

III

In his essay "Negro Contributions to America," Locke examined the ways in which slavery, which he called a "negative merit," created the oppressive conditions for Blacks who were the primary source of labor and thus made significant material contributions to America. Furthermore, because of slavery Blacks also contributed to the cultural and spiritual dimensions of American life. In perceiving Blacks primarily as sources of labor, as little more than animals, Americans were reluctant to recognize Blacks' cultural contributions. The reason was largely that slavery forced Blacks into a condition of dependence, a condition that excluded them from the mainstream of American life. Despite their dependence, Blacks still introduced creative elements into American culture.

Because of this condition of dependence, most Americans came to regard Blacks as passive receivers, more as liabilities than as assets. Locke believed that even those white Americans who regarded themselves as friends and benefactors of Blacks shared this attitude: "Many of the Negro's best practical friends and benefactors share this view, and the major premise of most missionary efforts in his behalf has been an assumption of his dependence upon a civilization in which he is merely a consumer."[34] Locke devoted most of his career to demonstrating that the above attitude had no basis in fact.

Locke was careful not to exaggerate or distort the facts: "Let us be realists and not presume that the gifts we shall mention were conscious, deliberate, or wholly original."[35] His point was that the Blacks' cultural contributions have been not so much a conscious effort as a result of the Blacks' reactions to American ideals and institutions under which they were forced to live. Among these Locke included "Christianity, the plantation, freedom, democracy, [and] justice. . . ."[36] Blacks exerted a twofold influence on these ideals: "first, as a passive presence influencing the institutional development of each of these basic social ideas; in the second place, actually making, in many instances, a constructive contribution to these same ideas."[37]

In analyzing how slavery provided the conditions for the Blacks' cultural contributions, Locke called attention to the negative power which the Black slaves possessed but did not exercise because of their willingness to conform to the American way of life. As slaves, they could have reacted in a much more aggressive manner to the American life-style; they could have introduced "factors of non-conformity into the very heart of American civilization which would have prevented on the one hand, his rapid cultural assimilation, and, on the other, would have put the basic values of American life on the defensive."[38] If the Black slave had exercised such "negative power," American civilization would have been quite different from what it now is and the institution of slavery may have been abolished before 1865. American civilization would not have benefited from the positive cultural contributions Blacks made. Locke was on the trail of another paradox here: that slavery was both good and bad for Blacks.

Locke named Christianity as one of the ideals to which Blacks reacted in constructive ways, both emotionally and artistically. The Black spirituals, associated with church music and song, combined both emotional and artistic factors. The spirituals represented the Blacks' own unique emotional interpretation of Christianity. Most people failed to appreciate the emotional aspects of the spiritual; they regarded them as merely an artistic expression of Blacks and "have been lauded as 'America's most notable folk music.' "[39] The spirituals went much deeper than the mere artistic; they had their roots in Black American feelings and elemental moods, which Americans may come to recognize in the future.

The notion of "spirituals" was customarily associated with the folk music which Blacks created,[40] but Locke did not limit the notion to folk music alone. He extended it to include the full range of Black Americans' artistic and cultural heritage, the cultural features that set Blacks apart from their European counterparts: "the Uncle Remus body of folk-lore, the spirituals, and the basic idioms of American popular music and dance to the extent that these are distinctively different from the borrowed forms of the ancestral European cultures."[41] There is an irony here. Although Blacks introduced many folk elements—folklore, folksong, folkdance, and popular music among them—into American culture, Blacks were not given proper credit. As Locke contended, however, the cultural features that are now regarded as distinctively American "are products of the despised slave minority."[42]

Although, as Locke maintained, our spiritual heritage arose out of the experience of Black slaves, present-day Blacks, drawing on the works of their African ancestors, elevated the artistic experience, especially in the areas of folk-dance and popular music, "from the level of instinctive folk-art to that of formal art."[43] This was attested to by the Harlem Renaissance movement, which was not only "an important aspect of minority self-expression, it [was] a movement that has already made substantial contributions of general artistic significance and value."[44]

Blacks have already made enormous contributions in music, and they have the potential to make similar headway in fields such as painting and sculpture. Here, Locke attempted to dispel the old myth that Blacks had special innate artistic endowments that enabled them to make such strides in creating culture. Locke denied that Blacks had an instinctive ability to create art. Rather, he appealed to environmental factors: Black Americans were good artists because of "the simple fact of the intensification of the emotional side of his life by persecution and suffering, and the concentrating of the group life-force at a point and in channels where the practical disabilities of social and economic handicaps are relatively powerless and inoperative. This is the Negro's compensation for his hard lot and generation-long sacrifice."[45] The next chapter shows that Locke was inconsistent in his position on Blacks' artistic abilities. In some passages, as will be seen, he agreed that these abilities were instinctive; in others, as in the above passage, he claimed that they were acquired.

In the latter part of "Negro Contributions to America," Locke mentioned how Blacks influenced the psychology, customs, and spirit of Southern whites: "The South is different in many vital ways because of its black peasant matrix."[46] The elements that were distinctively Black and had affected Southern whites included: "Southern amiability, nonchalance, familiarity, impracticality, self-pity, and sentimentalism."[47] Speaking more specifically of the ways in which Southern psychology had been shaped by the silent presence of Blacks, Locke noted that "deeper

traits, moods, and attitudes have come from his contagious presence."[48] Such a Black presence had modified the psychology of
the South both directly and indirectly, although whites were not
willing to admit it. Locke, however, was careful to note that
such an influence had not been desirable in every respect: "An
influence, especially that of a generally illiterate and exploited
mass cannot be wholly beneficent."[49]

Locke never made an explicit statement about which traits he
found desirable and which were undesirable, but in the following passage he spoke approvingly of certain emotional traits:
"Indeed it is a marvel and much to his credit that the Negro's
emotional influence in the South and on the South has been so
kindly, sweet-tempered, and humane."[50] Even though Locke
seemed to praise Blacks for this influence, manifested as the
"mammy tradition," he also indicated that the generation of
intelligent Blacks repudiated this tradition. Locke never stated
in "Negro Contributions to America" why they opposed this
tradition. In "Beauty Instead of Ashes" (1928), however, he offered reasons why many Blacks sought to repudiate the mammy
tradition and the folk culture generally. Many Black artists felt
that it was more fitting and proper for Black artists to draw not
from the folk experience, but from the genteel tradition, to depict
the experience of Blacks. They found the folk experience too
primitive, too condescending. Obviously, Locke wanted to move
the Black artists in the direction of the folk: "For folk temperament raised to the levels of conscious art promises more origi-
nality and beauty than any assumed or imitated class or national
or clique psychology available."[51]

Locke did not ignore the Blacks' contributions to the economy
of the South and the nation generally. If in the early history of
this country, Blacks had refused to labor as willingly as they
did, "the whole course of American History might have been
different and this difference on the negative side of the ledger."[52]
Although Locke, like Du Bois, acknowledged the Blacks' economic contributions, he did not encourage future Blacks to devote their energies exclusively to economic matters, with the
hope of improving conditions. Rather he told Blacks to devote
their energies in the future to developing culture. "Because of
the complementary character of such [cultural] contributions in

contrast with the predominantly practical, economic, and scientific trend of the nation, the part which the Negro will play is all the more desirable and promising."[53] Locke was convinced that because of the Blacks' unique experience and heredity, it was their duty to perform a "special creative rôle in American life as an artist class, as a social re-agent, and as a spiritual leaven."[54]

IV

In "Negro Contributions to America, Locke was concerned mainly with explaining the character of the Black Americans' folk heritage, their informal artistic expressions. In "The Negro's Contribution to American Art and Literature," Locke explained the more formal side of Black cultural achievements. He began by noting the two distinct elements out of which Black formal culture arose: "one, his primitive tropical heritage, however vague and clouded over that may be, and second, the specific character of the Negro group experience in America both with respect to group history and with regard to environing social conditions."[55] Such conditions were not limited to the Southern states, but were pervasive throughout the Black population, and functioned emotionally and intellectually to intensify group feelings, group reactions, and group traditions. Thus out of these group conditions, rooted in the African heritage, a unique culture arose that was distinctively Black.

"Negro Contributions to America," as was seen, devoted much attention to pointing out how readily the first generation of Blacks accepted American civilization and ideals. In "The Negro's Contribution to American Art and Literature," Locke noted that, although the early generations of Blacks conformed easily to American culture and rapidly assimilated its basic elements, such conformity and assimilation did not materially give Black culture its characteristic qualities. Rather, "it was the African or racial temperament, creeping back in the overtones of his half-articulate speech and action, which gave to his life and ways the characteristic qualities instantly recognized as peculiarly and representatively his."[56] If these African qualities were manifest in the slaveholding South, it follows then that Southern whites, whether or not they realized it, were also heirs to "the African heritage." Spiritually, the slaves conquered their masters, as Nietzsche would insist.

When Locke turned to a consideration of jazz music, he indicated that Black culture out of which jazz arose influenced not only the South, but also the nation generally:

The Negro has exerted in no other way since so general an influence, [as he had done in creating the folkways in the South] but in passing, we must note a near approach to a similar influence, nation-wide though more superficial, in our own generation,—the contagious influence of the "jazz-spirit," a corrupt hybrid of the folk-spirit and modern commercialized amusement and art.[57]

If American culture has its origin in Black folk culture, and because this folk culture preceded the more formal, articulate artistic expressions of Black culture, it would be instructive to consider the history of such developments. Locke divided the cultural history of Blacks in America into two periods:

a long period of sustained but unsophisticated expression at the folk level dating from his introduction to this country to half a generation after Emancipation, and a shorter period of expression at the cultural, articulate level, stretching back in exceptional and sporadic instances to 1787, but becoming semi-literary with anti-slavery controversy from 1835–1860, and literary in the full sense only since 1890.[58]

Between these two main historical periods lay a gap during which Blacks made a conscious effort to imitate white American standards and ideals and turned away from their own distinctive racial elements in their effort to achieve cultural conformity. Locke did not condemn Blacks for such conforming behavior because at that time it was "inevitable and under the circumstances normal."[59] This practice of cultural conformity did not last; Locke said that it was through the efforts of Paul Lawrence Dunbar and "the younger contemporary school of 'racial self-expression' "[60] that the practice of conformity was reversed. In conscious reaction to the American way of life, they placed a greater emphasis on the racial elements of Black life. By the phrase "racial self-expression," Locke meant the New Negro movement, the Harlem Renaissance, whose body of literature began to grow by 1917 and "in a decade produced the most outstanding formal contribution of the Negro to American literature and art."[61]

In a similar way, Locke outlined the history of white American attitudes toward Black culture: "First a long period of unconscious absorption and exchange, beginning in sentimental curiosity and growing with institutionalized slavery into a sentimental, condescending disdain."[62] This was followed by a "transitional period of formal revulsion, in part a natural reaction, in part a definite accompaniment of the Slavery-Anti-slavery controversy."[63] This was a time in which whites attempted to establish some psychological and cultural distance between themselves and Blacks. This phase of disinterestedness did not last very long; by 1895, in white American literature, a new, more objective interest in Black culture developed. Whites began to take Blacks more seriously, as whites began to incorporate Black folk themes into their materials. Among American works that introduced Black themes into American formal culture, Locke included Eugene O'Neill's plays of Negro life, DuBose Heyward's "Porgy," Mrs. Peterkin's "Green Thursday" and "Black April," and George Gershwin's adapted "jazz," along with University of North Carolina studies in Negro folk song and folklore.[64]

If slavery stimulated Blacks' artistic faculties, the antislavery movement sharpened Blacks' intellectual skills. The first popular Black American poets, Jupiter Hammon and Phyllis Wheatley, called attention to the contradictions of slavery and played key roles in the anti-slavery movement. In the area of prose, Locke included the anonymous "Othello" as early as 1799, followed by David Walker's famous "Appeal" in 1829, as examples of Blacks' intellectual and artistic achievements. Locke said that the literature dating from 1829 which focused on the slavery controversy was second rate, but in this and the allied field of oratory, Blacks made exceptional contributions, equalling their white contemporaries, including William Lloyd Garrison, Gerritt Smith, and Sumner Phillips. Other Black writers of that period included Martin Delaney, Samuel McCune Smith, Thomas Remond, Ringgold Ward, Henry Highland Garnett, Edward Wilmot Blyden, and Frederick Douglass.

Although most of the anti-slavery literature by both whites and Blacks at this time was not of high quality, "no one can deny its representativeness of its historical period."[65] Locke did not explain why most of the anti-slavery writings were below par artistically, but he offered a clue when he said that most Black writers at that time were conformist imitators of whites. Exceptions were Frederick Douglass, Josiah Henson, and Moses Roper, each of whom authored slave narratives.

Although Blacks have been contributing to American culture since their early years in this country, their most significant cultural "output and recognition [was] achieved in less than a decade [during the Harlem Renaissance] than in all the range of time since 1619."[66]

Although Blacks have enjoyed an extended history of achievement in the areas of music, literature, and poetry, they have not, according to Locke, achieved status in the area of art. Locke offered an explanation in "The Negro's Contribution in Art to American Culture" and in other works focusing on African art. In "The Negro's Contribution in Art to American Culture," Locke began by recounting his own experience when he set out to collect materials for *The New Negro*. At that time, he observed that whereas he found there was "a rich selection of poetry, fiction, music and social criticism available, there was almost nothing equally representative and racial in the field of art."[67] He offered the following explanation of this shortage of Black art.

The Negro artist was still in the eclipse of chilly disparagement, while the poets and playwrights and writers and musicians were in the sunlight and warmth of a proud and positive race consciousness. Why? Because social prejudice had seized on the stigma of color and racial feature, and had made the average Negro negatively color conscious.[68]

Of course, a number of Black artists produced works of art, but there was little or no Black art. "At that time most of our artists went in for the creed of being 'artists in general,' and either avoided racial subjects or treated them gingerly in what I used to call "Nordic transcriptions.' "[69]

The Black artist did not want to deal with racial themes, but rather sought to be an artist in general, and in "this general frame of mind, his pictures were bound to be weak and apologetic in spirit and conception, even if technically proficient."[70] Locke observed that in order to provide a balance of selections for *The New Negro*, so as not to exclude art that reflected Black elements and themes, "it was decided to turn to a white European artist, with a sympathy for, and background of experience in, the delineation of folk types."[71] That artist was Winold Reiss, who, according to Locke, did a remarkable job in the portrayal of Black types. When Locke decided to include Reiss, Locke correctly anticipated that he would be criticized.

Race consciousness in the 1920s had already begun to pervade the works of Black poets and race leaders. Of the latter Marcus Garvey was a case in point; many regard him as among the earliest to speak of race-pride. But the artists were relatively slow in making race a dominant theme in their works; shortly thereafter, at least three Black artists began to achieve a level of race awareness, comparable to their poet and race-leader counterparts. "They were trying to win recognition as 'Negro artists' and were stressing 'African design,' 'race types,' and 'racial symbolism.' "[72] Locke saw this as marking the beginning of Black artists who were attempting to free themselves from imitating whites, as well as from the belief, to which Locke himself once subscribed, that art should be for art's sake, independent of any social message or political overtone.

Thus, Black artists were becoming more race conscious. Locke welcomed this change as having great social benefits: "I see a double—in fact, a triple—gain in the further spread of the very real and vital racialism that is stirring in the world of the Negro artist, and for that matter in the white artists, interested in the truly serious portrayal of Negro life in the fine arts."[73] Among the social benefits of racialism on the part of Black artists, Locke included: (1) "the galvanizing of the Negro artist himself," so that he may be freed from imitating white artists and standards; (2) the education of the Black community so that it may come to appreciate the beauty and dignity of Black people, which in turn may serve as a specific antidote to the "blighting effects of subconscious race prejudice"; and (3) the education of the white community of the value and dignity of Black people, from which a deeper sympathetic understanding among the races might be advanced.[74]

To this point, it seemed that Locke had been suggesting that, until the 1920s, no Black person had picked up a paint brush. This was not his point; rather, he wanted to make a distinction, already mentioned, between Black artists who were "artists in general"and Black artists who were race conscious, who paint with a racial theme and a social message. The Black artists of the first type have always existed. As he wrote, "If we mean by the Negro artists just the Negro who paints or 'sculpts,' then he has a long, even though tenuous, history."[75] That history coincided with the history of American art and included such artists as Edward Bannister (1850s), Edmonia Lewis (1860–1870s), and James Duncanson (1880s). Locke added, however, that until Henry O. Tanner there was no Negro painter of decidedly international stature and affiliation. Even Tanner's work, great though it was, did not sufficiently emphasize racial themes of "social significance."[76] Not until the first and second decades of the twentieth century did racial elements begin to be reflected in the works of Black artists, in both sculptors and painters. Among the sculptors, Locke included Meta Warrick Fuller and May Howard Jackson, and among the painters, Henry Edouard Scott, a pupil of Tanner's. Other Black painters of what Locke called the younger generation were as follows: Aaron Douglas, Edouard Scott, Laura Wheeler Waring, Hale Woodruff, Archibald Motley, and James Lesesne Wells, each of whom reflected racial themes in their works.[77] Locke speculated that these artists and the future generations of Black artists would constitute what he called the school of Black art. Their aim would be to concentrate on racial themes.

In "Beauty Instead of Ashes," Locke again considered the relationship between Black arts and racial themes. He began the essay by exploring whether Black artists had a duty to focus almost exclusively on racial themes.

Locke wanted Black artists to create a school of Black art, and to do so required focusing on racial themes. At the same time he was aware that if the themes were forced on the artists or if the artists were not attracted to such themes by their creative urge, most Black artists would resent this task, and they would have the right to do so. As Locke put it, "Yet most Negro artists would repudiate their own art program if it were presented as a reformer's duty or a prophet's mission, and to the extent that they were true artists be quite justified."[78] On the other hand, Locke maintained that they had an obligation to fulfill their mission. This is where the ambiguity emerged: he suggested that he wanted to leave it up to the Black artists to express racial materials, although in fact he wanted to urge them to oblige themselves to this task.

By the phrase "reformer's duty or prophet's mission," Locke seemed to be reverting to his own views on values as expressed in "Values and Imperatives" in order to evade his ambiguous message to the Black artists. In explaining the relation between beauty or art and duty, Locke wrote:

The artist may feel duty toward his calling, obligation toward his unrealized idea, because when he feels conflict and tension in that context, he occupies an entirely different attitude toward his aesthetic material. Instead of repose or ecstasy of contemplation or the exuberant flow of creative expression, he feels the tension and pull of an unrealized situation, and feeling obligation and conflict, senses along with that a moral quality.[79]

Thus, if Black artists are psychologically necessitated to create Black art, they have the *moral obligation* to create Black art. This is their duty. Locke was aware that white artists, Eugene O'Neill, Ridgely Torrence, Paul Green, and Vachel Lindsay among others, were already including Black themes in their materials. This was an indication that, "the turbulent warm substance of Negro life seems to be broadening out in the main course of American literature like some distinctive literary Gulf Stream."[80] It was now time for the Blacks to catch up with their white counterparts.

Locke did not address the question of whether white artists, too, had a moral duty to focus on Black themes; yet, he praised white artists and the larger society generally for having an interest in the Black experience. In fact, he regarded the effort of white artists not as a mere passing interest, but as serious collaboration with Black artists which had resulted in what he called a division of labor.[81] White artists have generally taken the descriptive approach to drama and fiction, whereas Black artists have focused mainly on poetry and music. These approaches are analytic and emotional, respectively. And the two different orientations are complementary. Both white and Black artists have begun to subscribe to the principle of reciprocity, opening up a double channel through which the cultural contributions of Black Americans have begun to flow, and of which Americans have begun to gain a deeper appreciation.

Locke repeatedly stated that Black American artists had not made sufficient contributions in the area of painting and sculpture. He speculated that future Black artists, if they allowed themselves to be inspired by African art and culture, would make significant contributions in this area.

In "The Negro in American Culture" (1944), Locke found evidence to support this speculation. He said that America was beginning to witness a new development in American cultural history in which Black artists were expressing themselves in painting and sculpture. Among these Black artists Locke included "Horace Pippin and Jacob Lawrence, in addition to whole constellations of Negro artist groups like those now in Harlem, Chicago, and Atlanta."[82]

In "The Negro in American Culture," one also detects a terrific ambiguity in Locke's thought. Throughout his works, he praised Black artists for including in their works racial themes, the importance of which promoted both racial understanding and the development of Black American culture. In this essay, however, Locke seemed to abandon the notion that Black artists should focus on Black themes. He seemed to have reverted to his previous view that art should be for art's sake. As he wrote,

Another outstanding trend with Negro artists has been the gradual subordination of racialism in expression as a dominant motive to more technical motivations of art-style, and also to ideological alignments with various schools of social thought. It is largely in such ways that the Negro artists of today have so rapidly integrated themselves in the various arts with their fellow American artists.[83]

Here Locke was echoing the views of an integrationist, not a cultural pluralist. On close analysis, it is evident that Locke approved of this new trend whereby Black artists were beginning to give less emphasis to racialism, for it conformed to his view that there must be reciprocity between Black and white artists. Through this collaborative effort, he maintained the principle of cultural democracy and pluralism could be realized in America.

NOTES

1. Alain Locke, *The New Negro* (New York: Atheneum, 196?; originally published in 1925), p. ix.

2. Ibid.

3. Ibid.

4. Ibid.

5. Alain Locke, "Negro Education Bids for Par," *The Survey* 54 (September 1, 1925): 570.

6. Ibid.

7. Ibid.

8. Locke, *The New Negro*, pp. x-xi.

9. Ibid., p. 6.

10. Ibid., p. 7.

11. Ibid.

12. Ibid.

13. Ibid.

14. Ibid.

15. Ibid., p. 8.

16. Ibid., p. 9.

17. Ibid.

18. Ibid., p. 10.

19. An unnamed poem from *The Selected Poems of Claude McKay* (Boston: G. K. Hall & Co., 1981).

20. Locke, *The New Negro*, p. 13.

21. Ibid.

22. See McKay's poem "If We Must Die."

23. Locke, *The New Negro*, p. 13.

24. Ibid., p. 14.

25. Ibid., p. 15.

26. Alain Locke, "The Contribution of Race to Culture," *The Student World* (October 1930): 349.

27. Joseph E. Harris, *Africans and Their History* (New York: New American Library, 1972), p. 191.

28. Locke, "The Contribution of Race to Culture," p. 350.

29. Ibid.

30. Ibid.

31. Ibid.

32. Ibid., p. 351.

33. Ibid., p. 353.

34. Alain Locke, "Negro Contributions to America," *The World Tomorrow* 12 (June 1929): 255.

35. Ibid.

36. Ibid.

37. Ibid.

38. Ibid.

39. Ibid., p. 256.

40. The ethnomusicologist Jacqueline Cogdell Dje Dje of the University of California, Los Angeles, offers the following as a definition of the spiritual, which involves the "religious song that was created by American Blacks during slavery in the United States." She defines gospel music as religious songs created by Blacks during the early twentieth century. See Dje Dje, *American Black Spiritual and Gospel Songs from Southeast Georgia: A Comparative Study* (Los Angeles: University of California, Center for Afro-American Studies, 1978).

Locke's conception of the spirituals is a bit broader than Dje Dje's, as in this context he undoubtedly failed to draw a fine distinction between the spirituals and gospel songs.

41. Locke, "Negro Contributions to America," p. 256.

42. Ibid.

43. Ibid.

44. Ibid.

45. Ibid.

46. Ibid.

47. Ibid.

48. Ibid.

49. Ibid.

50. Ibid.

51. Alain Locke, "Beauty Instead of Ashes," *The Nation*, 126 (January 4, 1928–June 27, 1928): 434.

52. Locke, "Negro Contributions to America," p. 257.

53. Ibid.

54. Ibid.

55. Locke, "The Negro's Contribution to American Art and Literature," *Annals of the American Academy of Political and Social Science* 140 (November 1928): 234.

56. Ibid.

57. Ibid., p. 235.

58. Ibid.

59. Ibid.

60. Ibid., p. 235.

61. Ibid., pp. 235–236.

62. Ibid., p. 236.

63. Ibid.

64. Ibid.

65. Ibid., p. 238.

66. Ibid., p. 242.

67. Locke, "The Negro's Contribution in Art to American Culture," *Proceedings of the National Conference of Social Work* (Chicago, 1933), p. 316.

68. Ibid.

69. Ibid.

70. Ibid.

71. Ibid.

72. Ibid., p. 317.

73. Ibid., p. 318.

74. Ibid.

75. Ibid., p. 319.

76. Ibid.

77. Ibid., p. 320.

78. Locke, "Beauty Instead of Ashes," p. 432.

79. Locke, "Values and Imperatives," in *American Philosophy,Today and Tomorrow*, eds. Sidney Hook and Horace M. Kallen (New York: Lee Furman, 1935), pp. 321–322.

80. Locke, "Beauty Instead of Ashes," p. 432.

81. Ibid., p. 432.

82. Alain Locke, "The Negro in American Culture," *New Masses* (January 18, 1944): 6.

83. Ibid.

11 AFRICAN ART AND CULTURE

I

Although Alain Locke spent much of his career emphasizing how Blacks contributed to the development of American culture, he also devoted a number of articles to explaining how Africans developed culture on their own continent, and how they contributed to the growth of culture in Europe and other parts of the world. There are significant cultural differences between Africans, Black Americans, and Europeans; these differences, as well as the similarities, are considered shortly.

This chapter, first, explores Locke's view of the cultural kinship and differences between Africans, Black Americans, and modern Europeans, and, second, examines Locke's views on African art. In comparing African culture with Black American culture, Locke entertained conflicting views. These are pointed out as the occasion arises.

As noted in the previous chapter, Locke suggested that the uniqueness of the earliest stages of Black American folk culture was due in part to the African heritage. Locke called this the primitive tropical heritage. That he identified the African heritage with the initial stages of Black American folk culture was made explicit in this previously cited passage: "it was the African or racial temperament, creeping back in the overtones of his half-articulate speech and action, which gave to his life and ways the characteristic qualities instantly recognized as peculiarly and representatively his."[1]

Yet in at least two other articles, "The Legacy of the Ancestral Arts" (1925) and "The American Negro as Artist" (1931), Locke made statements that are at odds with the above observation, according to which Black Americans' artistic or cultural endowments are rooted in African culture. In the following passages, Locke suggested that there were no affinities at all between African and Black American cultures. In fact, he anxiously pointed out that American Blacks in relation to Africans had made a complete turn:

Between Africa and America the Negro, artistically speaking, has practically reversed himself. In his homeland, his dominant arts were the decorative and the craft arts—sculpture, metal-working, weaving—and so the characteristic African artistic virtuosities are decoration and design. But in America, the interpretive, emotional arts have been the Negro's chief forte, because his chief artistic expression has been in music, the dance, and folk poetry.[2]

In elaborating on the differences between African and Black American arts, Locke claimed that "the characteristic African art expressions are rigid, controlled, disciplined, abstract, heavily conventionalized; those of Aframerican,—free, exuberant, emotional, sentimental and human."[3] If there existed a cultural kinship between African and Black American, such kinship was mistakenly derived: "Only by misinterpretation of the African spirit, can one explain any emotional kinship between them— for the spirit of African expression, by and large, is disciplined, sophisticated, laconic and fatalistic. The emotional temper of the American Negro is exactly opposite."[4]

Historians and other authorities contend that the relocation caused by slavery forced Black Americans to break all cultural ties with Africa. Hence, one would expect Locke to share such a view; however, he had just the opposite view:

But even with the rude transplanting of slavery, that uprooted the technical elements of his former culture, the American Negro brought over as an emotional inheritance a deep-seated aesthetic endowment. And with a versatility of a very high order, this offshoot of the African spirit blended itself in with entirely different culture elements and blossomed in strange new forms.[5]

There are inconsistencies in Locke's remarks on the kinship between African and Black American cultures: at various times he said that the kinship both existed and did not exist. The above passage also suggests that this kinship was rooted in the African's genetic makeup.

With regard to why this African-Black American kinship resulted in these conflicting views, an essayist on Black culture, James B. Barnes, wrote:

Locke was misled when he compared the character of Afro-Americans and Africans, as he relied too heavily on nineteenth century thinking and theories of racial and ethnic personalities. He drew many of his conclusions from an analysis of African art, especially sculpture, a brief visit to Egypt (the only African country he ever visited), and the sober, dignified African visitors he encountered when they visited Howard University. Certainly his limited exposure to the African reality and his failure to observe African music and dance affected his judgments.[6]

Barnes' explanation is only partially correct, although it does shed some light on questions about the inconsistencies of Locke's views. Locke's inconsistencies stem not so much from his limited knowledge of African reality, but more from the paradoxical conditions engendered by the slavery under which Blacks lived. The core of the paradox is this: Whites attempted to force Black Americans during slavery to abandon their African culture and also attempted to prevent them from being fully integrated into the American culture. People cannot live in the absence of a culture. If slaves or any other group are stripped of their cultural heritage and are barred access to an alien culture, they will create their own. While remaining on the periphery of American culture, African-Americans created their own folkways which played a key role in the formation of American culture. As Locke stated, the negative effects of slavery, paradoxically, were a positive value for Blacks and the country generally. Slavery's positive value is that it forced Blacks as an isolated and oppressed group to create a unique culture of their own, and this Black culture influenced that of the larger society.

By calling attention to conditions of oppression and the working of environmental forces, Locke thought he provided evidence to support his claim that the existence of spiritual kinship between African and Black American cultures has been understood as nothing more than a mere appearance—a misinterpreted semblance. This kinship, this so-called similarity between the two cultures, is "the result of his [the Black American] peculiar experience in America and the emotional upheaval of its trials and ordeals."[7] Here Locke was clearly stating that the traits characterizing Black Americans' art and culture originated not in any African gene pool or race psychology, "but they represent essentially the working of environmental forces . . . they are really the acquired and not the original artistic temperament."[8]

In an effort to strengthen his claim of no genetic link between African and Black American artists, Locke compared the minds of the Black Americans to European minds: "When he [the Black American] confronts the various forms of African art expression with a sense of its ethnic claims upon him, [he] meets them in as alienated and misunderstanding an attitude as the average European Westerner."[9] Thus, if it is ridiculous to say that European Westerners possessed a common "race psychology" out of which their respective cultures emerged, it follows, in Locke's view, that it is equally absurd to say that Africans and Black Americans possessed a common race psychology.

Although Locke wanted to reject this notion of a common race psychology, when he considered sculpture as an area in which Black Americans might make great contributions, he suggested that there did exist a race psychology between Black Americans and Africans. If Africans had already done so well in the field of sculpture, Blacks in the future would likely do well in this area too. Witness this statement:

The Negro artist's great forte will be sculpture. This is not merely a belief in some dormant plastic sense, surviving in the late generations of the descendants of the admittedly superb African craftsman and wood sculptors. It is rather the feeling that there is some connection between unusual plastic sense and skill and the naïve emotional approach to life. It is the primitive skill of being *immersed by instinct* in the experiences of the senses in this case with the eyes that see [emphasis added]. And here, if it is not too stifled by academism, the Negro artist will give good account of himself, and is already promising to.[10]

This shifting back and forth between the position, on the one hand, that there was no spiritual affinity between Black American artists and their African forefathers, and, on the other, that there existed some intrinsic psychological or instinctive ties between them, indicates that Locke was trying to straddle the questions of what African and Black American artists had in common and of whether the Black American's artistic endowments were environmentally derived or transmitted genetically from the African ancestors. Locke may well have wanted to subscribe to both the environmental factors and the genetic transmission explanations. It is not clear why he shifted between the two positions.

Locke was quite straightforward, however, in his claim that African art influenced both Black American and European culture. At the time Locke was writing in the 1920s, he suggested that, heretofore, the African influence on Black American artists was channeled indirectly through European art. African art has had a greater direct influence on European culture than on American culture; because Black American artists were influenced by European culture, they were, in turn, influenced by African art and culture.

Locke encouraged Blacks to take a greater interest in African culture and to allow it to have more than a passing influence on them, "but a profound and galvanizing influence." Such an influence, Locke suggested, could be achieved because Blacks could draw on this ancestral legacy: "The legacy is there at least, with prospects of a rich yield. In the first place, there is in the mere knowledge of the skill and unique mastery of the arts of the ancestors the valuable and stimulating realization that the Negro is not a cultural foundling without his own inheritance."[11]

Although the Black Americans' African forefathers made great achievements in sculpture, painting, and decorative arts, Black Americans, as noted in the previous chapter, have made little contributions in these areas. If Black Americans allowed the African legacy to inspire them, as they began to in the 1920s, they could also excel in sculpture, painting, and the decorative arts: "If the forefathers could so adroitly master these mediums, why not we?"[12] Already contemporary European artists, Locke maintained, had benefited by studying African art and incorporating the African technique into their own art.

As Locke told Black artists, they needed to develop a greater appreciation of the legacy of the ancestral arts, so that they could be inspired by them. Locke also told Black artists to incorporate the African technique into their own mode of creating art. However, he told them that African art offered something more important: "the lesson of a classic background, the lesson of discipline, of style, of technical control pushed to the limits of technical mastery."[13]

Locke was suggesting that these lessons were lacking in the American art tradition. In fact, he suggested that American culture, as a young culture, did not offer much of an art tradition to Black artists or any other artists. Black American artists had absorbed the content of American life and experience; they now needed to integrate into their artistic activities the new patterns of art that the African art offered. In that way, "the Negro may well become what some have predicted, the artist of American life."[14]

II

Locke's "The Legacy of the Ancestral Arts" has two themes. In the first half of the essay, he compares African and Black American culture, contending that, in the past, African culture had not exerted much influence on Black American culture. The little African influence felt by Blacks had been channeled, indirectly through European culture. Blacks were more familiar with European culture than with its African counterpart because slavery placed them in a white America that derived its culture from European influences.

In the second half of "The Legacy of the Ancestral Arts" and in a number of other works, Locke emphasized the importance of African art to the modern world as a whole, not just to Black Americans. Moreover, in relation to this he pointed out in great detail how African art had been "the most influential exotic art of our era, Chinese and Japanese art not excepted."[15]

Locke asked why African art, previously regarded as not worthy of being called art, had achieved worldwide attention and exerted such a universal influence, especially in Europe. What was "previously regarded as ridiculously crude and inadequate, appeared [in the time Locke wrote] cunningly sophisticated and masterful."[16] Locke tried to explain this reversal of attitude. At the time African culture became recognized "there was a marked decadence and sterility in certain forms of European plastic art expression, due to generations of the inbreeding of style and idiom."[17] Locke's explanation continued: "Out of the exhaustion of imitating Greek classicism and the desperate exploitation in graphic art of all the technical possibilities of color by Impressionists and Post Impressionists, the problem of form and decorative design became emphasized in one of those reactions which in art occur so repeatedly."[18]

Locke documented in more detail how African sculpture influenced particular European artists who were representative of French and German Modernist art. Among the French painters Locke included Matisse, Picasso, Derain, Modigliani, and Utrillo. He wrote, "In Paris, centering around Paul Guillaume, one of its pioneer exponents, there has grown up an art coterie profoundly influenced by an aesthetic developed largely from the idioms of African art."[19] Of the German artists influenced by African art, Locke included Max Pechstein, Elaine Stern, and Franz Marc, who were representative of the German Expressionists; among the German sculptors were Modigliani, Archipenko, Epstein, Lipschitz, Lembruch, and Zadkine and Faggi.

In addition to the African sculpture which influenced European art, Locke noted that other African art forms had also shaped European culture. Among these he included the African decorative designs, musical rhythms, dance forms, verbal imagery, and symbolism. Even certain European poets, such as Guillaume Appolinaire and Blaisé Cendrars "have attempted artistic re-expression of African idioms in poetic symbols and verse forms." "The bible," Locke continued, "of this coterie has been Cendrars' *Anthologie Nègre*, now in its sixth edition."[20]

The European artists did not ignore African music. In fact, they were inspired by the study of both African and Black American music. Among the artists who drew on this double source, Locke included Berard, Satie, Poulenc, Auric, Honneger, and

Darius Milhaud, the last-named of whom "is an avowed propagandist of the possibilities of Negro musical idiom."[21] Locke commented on the significance of African and Black American art for world art:

The importance of these absorptions of African and Negro material by all of the major forms of contemporary art, some of them independently of any transfer that might be dismissed as a mere contagion of fad or vogue, is striking, and ought to be considered as a quite unanimous verdict of the modern creative mind upon the values, actual and potential, of this yet unexhausted reservoir of art material.[22]

If Europeans had so much interest in African art, he asked why such an interest in African art was not evident among Black American artists or, for that matter, American artists generally? In 1925, when Locke published *The New Negro*, there was a growing sense of racial consciousness among Black Americans as expressed in their art. But one may inquire to what extent they expressed what Locke called the African idiom in their art works and how much influence African art had on Black artists. What, if any, was the connection between "the African idiom and the natural ambition of Negro artists for a racial idiom in their art expression"?[23] Locke replied, "To a certain extent contemporary art has pronounced in advance upon this objective of the younger Negro artists, musicians and writers."[24] Locke did not elaborate on what he meant by "this objective of the younger Negro artists, musicians and writers." However, by "objective" he seemed to have meant that Black artists were beginning to combine in their expressions both African and Black American racial idioms. Although they aspired toward this objective, racial prejudice frustrated their efforts.

Only the most reactionary conventions of art, then, stand between the Negro artist and the frank experimental development of these fresh idioms. This movement would, we think, be well underway in more avenues of advance at present but for the timid conventionalism which racial disparagement has forced upon the Negro mind in America.[25]

Although Black artists and musicians were better known in America than in Europe, in America where racial prejudice was most virulent, American art scarcely reflected the Black experience: "Whereas in Europe, with the Negro subject rarely accessible, we have as far back as the French romanticists a strong interest in the theme, an interest that in contemporary French, Belgian, German, and even English painting has brought forth work of singular novelty and beauty."[26] Of the German painters who have incorporated the Black subject into their works, Locke noted Julius Hüther, Max Slevogt, Max Pechstein, Elaine Stern, and von Reuckterschell; of the French painters, Dinet, Lucie Cousturier, Bonnard, and Georges Rouault; of the Dutch, Klees van Dongen; of the Belgians, Auguste Mambour; and of the English, Neville Lewis, F. C. Gadell, John A. Wells, and Frank Potter.

Locke maintained that these European artists should serve as "the inspiration and guide-posts of a younger school of American Negro artists."[27] An irony here is that Black artists and American artists generally, with the Black subject at their disposal in America, needed to turn to European art to understand themselves and their subject. Black Americans, as a Marxist would say, were alienated from their own and the African cultural heritage. Although American art provided Black American artists only with "a Nordicized transcription, European art has gone on experimenting until the technique of the Negro subject has reached the dignity and skill of virtuoso treatment and a distinctive style."[28] Locke was suggesting that racism had a lesser grip on the minds of European artists than on their American counterparts. Because in America this racism had been forced on Black American artists who for the most part merely imitated white American artists, a distinctive school of Black artists had not arisen, although there was an urgent need for such a school: "We ought and must have a school of Negro art, a local and a racially representative tradition."[29] Locke was careful to point out in this context that there have been Negro artists, among whom Henry O. Tanner stood out, "but no development of a school of Negro art."[30] Instead of concentrating on the Black subject, Tanner "devoted his art talent mainly to the portrayal of Jewish Biblical types and subjects, and has never maturely touched the portrayal of the Negro subject."[31]

The generation of Black artists following Tanner was inspired by him as an artist, but because Tanner did not focus on the

Black subject, these artists had no guide for creating a Black school of art. Consequently, Locke said they fell short of Tanner's international stride and reach. Among the Black painters who were handicapped in this way, Locke included Henri Scott, Edwin A. Harleson, and Laura Wheeler; among the sculptors were Meta Warrick Fuller and May Howard Jackson. Locke added: "Lacking group leadership and concentration, they were wandering amateurs in the very field that might have given them concerted mastery."[32]

Locke, however, was not without hope, for he sensed the rise of a Black school of art. He also considered the works of such young artists as Archibald Motley, Otto Farrill, Cecil Gaylord, John Urquhart, Samuel Blount, Charles Keene, and Aaron Douglas. This younger generation of artists, according to Locke, was breaking with the old order and was following through on the lesson that contemporary European art had already learned—"that any vital artistic expression of the Negro theme and subject in art must break through the stereotypes to a new style, a distinctive fresh technique, and some sort of characteristic idiom."[33]

Although Locke devoted much of "The Legacy of the Ancestral Arts" to explaining the connection between European, Black American, and African arts, and although he encouraged Black artists to allow themselves to be inspired by European art, in this essay, he gave the Black artists a different message. Here he played down the importance of European art and reemphasized the importance of African art as the source of inspiration for Black American artists: "The African spirit, . . . is at its best in abstract decorative forms. Design, and to a lesser degree, color, are its original *fortes*. It is this aspect of the folk tradition, this slumbering gift of the folk temperament that most needs reachievement and reexpression."[34] For if African art has exerted the influence it has already exerted on contemporary art, "surely this is not too much to expect of its influence upon the culturally awakened Negro artist of the present generation."[35]

III

In his essays "A Collection of Congo Art" (1927), and "African Art: Classic Style" (1927), Locke went beyond a mere comparative analysis and sought to examine the importance of African art in its own right. He wanted to disclose its intrinsic value. In doing so, he also pointed out how African art is different from European art.

"A Collection of Congo Art" is an analysis of the Blondiau collection which was exhibited at the galleries of the New Art Circle in New York, presumably in 1927, under the auspices of *Theatre Arts*. That collection focused on the art of the Belgian Congo, as the title suggested. This collection was unique in its combination of the "artistic and scientific approach to African art." He added:

It is a collection drawn from the extensive and varied region of the Belgian Congo, selected over a period of twenty-five years on a rather rigid standard of fine workmanship, yet sufficiently inclusive as to the various types and intensive as to regional representativeness to give a really organic impression of one of the great schools of primitive Negro art.[36]

Thus, this Blondiau collection was the greatest and most extensive collection of African art, supplemented by the American collections, among which are the Ward at the Smithsonian in Washington, the Barnes Foundation at Merion, the University of Pennsylvania Museum, the Brooklyn Museum and the Museum of Natural History in New York. In addition to Belgium, France, Germany, and England had sizable acquisitions of African art. Among the European countries, however, the Belgium collection stood out, and collectively, the European collection dwarfed the holdings in America. These European countries, in contrast to America during the colonial era, exploited and appropriated most of African culture. This partly explains why Blacks and Africans are alienated from their own cultural heritage. This also explains why the European's African art collections are greater than those of their American counterparts. This greater access to African art might also elucidate why African art, as Locke claimed, had a greater influence on contemporary Europe than on America.

Locke began "A Collection of Congo Art" by attempting to dispel the myth that Congo art was inferior to that of Benin, the

Ivory Coast, and the Guinea Coast. People have usually been led to attribute a utility or instrumental value to Congo art, thus distinguishing it from art of the so-called higher type that possesses intrinsic value. Such a distinction, in Locke's mind, was not applicable in African culture. As Locke wrote, "In this we fail to see how irrelevant such a distinction is for a culture where fine and decorative art[s] have never been separated out, and where things can be superlatively beautiful and objects of utility at the same time."[37] Thus, in order to adequately appreciate African culture, we must come to realize that in art objects beauty and utility coincide; they are organically related to the Africans' day-to-day life.

Of all the African societies, the Congo provided the richest samples of African art objects, which included "work in all possible art media and art forms—large and small scale carving in ivory, horn and wood, forged and decorated work in iron and other metals, metal inlay work, carved and appliqué masks, pottery, woven and decorated textiles, all existing side by side, each in a relatively high state of artistic development."[38] Such a development had lasted without signs of decay for at least three or four centuries, until the presence of Europeans. When they arrived in Africa, they all but destroyed its culture. In this connection, Locke agreed with "Herbert Ward's original impression that the Congo epitomizes Africa, that its culture is one of the oldest and most typical, and that nowhere else do we find an equivalent or more characteristic flowering of the several handicrafts."[39]

In making judgments about the aesthetic quality of Congo art, Locke offered the cross-cultural approach, insisting that specimens of art objects be gathered from the various groups within the Congo for purposes of comparison. These groups included examples of Bukuba, Baluba, Bangongo, Bayaka, Kasai, Bena, Lulua, Azandé, and Basonge specimens. "Thus both the art of the dominant Bantu and of the subjugated nonBantu stocks are represented"[40] in the Blondiau collection.

Here it would be instructive to note another misconception about African art, particularly that of the Congo, which Locke attempted to dispel: "most persons are disposed to concede to African art its characteristic virtuosity of surface ornament and design."[41] Locke admitted that such an opinion was largely true. "But in the larger plastic technique, and the recognition of its values, there is often hesitancy, especially for Congo works."[42] It isn't clear what Locke meant by the phrase "there is often hesitancy." He presumably wanted to promote the notion that the Congo artists often hesitated to follow the traditional pattern of creating art by focusing merely on surface ornament and design. They went beyond the established pattern. They, especially Bushongo artists, did so by combining sculptural heads with ornamental forms, the fetish statuettes, and the semi-portrait figurines. "Particularly surprising in view of prevalent conceptions, is the subtle, placid tone and smooth flow of surface, and the austere economy of decorative elements."[43] Locke claimed that the African art represented in the Blondiau collection not only contradicted, but also was the opposite of the above discussion of Congo art: 'The vast majority of objects produced here are unimpressive plastically, tending either to extreme crudity of workmanship, to unimaginative naturalism, or to overcrowding with superficial decoration.'[44] Thus, the Congo art specimens were not art of a lower order, of a backward people, as popular myths would have us believe. The opposite was the case:

Really they exemplify, along with a number of ceremonial objects, scepters, staffs of office and other insignia, jewel-boxes and articles of fine personal adornment, an apparent aristocratic strain in Congo art, with a characteristic refinement and subtlety that marks it, for all the diversity of the objects themselves, as a distinct tradition in itself—a proud art of the ruling and conquering cast.[45]

In addition to the ceremonial art associated with the courts of chiefs and kings, Locke also considered the art of the common people. He described this type of art as having modes of expression that run "consistently through the characteristic tribal differences, a bizarre and grotesque strain and another, crudely rustic and realistic."[46] One pertains mainly to religious art, the other, "particularly the small circumcision masks of ivory and the body fetishes, are of exquisite workmanship, linking up with the sophisticated court style, but the large masks are for the most part broad and powerful in treatment, and achieve their effect more through emotional than plastic appeal."[47] Locke went on to say that the aesthetic value of Congo masks lay not so much in their intrinsic beauty but in their variety. The Congo masks were more grotesque than beautiful in form, "but this is often compensated by unusual decorative values in color and surface contrasts."[48] The accessory articles and the ritual ceremonies in which the masks were used were more beautiful than the masks themselves: "Anklets, collars, rings, pendants, rattles, gongs, whistles, diviningblocks, drums and other musical instruments are so finely conceived and executed that their sheer beauty and abstract decorative appeal lift them quite out of the class of the minor arts."[49]

Locke proposed that the accessories were more beautiful than the masks themselves, for the following reason: "The only explanation plausible is that symbolic requirements and the religious and ceremonial necessity for evoking terror and awe dictate the latter, but that in subordinate details the inhibited instinct for pure beauty seizes upon its only opportunity for free play."[50] This relation between the beautiful and the grotesque parallels the relation between good and evil. The ugliness of the masks, as Locke suggested, was needed to heighten the beauty of the accessories. Similarly, some people felt that physical and moral evil in the world were needed to appreciate moral goodness. Whitehead said that truth and falsehood are yoked together; the same may be said of good and evil, and of the beauty and ugliness seen in the African masks.

An alternate explanation of why the Congo masks appeared ugly and the accessories beautiful can be found in Locke's own theory of values, explained in "Values and Imperatives." Here, it will be recalled, he reduced all values and judgments about values to feelings, attitudes, or preferences. Assuming the truth of his theory of values, it follows, from the previous discussions, that whether or not the masks are beautiful depends on the sort of feeling the masks evoke in the judging person. If the masks evoke the feeling of exaltation, then they take on a religious value; if they evoke tension, a moral or ethical value; if acceptance or agreement, a scientific or logical value; and if repose or equilibrium, an aesthetic or artistic value is assigned. For the introverted person, the masks are of the aesthetic type, and the predicates are beautiful and ugly; the positive value is satisfaction, and the negative value is disgust. For the extroverted person, the masks are of the artistic type, and the predicates are fine and unsatisfactory; the positive value is joy, and the negative value is distress.

It is curious that Locke did not utilize his own values theory to explain the nature of values and value judgments as they pertained to African art culture.

The masks are not the only art objects that are less beautiful than accessories and other objects of the higher order. Locke called attention to other art objects in the Congo that "smack of the jungle, and reflect its crude, primitive realities."[51] Within this class of objects he included "the totemic fetishes, the funerary statuettes and the nail and fertility fetishes with their direct practical appeal to sympathetic magic."[52] Locke speculated that these objects were expressed in such a crude and weird idiom because "the rationale of the style is after all superstitiously motivated, and . . . the salient symbolism expressed at the expense of artistic balance and restraint is sensed as making the object more potent and effective."[53]

Previously, we considered Locke's view on the influence of African art on European art. When Locke discussed this crude, primitive strain of Congo art, he noted that this art had been affected by the "infiltration of European idioms, as is shown by the many examples of this style registering in ludicrous combinations the superimposing of European hats, boots, and whatnot upon African fundamentals."[54] This European infiltration had corrupted and degenerated the most indigenous and possibly one of the earliest of the African styles. Although Locke said this art was possibly of the most basic of African art, he was not sure about this and said that it could be a European assumption. He went on to explain: "The crude styles may just as well be themselves degenerated strains, or more possibly even, with the criss-crossings of endless tribal warfare, parallel ethnic strands of other tribal traditions, and not the basis from which the fine tradition built itself up."[55] Although the date of the rise of this crude art is unknown, one can be certain that

"Bushongo and other varieties of African art reached a classic stage of expression very early indeed, and then remained stable over many generations."[56] Locke believed that the classic style of Congo art was achieved 300 to 600 years ago. Evidence for this claim was found both in the registration of early European influence and in the dynastic dates of the Bantu chronicles. At this point in his discussion, Locke cast suspicion on the judgments which many European African art enthusiasts (Matisse was representative of these) made about African art. Locke said that, although they incorporated African art into European culture, they were not authorities on African art, suggesting that they knew little of its intrinsic value. Many of the examples which the Europeans used to introduce into Europe were relatively poor specimens; according to Locke, they introduced its strange values and generalized on its idiom. Now that a more adequate knowledge had been acquired about African art, the time had arrived to engage in "a more intensive study of African art in its first principles."[57]

By studying the historical development of African art more closely, the greater understanding we will acquire of both European art and American art, especially that of Black Americans. African art, as noted earlier, is organically related to our own art tradition in many ways.

Locke pointed out that a fuller understanding and appreciation of African art was especially important for the future development of Black American art: "With the particular appeal of a rediscovered race heritage, it cannot fail to stimulate a generation of artists who are already in the swing of a program to express their racial life and experience in intimate and original ways."[58]

Inspired by African culture, plastic and decorative arts have already had an impact on contemporary Western art; the field of plastic and decorative arts which the African ancestors perfected represents an inspiring model for the future development of Black American art. Here Locke was suggesting that African art could play the roles of gadfly and midwife in stimulating the creative effort of Black American artists so that they could rehabilitate their culture. Let us recall, however, that in "The New

Negro," he assigned Black artists in America the task of rehabilitating African culture. One may well ask whether he was
being consistent here.

IV

"An African Art: Classic Style" presented a much broader
spectrum of African art collections than either "The Legacy of
the Ancestral Arts" or "A Collection of Congo Art." "An African
Art" was a report on the exhibition of the Museum of Modern
Art presumably held in 1935.

In "A Collection of Congo Art," Locke focused on art specimens obtained from the Congo and "In African Art: Classic
Style," he presented a master lesson in the classic idioms of at
least fourteen of the great regional art styles of the African continent. This 1935 exhibition drew from "seventy-two collections . . . from which a selection of six hundred items has been
chosen."[59] A number of sources from which these collections
were drawn have already been mentioned above. The traditions
of the French Sudan, French Guinea, the Upper Volta, Sierra
Leone, Dahomey, Ashanti, French Ivory Coast, Gold Coast, Ca-
meroon, Gabun, Pahouin, Mpongwe, French and Belgian Congo,
and Angola were among those Locke said were represented in
this 1935 exhibition.

In addition to comparing and contrasting the various specimens on display in this 1935 exhibition, Locke took a position
here that was apparently in direct conflict with the thesis he had
advanced earlier, that contemporary European art was influenced by African Art. He in effect accepted James Johnson Sweeney's position that these two art movements—the new
appreciation of African art and of the Negro plastic tradition,
and the working out of the new aesthetic in European art—were
coincidental rather than cause and effect. Sweeney had made
this exhibition possible:

Mr. Sweeney draws deductions leading to the glorification rather than
the belittlement of African art. He believes that African art is best understood directly, and in terms of its own historical development and
background, and that it should be recognized in its own idiom and

right, rather than in terms of its correlation with modern art or its admitted influence upon modern art. The exhibition vindicates this thesis and the claim that "today the art of Negro Africa has its place of respect among the aesthetic traditions of the world."[60]

Although in light of Sweeney's observation on relations between African and European art Locke may have wanted to renounce his previously held view that Africa played an important role in inspiring modern European art, he probably did not want to reject it completely. As evidence, let us consider the last half of the last sentence in the above cited passage, that "today the art of Negro Africa has its place of respect among the aesthetic tradition of the world." He seemed to be anxious to note that the thesis in question proved his own point, which he had made repeatedly, that African art was of a high order in its own right.

Locke seemed to be saying that he had accepted Sweeney's view, not because such a thesis had shown that African art had no influence on Europe, but rather because such a thesis had thrown light on parallels between the two traditions. A major weakness in Locke's position on African art follows.

Locke should not have so easily downplayed his earlier position that African art influenced modern European art and artists, as he nearly did when he evoked Sweeney's view. Because Europeans had had contact with African culture since colonial rule they were obviously influenced by that culture, just as Africans were influenced by European culture. This was evidenced by the Africans superimposing the images of hats and boots on their art objects. The cultural exchanges did occur.

Locke's argument that African art had influenced European art and artists was weak because he did not delve far enough into the history of both African and European cultures. His focus was mainly on the culture of modern and contemporary Europe and the available collections of African art which were gathered and interpreted mainly by Europeans.

Locke could have strengthened his position by tracing the historical developments of European culture from antiquity onward and by focusing on the earliest contacts between African and Western cultures. He would have discovered that according to certain authorities, much of Western culture had its origin in Egypt, Ethiopia, and other African nations. Among the authorities who make this claim are Frank Snowden, *Blacks in Antiquity: Ethiopians in Greco-Roman Experience*; Cheikh Anta Diop, *The African Origin of Civilization*; Joseph E. Harris, *Africans and Their History*; and William Leo Hansberry, *Pillars in Ethiopian History, Vol. I.*, and *Africa and Africans as Seen by Classical Writers, Vol. II.* In the following passage, for example, Hansberry claimed that the origin of Greek drama and poetry lay directly in Ethiopia:

There is much archeological evidence and many ancient traditions which link Ethiopia and its African environs with the world of the heroes reflected in the Homeric and the later poems, and since the sources of the traditions used by the poets were essentially the same as those which were utilized by the dramatists, it is not surprising that the works of Aeschylus, Sophocles, and Euripides contained occasional notices of Ethiopia and Ethiopians.[61]. . . It will, however, be somewhat surprising when we say that there are certain indications that the Dionysian festival which provided the foundations of Greek drama may have had its origin in the inner or Ethiopian areas of Africa.[62]

This claim undermines Sweeney's thesis that African art had little if any influence on European culture and art. Like Locke, Sweeney himself failed to go far enough into history to arrive at an adequate assessment of African art and culture. Ironically, this is true even though both Sweeney and Locke claimed that a deeper understanding of the relationship between African and European culture required close attention to their historical development.

One final point merits consideration. Locke focused on African art largely to heighten the world's awareness of the intrinsic value of African art and to encourage Black American artists to allow themselves to be inspired by African art. However, art cannot be studied as an isolated item, apart from its historical settings and ancient roots. Locke's investigation is guilty of this limitation. In order to have a more adequate understanding of both African and European art, we need to consult the ancient texts and traditions and to examine not only the development of art but also science, philosophy, mythology, religion, magic, and engineering. Thus, the history of both African and European art, like the history of philosophy, religion, and science, has its roots in the world's earliest civilizations, which include Egypt and Ethiopia and other parts of Africa.

NOTES

1. Alain Locke, "The Negro's Contribution to American Art and Literature," *Annals of the American Academy of Political and Social Science* 140 (1928): 234.

2. Alain Locke, "The American Negro as Artist," *American Magazine of Art* (September 1931): 211.

3. Alain Locke, "The Legacy of the Ancestral Arts," in *The New Negro*, ed. Alain Locke (New York: Albert and Charles Boni, Inc., 1925), p. 254.

4. Ibid.

5. Ibid.

6. *Alain Locke: Reflections on a Modern Renaissance Man* ed. Russell J. Linnemann (Baton Rouge: Louisiana State University, 1982), p. 107.

7. Locke, "The Legacy of the Ancestral Arts," pp. 254–255.

8. Ibid.

9. Ibid.

10. Locke, "The Negro's Contribution in Art to American Culture," *Proceedings of the National Conference of Social Work* (Chicago, 1933), pp. 320–321.

11. Locke, "The Legacy of the Ancestral Arts," p. 256.

12. Ibid.

13. Ibid.

14. Ibid., p. 258.

15. Ibid.

16. Ibid., p. 259.

17. Ibid., p. 258.

18. Ibid., pp. 258–259.

19. Ibid., p. 261; Locke included Modigliani in the categories of both French and German artists.

20. Ibid.

21. Ibid.

22. Ibid., pp. 261–262.

23. Ibid.

24. Ibid., p. 262.

25. Ibid.

26. Ibid.

27. Ibid., p. 264.

28. Ibid.

29. Ibid., p. 266.

30. Ibid., p. 264.

31. Ibid.

32. Ibid., p. 266.

33. Ibid., p. 267.

34. Ibid.

35. Ibid.

36. Alain Locke, "A Collection of Congo Art," *Arts*, 2 (February 1927): 61–62.

37. Ibid., p. 62.

38. Ibid., p. 63.

39. Ibid., pp. 63–64.

40. Ibid., p. 64.

41. Ibid., p. 65.

42. Ibid.

43. Ibid.

44. Ibid.

45. Ibid.

46. Ibid., p. 66.

47. Ibid.

48. Ibid.

49. Ibid.

50. Ibid., p. 67.

51. Ibid.

52. Ibid.

53. Ibid., pp. 67–68.

54. Ibid., p. 68.

55. Ibid.

56. Ibid.

57. Ibid., p. 69.

58. Ibid., p. 70.

59. Alain Locke, "African Art: Classic Style," *American Magazine of Art* 27 (May 1935): 271.

60. Ibid.

61. Joseph E. Harris, ed., *Africa & Africans As Seen by Classical Writers: The William Leo Hansberry African History Notebook*, vol. II (Washington, D.C.: Howard University Press, 1977), p. 89.

62. Ibid.

12 ALAIN LOCKE, YESTERDAY AND TODAY

This final chapter is concerned with Alain Locke's reputation as a philosopher, briefly considering the American philosophic community's attitude toward Locke, as well as the appreciation that African intellectuals during the 1920s and 1930s extended to him. This chapter also returns to the problem of desegregation in higher education, taking as a case study Tennessee State University, a predominantly Black school in Nashville, Tennessee. In addition to shedding further light on the desegregation problem, it is hoped that this case study will demonstrate the relevance of Locke's approach to some of the problems that the country faces today. One such problem focuses on the question of the identity of historic Black educational institutions; desegregation efforts have thrown into question the identity of these institutions.

Similarly, both the Black American and the African philosophic communities have raised serious questions regarding the identity of their respective disciplines. Again we show the relevance of Locke by showing that his recommendations, which enabled the Black artists of the 1920s to find themselves, apply equally to the identity problem of Black and African philosophers of today. This is a derivation of the more basic problem concerning the identity of the New Negro.

I

To the Black audience it should be evident that Locke was more than part of the Harlem Renaissance and more than a literary critic. If Locke had taken himself seriously and had been less modest, he would have realized that he was more than a Socratic or philosophic midwife. He was more than a midwife, as his intellectual achievements speak for themselves. A number of leading American philosophers who were Locke's contemporaries held Locke in the highest esteem. As Ernest D. Mason notes, such philosophers "thought him important enough to include several of his philosophical articles in their publications."[1] Among them were Sidney Hook and Horace M. Kallen, Edgar S. Brightman . . . and professional philosophers who organized the yearly Conference on Science, Philosophy and Religion—John Dewey, Roy Wood Seelers, [sic] F.S.C. Northrop, and Richard McKeon to mention only a few."[2]

It is difficult to determine the extent to which Locke influenced the American philosophic tradition generally or a particular American philosopher. We do know that there was much philosophic correspondence between Locke and Dewey, between Locke and Kallen, and between Locke and Santayana, among others. Locke regularly visited Santayana in England after Santayana retired from Harvard. In addition, Locke carried on an extensive correspondence with Du Bois and the Harlem Renaissance participants.

Throughout his career Locke was in heavy demand by academic communities, both Black and white, both at home and abroad. Abroad he was a visiting professor in institutions in Haiti, Latin America, Paris, Rome and Salzburg, and in the United States at the University of Wisconsin, the University of California, Northwestern University, the New School of Social Research, and Fisk University.

That Locke was highly regarded by his contemporaries is evident by the funeral orations mentioned in the Introduction. Most of the recent works about Locke confirm the sentiments and perceptions reflected in the funeral orations. One such work is Russell J. Linnemann's *Alain Locke: Reflections on a Modern Renaissance Man* (1982) which includes essays by both white and Black authors from various disciplines. Linnemann captured the considered judgment of each of the contributors when he wrote: "Locke was no dilettante; he was an incisive, fertile, creative thinker who made significant contributions to each of the modes of thought that came under his scrutiny."[3]

A number of African intellectuals thought highly of Locke, especially Leopold Senghor, the former president of the Republic of Senegal. They acknowledged Locke's influence: "Senghor, who paid explicit tribute to Alain Locke as one of the 'pioneer thinkers who lighted our road' in the years when Senghor and Aimé Césaire were developing their philosophy of négritude, explained the views of the complementary characteristics of Africans and Anglo-Saxons."[4] Clare Bloodgood Crane demonstrates that Locke and other members of the Harlem Renaissance not only influenced the *négritude* movement from a distance through literature, but also they often visited the literary salons in Paris where African intellectuals, including Senghor, gathered:

Senghor wrote that from 1929 to 1934 he and his fellow African students "had contact with the Negro-Americans through the intermediary of Mademoiselle Andrée Nardal. . . . [who] held a literary salon where Negro-Africans, Antillians and Negro-Americans met." This salon, so important in drawing together black artists and intellectuals from various parts of the world, recalled Senghor, "was frequented notably by the celebrated Professor Alain Locke."[5]

Inspired by Locke and others, these African intellectuals subsequently initiated the decolonization movement on the continent of Africa.

Many African philosophers and others received their inspiration from Black American thinkers such as Garvey, Du Bois, and Locke. The same is true for the second generation of the New Negro, who arrived on the scene in the 1960s and who is achieving maturity in the 1980s.

Locke was among the brightest stars in the galaxy of Black intellectual leaders during the first half of the twentieth century. The principles for which Locke stood are as "relevant" for the second generation of the New Negro as they were for the first, and in the distant future his vision will continue to illuminate paths.

this should have been left out

II

Some of the same problems with which Locke struggled have reasserted themselves today, and a number of leaders, especially Blacks, are appealing to some of the same principles Locke introduced more than seventy-five years ago. One of these problems is the desegregation of state colleges, or what may be termed the reverse desegregation of state colleges.

When Locke wrote about desegregation some fifty years ago, his focus was on the public elementary and secondary schools, and the effort to desegregate them was met by resistance from most whites. Since then, history has taken many odd twists and turns. Today many whites continue to resist the dismantling of the dual system of elementary and secondary public schools. At the same time, however, in the past decade or so many whites have reversed their attitudes toward desegregation and are now making a concerted effort to desegregate the historic Black colleges, although they do not talk much about the need to desegregate the historic white state colleges. It is not clear why whites have made this complete turn about. Some claim that job security is behind the whites' changed attitude. It is far easier to understand why Blacks are reluctant to desegregate historic state institutions. First, many Blacks have been disillusioned by the integration efforts. Second, many Blacks believe that the desegregation of these institutions may destroy the identity of the historic Black institutions and ultimately discourage a large percentage of Black youths from receiving a higher education. They would not be able to attend the traditionally white institutions, neither private nor public, for such institutions would then begin to raise their admissions standards. There is also the fear that if the white desegregationists had their way, the effort to raise admission standards would also be applied to the historic Black-state institution; this, too, it is argued, would bar Black youths from acquiring higher education. Such concerns have been raised by the movement to desegregate Tennessee State University,[6] which in 1979, on orders of the U.S. District Court, merged with the traditionally white institution, the University of Tennessee at Nashville. This merger has generated a great deal of controversy and has increased tensions between Blacks and whites. In

August 1984 the dispute was settled, as reported by the students' newspaper:

The stipulation of settlement calls for the immediate interim objective of TSU [Tennessee State University] having 50 percent white faculty and at least 50 percent upper level administrators, (president, vice presidents, deans and department chairs), by 1987. TSU must also immediately establish a 1993 interim objective of 50 percent white full-time students.[7]

Many Blacks have opposed the notion of a quota, which they believe will apply only to TSU and not to other state colleges and universities, especially the white ones.[8] The University of Tennessee at Knoxville, Memphis State, and the University of Tennessee at Chattanooga are white state institutions, but the settlement did not establish any quota for these as it did for TSU. Hence, many opponents of the settlement believe that the Court was singling out TSU. As one student observed, "For the judge not to place an interim objectives [sic] on any of the predominantly white institutions is purely racist."[9] Another point merits mentioning in this context: whereas many whites want to desegregate TSU, they want to do so on the basis that TSU no longer be called a Black institution. They want it to be a "university in general."

The TSU desegregation case is important because the Court's final ruling on the matter will affect public institutions of higher learning not only in the state of Tennessee, but also throughout the nation. Furthermore, this case is of interest because it calls attention to a problem with which Locke struggled most of his life: the question of the proper role and purpose of the Black college in a pluralistic society. He would likely have urged TSU and other Black institutions, both public and private, to maintain their Black identity by keeping Black administrators in control, by teaching Black courses along with other courses, and by maintaining a predominantly Black faculty, staff, and student body. He would also have encouraged such institutions to subscribe to the principle of reciprocity so that a proportionate number of white administrators, faculty, and staff could be employed and white students be allowed to attend. As discussed in Chapter

7, Locke spelled out the formula for establishing parity between Black and white educational institutions with regard to the number of Black students who should attend Black colleges and the number of Black students who should be allowed to attend white colleges. He stipulated a three to one ratio for undergraduate education: that is, for every three Black youths who attend the Black college, one Black youth should attend the white college, both state and private. In graduate education, Locke reduced this formula to a two to one ratio: that is, for every two Black youths who attend the Black college, one should attend the white college. Locke's formula for achieving a racially balanced student body in both Black and white educational institutions worked around the notion of the quota which so many Blacks in the TSU case find objectionable but which many whites do not. This Lockean formula is equally applicable to apartheid in South Africa. Locke's formula approximates the ideal of a desegregated educational system without any attempt to undermine the identity and historic character of Black institutions.

When the Reverend Jesse Jackson spoke at TSU in 1984,[10] he addressed the TSU desegregation problem; he, like Locke, appealed to the principle of plurality, arguing that because we live in a pluralistic society, it is both fitting and proper for TSU to maintain its Black identity, just as the Catholics have Notre Dame University, the Jews, Brandeis University, and the Moral Majority, Bob Jones University. Jackson opposed the notion of racial quota, just as Locke probably would have done. Jackson suggested that TSU should retain its historic mission and Black identity and yet be open to other racial groups, just as Harvard University and Memphis State University should maintain their missions and identities and yet be open to other racial groups. Jackson's position here reflects his model of what he calls the "Rainbow Society."

As discussed earlier, the desegregation problem can best be approached by establishing an Arendtian type of federated council system. In this system there will be no need to make the state-private distinction, for the old notion of state will have been replaced by the council system. Insofar as the council system will in part be established along ethnic group lines, in keeping with the principle of pluralism, then TSU and Fisk University, whose histories are associated with the Black community, would be among the Black council systems in Nashville. Similarly, Vanderbilt University, a white private institution in Nashville, would be one of the larger society's council systems. Within a federated council system the principle of reciprocity will permit contacts and exchanges among such institutions within the respective council systems. Both Arendt and Locke would have seen this arrangement as a step in the direction of achieving a racially balanced society.

NOTHING takes priority over racial balance,

III

There are obvious differences between the first and second generations of the New Negro. In Locke's times, especially during the 1920s, Blacks for the first time launched a concerted search for their identity, an effort that was evidenced in cultural or artistic activities, and the emphasis was on cultural equality. In the 1960s, during the early phases of the second generation of the New Negro, Blacks again made a concerted effort to find out who they were; at that time greater attention was given to Africa as the home of their ancestors. But unlike the 1920s, this second generation of the New Negro in the 1960s did not strive so much for cultural equality as for political equality and equal job opportunities. (This movement also prompted white women to seek equal opportunity in the work world.) In the mid-1980s, this second generation of the New Negro seems to be achieving maturity; hence, the political aspirations of Blacks, other minorities, and women have increased. This stress on political equality is not new, for Frederick Douglass as well as W.E.B. Du Bois, and to a lesser degree Booker T. Washington, encouraged Blacks to seek political freedom and economic opportunities. These ideals were nurtured by Martin Luther King, Jr., the chief Socratic gadfly and midwife who helped usher in the second generation of the New Negro. (It will be remembered that Jesse Jackson played a major role in King's civil rights activities.) But with the exception of Jackson none of these men sought the presidency, although King and Du Bois encouraged Blacks to become registered voters and to exercise their voting rights. By contrast Locke, who never made a big issue out of voting, had

for J.W., but how about for A. L.?

little interest in party politics. He was loyal to no particular political party.

By introducing the notion of the Rainbow Coalition, it was Jesse Jackson who in his 1984 presidential election campaign cut across racial lines and thereby enlarged the Democratic party by encouraging a sizable mass of Black people, previously uninterested in voting, to vote in the national elections. Jackson encouraged Democrates to allow a white woman, Geraldine Ferraro, to be nominated as the vice-presidential candidate for the Democratic party. Jackson's political activities are described in detail here to demonstrate that the Rainbow political model on which he campaigned, and through which he stirred the political imagination of the Black masses, other minorities, and working-class white men and women, is nothing more than the pluralism-reciprocity model that Alain Locke advocated earlier. Jackson and other political leaders should now encourage the Kantian-Arendtian enlarged mentality, so that effective political thinking can be exercised in the realm of human affairs.

When Locke examined the problems of establishing an adult education program, he saw the need to devise a program that would know no color or racial barriers. Here Locke was trying to make his pluralism-reciprocity model effective at the grass-roots level. If he had been a good party politician, he would also have talked about the need for voter registration among the constituency of the adult education program, both Black and white, male and female. In any event, Locke was the forerunner of the notion of the Rainbow Coalition. Whereas he used the pluralism principle in his gadfly role in attempting to implement his program of adult education, Jackson used the Rainbow Coalition principle to enlarge the voting capacity of the Democratic party.

IV

Let us now return to another problem that Alain Locke and other Harlem Renaissance participants faced: that of identity, namely, the need to define the identity of the Black artist. It is not only the Black or African artist who is undergoing this identity crisis. A similar crisis, owing partly to the shifting roles and relations between men and women, is being experienced by women, and perhaps to a lesser degree by men as well. Women are leaving the home and entering the workplace in increasing numbers. But one may question whether the work world is the most appropriate place to search for one's identity. As observed earlier, in the 1920s Blacks in search of their identity turned to culture.

In the early 1920s, Locke maintained that Black American artists had a negative attitude toward their own culture and toward "Blackness" in general. The Black artists did not want to be identified with the Black race; they regarded themselves as "artists in general." (It should be remembered that Locke himself once believed that "art should be for art's sake.") The reason for this attitude was obvious: racial prejudice forced the Black artist to turn against himself and to become alienated from himself and his culture. Locke recognized that, of course, there had been Blacks who were artists, but in the absence of race consciousness there had been no Black artists proper and no school or tradition of Black art. This, then, raised questions about what constituted Black art and about who the Black artists were. Thus arose the identity problem. With regard to this perplexing issue, Locke suggested certain criteria, which, if satisfied, would point in the direction of a solution. An important element in those criteria was race consciousness, that is, the Black artists must incorporate racial themes or idioms into their works. The Black artists, however, must not limit themselves to their own racial or cultural field: "The point here . . . is that we do and should not expect Negro art or the Negro artist to grow in his own soil exclusively, but only to come back to that soil with its acquired perspective and endowment."[11] Locke seemed to be reverting here to Josiah Royce's principle of loyalty to loyalty: the Black artist must be loyal to his own culture, move beyond his culture so as to appreciate the culture of others, and return to his own culture. This also ties in with Locke's notion of cultural reciprocity, which stated that Black artists could enrich their own culture and the cultures of others by not limiting themselves to their own culture.

If Black artists have in the past regarded themselves as "artists in general," a similar attitude may be seen to haunt both Black

American and African philosophers, who are undergoing an identity crisis. In Chapter 1, it is suggested why this issue pertained to Black philosophy, as is described in that context. In this chapter we are concerned with the identity crises that Black and African professional philosophers face, crises that have received much attention within the past decade. This increased attention is due partly to the fact that within the past two decades a sizable number of Black Americans and Africans have received Ph.D. degrees in philosophy and are now making significant contributions to the field of academic or professional philosophy. Some of the most recent works that demonstrate their contributions are contained in the following two anthologies: Leonard Harris, *Philosophy Born of Struggle* (1983), and H. Odera Oruka and D. A. Masolo, *Philosophy and Cultures* (1983). Along the same axis we also have Kwasi Wiredu, *Philosophy and An African Culture* (1980) and Paulin Hountondji, *African Philosophy: Myth and Reality* (1983). But as was true of the Black artists of Locke's time, a number of contributors to these texts are uneasy about the use of the expression "Black or African philosophy." They give the impression that such usage compromises or undermines philosophy as "a universal intellectual activity." Nevertheless, a considerable number of contributions show a keen interest and bold confidence in Black and African philosophy.

Consider, for example, Black American philosophy. Various conferences have been held for the purpose of defining Black philosophy, and much has been written about the subject.[12] The debate has centered on the question of whether there is a Black philosophy. The responses are often divided or conflicting. The general sentiment seems to be that there is indeed a Black philosophy, but there are disagreements about the specifics involved in the criteria to be used in characterizing it. The same is true of African philosophy. Then, there is the related question of the relationship between African philosophy and Black philosophy. Should a Black American philosopher who writes about philosophic problems pertaining to the African experience be regarded as "merely a philosopher," a Black American philosopher, or an African philosopher? And the other way around? Or should a white European scholar who writes about African philosophic issues be regarded as an African philosopher? Equally important questions center on how African philosophers and Black American philosophers should collectively regard themselves and what term should be used to denote this unique combination.

If we accept Locke's criteria as to what is meant by Black artist, those criteria may be appropriately extended to the problem mentioned above—who is the Black philosopher? We may claim that a Black philosopher is one who is a philosopher who is Black and whose reflective inquiry incorporates elements or themes or idioms of the Black experience. A similar claim may be made for the African philosopher. Yet, as in the case of the artist, we cannot expect the Black philosopher or the African philosopher to be limited to his or her particular culture; nor should such a philosopher be limited to racial idiom. The basic tenets of science, religion, mysticism, magic, and so on—all have their place in Black or African philosophy. Although philosophic activities must begin with the particular culture involved, such activities must move beyond that culture and subsequently return to it with breadth and depth. This approach will not, however, solve the identity problem completely, because on a deeper analysis, the problem is beyond resolution: the identity problem is largely rooted in the Alain Lockean paradox discussed in his psychograph.

The question as to how to describe this philosophic community whose members include both African and Black American philosophers is too broad to deal with here. We should perhaps refer the reader to the contributions to the Africana Conference, held at Haverford, Pennsylvania in July 1982. These papers are currently being edited for publication by Professor Lucius Outlaw.

Finally, in passing a related issue should be mentioned, namely, the aims of Black or African philosophy. In addition to focusing on Black or African experiences, such philosophies must be concerned with value considerations, interpreting cultural experiences and seeking to understand conflicts that arise among human groupings, both in one's own and other cultures. The philosophers need not assume this task alone; in fact, the philosopher, artist, and statesman can undertake this task collectively and in the process engage in loving struggle. In pursuing this holy task, the philosopher may well allow himself or herself to be inspired by the philosophic legacy of Alain Locke.

NOTES

1. Russell J. Linnemann, ed., *Alain Locke: Reflections on a Modern Renaissance Man* (Baton Rouge: Louisiana State University, 1982), p. 1.

2. Ibid.

3. Ibid., pp. xi-xii.

4. Clare Bloodgood Crane, "Alain Locke and the Negro Renaissance" (Ph.D. dissertation, University of California, San Diego, 1971), p. 210.

5. Ibid., p. 212.

6. In 1912 Tennessee State University was established as a land-grant college to serve the Black youths of the state of Tennessee.

7. *TSU, The Meter*, October 25, 1984.

8. Of the white-Black student ratio at TSU, a local newspaper reported the following:

Now known as TSU's "downtown campus," the former UT-Nashville, maintained its mission to serve working adults through its broad offering of night classes.

But the Black-white student ratio at TSU, which was 2,556 white and 5,245 Black in the fall of 1980, has increased only slightly in the ensuing four years. Last fall, TSU enrolled 5,018 Black students and 2,595 white students.

The Freshman class at TSU last fall was 90.2% Black, compared to 69.7% Black in 1979. (*The Tennessean*, September 30, 1984).

9. *TSU, The Meter*, October 25, 1984.

10. Ibid.

11. Locke, "The Negro's Contribution in Art to American Culture," *Proceedings of the National Conference of Social Work* (New York, 1933), p. 320.

12. Noting the sequence of the various conferences on Black philosophy, Leonard Harris wrote:

Black philosophy conferences were held at The University of Chicago Circle, (1971), Tuskegee Institute, (1973/76), Wingspred, Michigan (1976), and Morgan State University, (1979). The urge to have a journal and an organization free of white domination sparked the creation of the standing American Philosophical Association's Committee on Blacks in philosophy; the New York Society for the Study of Black philosophy, and the Afro-American Society for philosophy." (pp. 104–5) (Harris, "Philosophy Born of Struggle," in *Philosophy and Cultures*, eds. H. Odera Oruka and D. A. Masolo. Nairobi, Kenya: Bookwise Limited, 1983).

SELECTED BIBLIOGRAPHY

WORKS BY ALAIN LOCKE

"Oxford Contrasts." *Independent* 67 (July 15, 1909), pp. 139–142.

"The Negro and a Race Tradition." *A.M.F. Quarterly Review* (April 1911), n.p.

"The American Temperament." *North American Review* 194 (August 1911), pp. 262–270.

"Emile Verhaeren." *The Poetry Review of America*. Ed. William S. Braithwaite (January 1917), pp. 41–43.

"The Role of the Talented Tenth." *Howard University Record* 12, No. 7 (December 1918), pp. 15–18.

"The Problem of Classification in the Theory of Value." Unpublished Ph.D. Thesis, Harvard University, 1918.

Review of Emmett J. Scott's *Negro Migration During the War. Journal of Negro History* 5 (October 1920), pp. 490–491.

"Steps Toward the Negro Theatre." *Crisis* 25 (December 1922), pp. 66–68.

"The Ethics of Culture." *Howard University Record* 18 (January 1923), pp. 178–185.

"Review of Goat Alley." *Opportunity*, 1 (February, 1923), 30.

"Professional Ideas in Teaching." *Bulletin*, National Association of Teachers in Colored Schools (April 1923), n.p.

"Portrait." *Current History Magazine of the New York Times* 18 (June 1923), 413.

Review of Abbot Lawrence Lowell's *Public Opinion in War and Peace. Opportunity* 1 (July 1923), 223.

Review of Roland Dixon's *The Racial History of Man. Opportunity*, 1 (September 1923), pp. 261–262.

"Problems of Race Classification." 1 (September 1923), pp. 261–262.

"The Colonial Literature of France." *Opportunity* 1 (November 1923), pp. 331–335.

"Roland Hayes: An Appreciation." *Opportunity* 1 (December 1923), pp. 356–358.

"Black Watch on the Rhine." *Opportunity* 2 (January 1924), pp. 6–9.

"Apropos of Africa." *Opportunity* 2 (February 1924), pp. 37–40.

"New Themes." *Crisis* 27 (February 1924), p. 178.

"The Younger Literary Movement." *Crisis* 28 (February 1924), pp. 161–163 (with Du Bois).

Review of Frank L. Schoel's *La Question des Nois aux Etats-Unis*. *Opportunity* 2 (April 1924), pp. 109–110.

"As Others See Us." *Opportunity* 2 (April 1924), pp. 109–110.

"Negro Speaks for Himself." *The Survey* 52 (April 15, 1924), pp. 71–72.

"A Note on African Art." *Opportunity* 2 (May 1924), pp. 134–138.

"Max Rheinhardt [sic] Reads the Negro's Dramatic Horoscope." *Opportunity* 2 (May 1924), pp. 145–146.

"The Concept of Race as Applied to Social Culture." *Howard Review* 1 (June 1924), pp. 290–299.

"Art of the Ancestors." *The Survey* 53 (March 1, 1925), p. 673.

"Enter the New Negro." *The Survey* 53 (March 1925), pp. 631–634.

"Youth Speaks." *The Survey* 53 (March 1, 1925), pp. 659–660.

"Harlem." *Survey Graphic* 53 (March 1, 1925), pp. 629–630.

"Internationalism: Friend or Foe of Art?" *The World Tomorrow* 8 (March 1925), pp. 75–76.

"Backstage on English Imperialism." *Opportunity* 3 (April 1925), pp. 112–114.

"To Certain of Our Philistines." *Opportunity* 3 (May 1925), pp. 155–156.

"The Command of the Spirit." *The Southern Workman* 54 (July 1925), pp. 295–299.

"The Art of Auguste Mambour." *Opportunity* 3 (August 1925) pp. 240–241, 252.

"Technical Study of the Spiritual." *Opportunity* 3 (November 1925), pp. 331–332.

"Negro Education Bids for Par." *The Survey* 54 (September 1, 1925), pp. 567–570.

"More of the Negro in Art." *Opportunity* 3 (December 1925), pp. 363–365.

"The Legacy of the Ancestral Arts." *The New Negro*. Ed. Alain Locke. 1925.

The New Negro. Ed. Alain Locke. New York: Albert and Charles Boni, Inc., 1925. (Reprinted by Atheneum, 1968.)

"The New Negro." *The New Negro*. Ed. Alain Locke. 1925.

"The Negro Spirituals." *The New Negro*. Ed. Alain Locke, 1925.

"Negro Youth Speaks." The New Negro. Ed. Alain Locke, 1925.

"Colen—A Review," by Countee Cullers. Opportunity 4 (January 1926), pp. 14–15.

"Nana Amoah: An African Statesman." *The Survey* 55 (January 1926), pp. 434–435.

"The Negro and the American Stage." *Theatre Arts Magazine* 10 (February 1926), pp. 112–120.

"American Literary Tradition and the Negro." *The Modern Quarterly* 3 (May-July 1926), pp. 215–222.

"The Drama of Negro Life." *Theatre Arts Monthly* 10 (October 1926), pp. 701–706.

"Review of the Weary Blues." *Palms* (October 1926), pp. 24–26.

"America's First Pacifist (Benjamin Banneker)." Letter to *The Nation* 123, No. 3204 (December 1, 1926), p. 560.

Review of Edwin Mim's *The Advancing South. Opportunity*4 (December, 1926), pp. 374–375.

"The Negro Poets of the United States." *Anthology of Magazine Verse for 1926 and Yearbook of American Poetry*. Ed. William S. Braithwaite. Boston: B. J. Brimmer Co., 1926, pp. 143–151.

"Adult Education for Negroes." *Handbook of Adult Education in the United States*. New York: American Association for Adult Education, 1926, pp. 121–131.

"The Gift of the Jungle." *The Survey* 57 (January 1, 1927), p. 463.

Review of Carter G. Woodson's *The Negro in Our History. Journal of Negro History* 12 (January 1927), pp. 99–101.

"Art Lessons from the Congo: Blondiau Theatre Arts Collection." *The Survey* 57 (February 1, 1927), pp. 587–589.

"A Collection of Congo Art." *Arts* 2 (February 1927), pp. 60–70.

Review of V. F. Calverton's *Sex Expression in Literature. Opportunity* 5 (February 1927), pp. 57–58.

"African Art in America." Letter to the Editor of *The Nation*, 124 (March 16, 1927), p. 290.

"The Negro Poet and His Tradition." *The Survey* 58 (August 1, 1927), pp. 473–474.

Review of *Fire. The Survey* 58 (August-September 1927), p. 563.

"The High Cost of Prejudice." *The Forum* 78 (December 1927), pp. 500–510.

"The Negro in the American Theatre." *Theatre: Essays in the Arts of the Theatre*. Ed. Edith J. Isaac. Boston: Little, Brown and Co., 1927.

Four Negro Poets. Ed. Alain Locke. New York: Simon and Schuster, 1927.

"Our Little Renaissance." *Ebony and Topaz.* Ed. Charles S. Johnson. New York: National Urban League, 1927.

Plays of Negro Life: A Source-Book of Native American Drama. Ed. Alain Locke and Montgomery Gregory. New York: Harper and Bros., 1927.

"The Drama of Negro Life." *Plays of Negro Life.* Eds. Alain Locke and Montgomery Gregory. New York: Harper and Bros., 1927.

"The Poetry of Negro Life." (Introduction to) *Four Negro Poets.* Ed. Alain Locke. New York: Simon and Schuster, 1927.

"Beauty Instead of Ashes." *The Nation* 126 (April 18, 1928), pp. 432–434.

"The Message of the Negro Poets." *Carolina Magazine* 58 (May 1928), pp. 5–15.

"Art or Propaganda?" *Harlem* 1 (November 1928), pp. 12–13.

"The Negro's Contribution to American Art and Literature." *Annals of the American Academy of Political and Social Science* 140 (1928), pp. 234–247.

"1928; A Retrospective Review." *Opportunity* 7 (January 1929), pp. 8–11.

"North and South: The Washington Conference on the American Negro." *The Survey* 61 (January 15, 1929), pp. 469–472.

"The Boxed Compass of Our Race Relations." *The Survey* 61 (January 15, 1929), pp. 469–472.

Review of Julia Peterkin's *Scarlet Sister Mary. Opportunity* 9 (June 1929), pp. 190–191.

"Both Sides of the Color Line." *The Survey* 62 (June 1929), pp. 325–336.

"Negro Contributions to America." *The World Tomorrow* 12 (June 1929), pp. 255–257.

"Beauty and the Province." *The Styles* (June 1929), pp. 3–4.

"The Negro in American Culture." *Anthology of American Negro Literature.* Ed. V.F. Calverton. New York: Modern Library Series, 1929, pp. 248–266.

"The Contribution of Race to Culture." *The Student World* (October 1930), pp. 349–353.

"This Year of Grace: Outstanding Books of the Year in Negro Literature." *Opportunity* 9 (February 1931), pp. 48–51.

"Slavery in the Modern Manner." *The Survey* 65 (March 1, 1931), pp. 590–593.

"The American Negro as Artist." *The American Magazine of Art* 23 (September 1931), pp. 210–220.

"The Negro in Art." *Christian Education* 13 (November 1931), pp. 210–220.

"Unity Through Diversity: A Baha'i Principle." *Baha'i World* 4 (Part Four, 1931) pp. 372–374.

"We Turn to Prose: A Retrospective Review of the Literature of the Negro for 1931." *Opportunity* 10 (February 1932), pp. 40–44.

"Black Truth and Black Beauty: A Retrospective Review of the Literature of the Negro for 1932." *Opportunity* 11 (January 1933), pp. 14–18.

"The Negro in Times Like These." *The Survey* 69 (June 1933), pp. 222–224.

The Negro in America. Chicago: American Library Association, 1933.

"The Negro's Contribution in Art to American Culture." *Proceedings of the National Conference of Social Work* (New York, 1933), pp. 315–322.

"The Saving Grace of Realism: A Retrospective Review of the Negro Literature of 1933." *Opportunity*, 13 (January 1934), pp. 8–11, 30.

"Some Lessons from Negro Adult Education." *Proceedings of the Sixth Annual Conference of the American Association for Adult Education* (May 1934), n.p.

"Reciprocity Instead of Regimentation: Lessons of Negro Adult Education." *Journal of Adult Education* 6 (October 1934), pp. 418–420.

"Toward a Critique of Negro Music." *Opportunity* 12 (November and December 1934), pp. 328–331, 365–367, 385.

"Sterling Brown: The New Negro Folk-Poet." *Negro Anthology.* Ed. Nancy Conard. London: Wishart and Co., 1934, pp. 111–115.

"The Eleventh Hour of Nordicism: A Retrospective Review of the Literature of the Negro for 1934." *Opportunity* 13 (January-February1935), pp. 8–12, 46–48, 59.

"Minorities and the Social Mind." *Progressive Education* 12 (March 1935), pp. 141–146.

"African Art:Classic Style." *American Magazine of Art* 28 (May 1935), pp. 270–278.

"The Dilemma of Segregation." *Journal of Negro Education* 4 (July 1935), pp. 406–411.

"Values and Imperatives." *American Philosophy, Today and Tomorrow.* Eds. Sidney Hook and Horace M. Kallen. New York: Lee Furman, 1935, pp. 313–333.

"Deep River, Deeper Sea: Retrospective Review of the Literature of the Negro for 1935." *Opportunity*, 14 (January and February 1936), pp. 6–10, 42–43, 61.

"Harlem: Dark Weather-vane." *Survey Graphic* 25 (August 1936), pp. 457–462, 493–495.

"Martyrdom to Glad Music: The Irony of Black Patriotism." 14 (December 1936), p. 38.

"Propaganda—or Poetry?" *Race* (Summer 1936), pp. 70–76, 87.

"Lessons of Negro Adult Education." *Adult Education in Action*. Ed. Mary L. Fly. New York: American Association for Adult Education, 1936, pp. 126–131.

The Negro and His Music. Washington, D.C.: Associates in Negro Folk Education, 1936.

Negro Art: Past and Present. Washington, D.C.: Associates in Negro Folk Education, 1936.

"God Save Reality! A Retrospective Review of the Literature of the Negro for 1936." *Opportunity* 15 (January and February 1937), pp. 8–13, 40–44.

"Spiritual Truancy." *New Challenge* 2 (Fall 1937), pp. 81–85.

"Jingo Counter-Jingo and Us. A Retrospective Review of the Literature of the Negro for 1937." *Opportunity* 16 (January and February 1938), pp. 7–11, 27, 39–42.

"With Science as His Shield the Educator Must Bridge Our Great Divides." *Frontiers of Democracy* (May 1938–April 1941), pp. 8–10.

"Freedom Through Art: A Review of Negro Art, 1870–1938." *Crisis* 45 (July 1938), pp. 227–229.

Review of Melville J. Herskovits' *Dahomey: An Ancient African Kingdom*. *Opportunity* 16 (November 1938), pp. 342–343.

"Negro Needs as Adult Educational Opportunities." *Findings of The First Annual Conference on Adult Education and the Negro*, 1938, pp. 5–10.

"The Negro: 'New' or Newer: A Retrospective Review of the Literature of the Negro for 1938." *Opportunity* 17 (January and February 1939), pp. 4–10, 36–42.

"What Every American Knows." Letter to *The Survey* 28, No. 2 (February 1939), p. 155.

"Advance on the Art Front." *Opportunity* 17 (May 1939), pp. 132–136.

"Negro Music Goes to Par." *Opportunity* 17 (July 1939), pp. 196–200.

"The Negro's Contribution to American Culture." *Journal of Negro Education* 8 (July 1939), pp. 521–529.

Americans All: Immigrants All. Ed. Alain Locke. Washington, D.C.: Office of Education *Bulletin*, 1939.

Forward to *Contemporary Negro Art*. The Baltimore Museum of Art. Exhibition of February 3–19, 1939.

"Dry Fields and Green Pastures: A Retrospective Review of Negro Literature and Art for 1939." *Opportunity* 18 (January and February 1940), pp. 4–10, 28, 41–46, 53.

"Ballard for Democracy." *Opportunity* 18 (August 1940), pp. 228–229.

"Negroes (American)." *Britannica Book of the Year* (1940), pp. 485–486.

"Popularized Literature." *Findings of the Second Annual Conference on Adult Education and the Negro*, 1940, pp. 48–50.

The Negro in Art: A Pictorial Record of the Negro Artist and of the Negro Theme in Art. Washington, D.C.: Associates in Negro Folk Education, 1940.

"Of Native Sons: Real and Otherwise." *Opportunity* 19 (January and February 1941), pp. 4–9, 48–52.

"Negroes (American)." *Britannica Book of the Year* (1941), pp. 486–487. Annual revision of 1940 article.

"Chicago's New Southside Art Center." *Magazine of Art* 34 (August 1941), pp. 370–374.

"Broadway and the Negro Drama." *Theatre Arts* 25 (October 1941), pp. 745–750.

"Three Corollaries of Cultural Relativism." In *Proceedings of the Second Conference on the Scientific Spirit and the Democratic Faith.* New York, 1941.

"Who and What Is 'Negro'?" *Opportunity* 20 (February and March 1942), pp. 36–41, 83–87.

"Democracy Faces a World Order." *Harvard Education Review* 12 (March 1942), pp. 121–128.

"Is there a Basis for Spiritual Unity in the World Today?" *Bulletin of America's Town Meeting of the Air* (June 1, 1942). George Denny, Jr., Moderator. Discussants: Mordecai W. Johnson, Alain Locke, Leon A. Ransom, and Doxie A. Wilkerson.

"The Unfinished Business of Democracy." *Survey Graphic* 31 (November 1942), pp. 455–461.

"Autobiographical Sketch." *Twentieth Century Authors.* Eds. Stanley Kunitz and Howard Haycroft. New York: Wilson Company, 1942.

When Peoples Meet: A Study of Race and Culture Contacts. Eds. Alain Locke and Bernhard J. Stern. New York: Committee on Workshops, Progressive Education Association, 1942.

"Negroes (American)." *Britannica Book of the Year* (1942), p. 472. Annual revision of 1940 article.

"Pluralism and Intellectual Democracy." *Second Symposium.* New York: Conference on Science, Philosophy, and Religion, 1942, pp. 196–211.

Le' role du Negro dans la culture des Ameriques. Port-au-Prince, Haiti: Imprimerie de l'état, 1943.

"Negroes (American)." *Britannica Book of the Year* (1943), pp. 491–492.

"The Negro in American Culture." *New Masses* (January 18, 1944), pp. 4–6.

"Understanding World Cultures." *Educational Leadership* 1 (March 1944), pp. 381–382.

"The Negro Contribution to American Culture." *Journal of Negro Education* 13 (Winter 1944), pp. 7–18.

"The Negro in the Three Americas." *Journal of Negro Education*13 (Winter 1944), pp. 7–18.

"Wither Race Relations? A Critical Commentary." *Journal of Negro Education* (Summer 1944), pp. 398–406.

"Cultural Relativism and Ideological Peace." *Approaches to World Peace.* New York. Conference on Science, Philosophy, and Religion, 1944, pp. 609–618.

"Negroes (American)." *Britannica Book of the Year* (1944), pp. 490–491. Annual revision of 1940 article.

"The Negro Group." *Group Relations and Group Antagonisms.* Ed. R.M. MacIver. New York: Harper and Bros., 1944, pp. 43–59.

"Understanding Through Art and Culture." *Africa Today and Tomorrow* (April 1945), p. 23.

"Areas of Extension and Improvement of Adult Education Among Negroes." *Journal of Negro Education* 15 (Summer 1945), pp. 453–459.

"A Contribution to American Culture." *Opportunity* 23 (Fall 1945), pp. 192–193, 238.

Diversity Within National Unity. Washington, D.C.: National Council for the Social Studies, 1945. Symposium with Alain Locke, Carey McWilliams, George B. Ford, Otto Klineberg, and Howard E. Wilson (Locke Presiding).

"The Negro and the War." *Britannica Book of the Year* (1945), pp. 486–487.

"Up Till Now." *Introduction to The Negro Artist Comes of Age; A National Survey of Contemporary American Artists.* Albany, N.Y. Albany Institute of History and Art 1945, pp. iii-vii.

"The Negro and World War II." *Britannica Book of the Year* (1946), pp. 517–518.

"The Negro Minority in American Literature." *English Journal* 35 (1946), pp. 315–319.

"Coming of Age." *Adult Education Journal* 6 (January 1947), pp. 1–3.

"More Than Blasting Brick and Mortar." *Survey Graphic* 36 (January 1947), pp. 87–89.

Review of John H. Franklin's *From Slavery to Freedom. Saturday Review of Literature* 30 (November 8, 1947), p. 16.

"The Armed Services." *Britannica Book of the Year* (1947), pp. 537–538.

"Pluralism and Ideological Peace." *Freedom and Experience.* Eds,. Milton R. Konvitz and Sidney Hook. Ithaca, New York: Cornell University Press, 1947, pp. 63–69.

"Reason and Race: A Review of the Literature of the Negro for 1946." *Phylon* 8 (1947), pp. 17–27.

"Education for Adulthood." *Adult Education Journal* 6 (July 1947), pp. 104–111.

"A Critical Retrospect of the Literature of the Negro for 1947." *Phylon* 9 (1948), pp. 3–12.

Foreword to *Witness for Freedom*, by Rebecca Barton. New York: Harper and Brothers, 1948.

"Dawn Patrol: A Review of Literature of the Negro for 1948." *Phylon*, 10 (First and Second Quarters, 1949), pp. 5–14; 167–172.

"The Need for a New Organon in Education." *Goals for American Education*. New York: Conference on Science, Philosophy, and Religion, 1950, pp. 201–212.

"Negroes (American)." *Britannica Book of the Year* (1950), pp. 481–482.

"The Negro and the American Stage." *Theatre Arts Anthology*. Ed. Rosamond Gilder. New York: Theatre Art Books, 1950, pp. 81–87.

"Self-Criticism: The Third Dimension in Culture." *Phylon* 11 (1950), pp. 391–394.

"Wisdom de Profundis: Literature of the Negro, 1949." *Phylon* 11 (1950), pp. 5–15, 171–175.

"Changing Values in the Western World." *American Scholar* (February 14, 1951), pp. 343–358. Forum with Alain Locke, Arthur Schlesinger, Jr., Walter Mehring, Frederick A. Weiss, Matthew Huxley, Hiram Haydn, Alan Gregg, and Simon Michael Bessie.

"The Arts and the Creative Integration of Modern Living." *Progressive Education* 28 (April 1951), pp. 182–183. (A response to and article by Alexander Dorner.)

"Cultural Ascendancy." *Encylopaedia Britannica*, Vol. 16 (1951), pp. 194–196.

"Harlem." *Encylopaedia Britannica*, Vol. 16 (1951), pp. 200–201.

"L'Apport Intellectual et Cultural du Noir American." *Les Etudes Americaines*, Cahier 29, Bimestriel (1951), pp. 3–6.

"Inventory at Mid-Century: A Review of the Literature of the Negro for 1950." *Phylon* 12 (First and Second Quarters, 1959), pp. 5–12; 185–190.

"Negro Art." *Encyclopaedia Britannica* Vol. 16. (1951), pp. 198–199.

"Negro Poetry." *Encyclopaedia Britannica*, Vol. 16 (1951), p. 200. (With James W. Johnson.)

"The Negro in American Literature." *New World Writing* 1, New York, 1952, pp. 18–33.

"Negroes (American)." *Britannica Book of the Year* (1952), pp. 495–497. Revision of 1950 article.

"The High Price of Integration: A Review of the Literature of the Negro for 1951." *Phylon*, 13 (1952)), pp. 7–18.

"From *Native Son to Invisible Man*: A Review of the Literature of the
Negro for 1952." 14 *Phylon* (1953); pp. 34–44.

"Negro in the Arts." *United Asia: International Magazine of Asian Affairs*
3 (June 1953), pp. 177–181.

"Our Changing Race Relations: Some Educational Implications." *Progressive Education* 30 (1953), pp. 75–76, 91–92.

"The Social Responsibility of the Scholar." *Proceedings of the Conference
of the Division of the Social Sciences.* Washington, D.C.: Howard
University Press, 1953, pp. 143–146.

"Values That Matter." *Key Reporter* 19 (May 1954), p. 4. Review of Ralph
Barton Perry's *Realms of Value.*

"Negroes (American)." *Britannica Book of the Year* (1954), pp. 498–499.
Revision of 1950 article.

"Impressions of Haifa." *Baha'i World* 3 (Part Four, n.d.), n.p.

"Lessons in World Crisis." *Baha'i World* 9 (Part Four, n.d.), n.p.

"Minority Side of Intercultural Education." *Education for Cultural Unity:
Seventeenth Yearbook*, California Elementary School Principals Association, n.d., pp. 60–64.

"The Orientation of Hope." *Baha'i World* 6 (Part Four, n.d.) n.p.

WORKS ABOUT ALAIN LOCKE

Braithwaite, William Stanley. "Alain Locke's Relationship to the Negro
in American Literature." 15 pp. Typewritten address delivered
in Locke's honor.

———. "Alain Locke's Relationship to the Negro in American Literature." *Phylon* 18 (1957), pp. 166–73.

Brewer, William. "Alain Locke." *Negro History Bulletin* 18 (November
1954), pp. 26–32.

Bunche, Ralph J., Krikorian, Y. H., Nelson, William, et al. "The Passing
of Alain Leroy Locke." *Phylon* 15 (1954), pp. 243–252.

Butcher, Margaret Just. *The Negro in American Culture.* New York: Alfred
A. Knopf. 1956.

Crane, Clare Bloodgood. "Alain Locke and the Negro Renaissance."
Ph.D. dissertation, University of California, San Diego, 1971.

Fennel, Robert. "From Cain's Other Side: An Informal View of Alain
Locke." *Recapit* 1 (February 1959), pp. 1–3.

Hay, Samuel A. "Alain Locke and Black Drama." *Black World* (April
1972), pp. 8–14.

Holmes, Eugene C. "Alain Locke: A Sketch." *Phylon* (Spring 1959), pp.
82–89.

————. "Alain Locke—Philosopher, Critic, Spokesman." *Journal of Philosophy* (February 28, 1957), pp. 113–118.

————. "The Legacy of Alain Locke."*Freedomways* 3 (Summer 1963), pp. 293–306.

Kallen, H. M. "Alain Locke and Cultural Pluralism." *Journal of Philosophy* (February 28, 1957), pp. 119–127.

Linnemann, Russell J., ed. *Alain Locke: Reflections on a Modern Renaissance Man.* Baton Rouge: Louisiana State University, 1982.

Long, Richard. "Alain Locke, Cultural Mentor." *Homage to Alain Locke.* Atlanta: Atlanta University Press, 1970.

Mason, Ernest D. "An Introduction to Alain Locke's Theory of Values." Ph.D. dissertation, Emory University, 1975.

Stewart, Jeffrey C. *The Critical Temper of Alain Locke: A Selection of His Essays on Art and Culture.* New York: Garland Publishing, Inc., 1983.

Wright, W. D. "The Cultural Thought and Leadership of Alain Locke." *Freedomways* (First Quarter, 1974), pp. 35–50.

The New Negro Thirty Years Afterward: Papers Presented to the Sixteenth Annual Spring Conference of the Division of the Social Sciences, April 20, 21, and 22, 1955. Washington, D.C.: Howard University Press, 1955.

Other sources that contain Locke's papers include: The Alain Locke Collection, Moorland-Spingarn Research Center, Howard University; Arthur Schomburg Collection, New York Public Library; Survey Associates Papers, Archives of Social Welfare History, University of Minnesota; Special Collections, Atlanta University Library, Atlanta, Georgia; and Special Collections, Fisk University, Nashville, Tennessee.

INDEX

About the Author

JOHNNY WASHINGTON is Associate Professor in the Department of Psychology, Philosophy, and Religious Studies at the
University of Tennessee at Martin. His areas of specialization
include ethics, social/political philosophy, and Afro-American
philosophy.

Recent Titles in
Contributions in Afro-American and African Studies
Series Advisers: John W. Blassingame and Henry Louis Gates, Jr.